Ports, Cities, and Global Supply Chains

Edited by

JAMES WANG
University of Hong Kong, China

DANIEL OLIVIER
University of Hong Kong, China

THEO NOTTEBOOM
University of Antwerp, Belgium

BRIAN SLACK
Concordia University, Canada

ASHGATE

Published by
Ashgate Publishing Limited
Gower House
Croft Road
Aldershot
Hampshire GU11 3HR
England

Ashgate Publishing Company
Suite 420
101 Cherry Street
Burlington, VT 05401-4405
USA

Ashgate website: http://www.ashgate.com

British Library Cataloguing in Publication Data
Ports, cities, and global supply chains. - (Transport and
    mobility series)
    1. Harbors 2. Shipping 3. City planning 4. Business
    logistics 5. International trade
    I. Wang, James
    387.1

Library of Congress Cataloging-in-Publication Data
International Workshop of Port Cities and Global Supply Chains (2005 : Hong Kong, China)
    Ports, cities, and global supply chains / edited by James Wang ... [et al.].
        p. cm.
    Papers from the International Workshop of [sic] Port Cities and Global Supply Chains held in December 2005 in Hong Kong.
    Includes index.
    ISBN-13: 978-0-7546-7054-4 1. Harbors--Economic aspects--Congresses.
2. Business logistics--Congresses. 3. Shipping--Economic aspects--Congresses. 4.
Infrastructure (Economics)--Congresses. 5. Globalization--Economic aspects--
Congresses. I. Wang, James Jixian. II. Title.

    HE551.I575 2007
    387.1'64--dc22

                                                                        2007002938
ISBN 978-0-7546-7054-4

Printed and bound in Great Britain by Antony Rowe Ltd, Chippenham, Wiltshire.

Contents

PART 3: INSERTING PORT-CITIES INTO GLOBAL SUPPLY CHAINS

PART 4: CORPORATE PERSPECTIVES ON THE INSERTION OF PORTS IN GLOBAL SUPPLY CHAINS

List of Figures

List of Tables

List of Contributors

Dr James J. Wang is associate professor at The University of Hong Kong. Born in Beijing, he received his Bachelor of Economics from the People's University of China, M.Phil. in Geography from the University of Hong Kong, and PhD from the University of Toronto. As a China port specialist, he has been involved in more than 12 research and planning projects on major ports in China since 1995, and published widely in various international journals on issues of port governance, competition, and port-city relationships. He contributed also chapters to recently published books such as *Global Logistics* edited by D. Waters (2006), and *Asian Container Ports* by K Cullinane, D-W Song (eds.) (2006).

Dr Daniel Olivier joined Transport Canada, Strategic Policy, in October 2006 after receiving his PhD in economic geography from the University of Hong Kong earlier that year. His doctoral research documented the emergence of transnational firms in the container port industry, with a special focus on corporate strategy, organizational change and spatial dynamics of global firms. His general areas of expertise include transnational firms, management theory, corporate governance, Asia and maritime logistics. Dr Olivier has published in journals such as *Transport Policy*, *Maritime Economics and Logistics*, *Environment & Planning A* as well as contributing chapters in books on the subject of port management and development. His current work at Transport Canada falls under the Asia-Pacific Gateway and Corridor Initiative.

Dr Theo E. Notteboom is president of ITMMA (Institute of Transport and Maritime Management Antwerp) of the University of Antwerp and is also affiliated with the Department of Transport and Regional Economics of the University of Antwerp. He lectures transport policy, port economics, inland transport and maritime technology at the University of Antwerp, ITMMA and some other universities and institutions. He holds visiting posts at Dalian Maritime University (China) and Nanyang Technological University (Singapore). He published widely on port and maritime economics, including market organization in liner shipping and inland transportation. Theo Notteboom is member of the Council of IAME (International Association of Maritime Economics) and active member of the Royal Belgian Marine Academy, the Royal Academy of Overseas Sciences and member of several editorial boards of academic journals. He has been involved as promoter or co-promoter about 35 academic research programs and consultancy studies on maritime and logistics topics.

Dr Brian Slack was born in England and obtained his bachelor's degree from the London School of Economics. He came to Canada to pursue post graduate degrees, and obtained masters and doctorate degrees from McGill University, Montreal. His professional career has been anchored by a position he held at Concordia University,

Montreal, for over 40 years. He has also held visiting positions at universities around the world. He retired in January 2005, and is Distinguished Professor Emeritus at Concordia. In 2003 he was awarded the Ullman Award for contributions to Transport Geography by the American Association of Geographers, and in 2004 was awarded an honorary doctorate by the University of Le Havre. Although he is officially retired, he continues to work closely with his colleagues of many years in Canada, Claude Comtois and Bob McCalla; is actively engaged in joint projects with Elisabeth Gouvernal at INRETS; contributes guest lectures to courses in Belgium and Hong Kong; and, encourages young scholars on three continents.

Prof Alfred Baird is Head of the Maritime Research Group at Napier University's Transport Research Institute in Edinburgh, Scotland. Prior to his academic career he worked for an international liner container shipping company. His doctoral research involved the study of global strategic management in liner container shipping, in collaboration with Sea-Land Service Inc. Professor Baird has researched, published, advised, and taught across a range of international maritime transport subjects, including port competition and privatization, strategic management in shipping, market analysis in the maritime industry, ship cost and service schedule modelling, assessing the feasibility of new shipping services and port developments, and promotion and marketing of shipping services and port facilities.

Dr Valentina Carbone is Professor in Supply Chain Management at ESCE (Ecole Supérieure du Commerce Extérieur, Paris) and lecturer at the International MBA, ESCP (Ecole Supérieure de Commerce de Paris). She joins different training programmes at Paris IX Dauphine University and Paris I – Sorbonne University. She is also associate researcher at SPLOT - INRETS (Institut National de Recherche sur les Transports et leur Sécurité). Her main research areas cover SCM, sustainable logistics and 3PL strategies. She did her PhD in logistics at ENPC (Ecole Nationale des Ponts et Chaussées) in Paris. She had attended an MBA in Italy, where she studied Business and Economics at the University of Naples.

Dr Claude Comtois is professor of geography at the Université de Montréal, Canada. He has a degree in political science, a M.Sc. in geography from Laval University and a PhD from the University of Hong Kong for his research in the field of transportation. He is affiliated with the Research Centre on Enterprise Networks, Logistics and Transportation of the Université de Montréal. He has over 10 years experience as transport project director for the Canadian International Development Agency in China. Visiting professorships include more than 15 foreign universities. His teaching and research are centred on transport systems with an emphasis on shipping and ports. He has been involved in consultancy studies on marine policy, intermodal transport and environmental issues. He is a co-author of the *Geography of Transport Systems*, published by Routledge and has published many articles in scientific journals on port and marine transport. He currently supervises a project on sustainable port and inland waterways.

Dr César Ducruet is post-doctoral research fellow at the Korea Research Institute for Human Settlements (KRIHS) in South Korea. He received his PhD in Geography at Le Havre University (2004) on the theme *Port cities, laboratories of globalisation*. His main research issues include port-city relationships through theoretical aspects, international comparison and quantitative approaches. Applications of his studies are various, for example, air-sea linkages within European port-cities, Europe-Asia port-city structures and dynamics, spatial modelisation of port-city interface, globalisation and regionalisation processes affecting port-cities, free trade zone development in Korea and China, spatial graphical modelling improvement. Future research is to be led from 2006 (KRIHS) with a joint France-Korea team on North Korea's industrial and port potential development.

Dr Antoine Frémont, is holder of the Agrégation in Geography, Doctor of Geography (PhD from Le Havre University in 1996) and has accreditation to supervise research (University of Paris Pantheon-Sorbonne in 2005). He is Associate Professor. He works at the INRETS (The French National Institute for Transport and Safety Research). He specialises in maritime transport issues, specifically on shipping lines strategies, maritime networks, hinterlands and the organisation of the combined transport chains and the development of logistics within the maritime sector. He is currently managing a research program on container inland navigation and the hinterland of the French ports. He cooperates with the OECD on the reliability and levels of service of the surface transport networks. He has published 3 books, 11 chapters of books and 27 papers in academic journals and professional reviews.

Dr Elisabeth Gouvernal is senior researcher in the French National Institute on Transport and Security, and head of the research unit 'Production Systems, Freight and Logistics'. She holds a doctorate in economics and planning. She has conducted research on the competitiveness of transport chains for the World Bank and the European Commission, and held a position in the shipping company, CMA-CGM. Her current research focuses on maritime transport, the organization of transport chains, multimodality and problems of inland haulage to and from ports. In 1989 she directed a very large survey of shippers and the transport chain employing a new methodology, a survey that was repeated in 2004. She lectures at the University of Paris I and the Ecole nationale des Ponts et Chaussées on the subject of maritime transport.

Dr Peter V. Hall is a professor in the Urban Studies Program at Simon Fraser University in Vancouver, Canada, where he is also the Associate Director of the Center for Sustainable Community Development. His research addresses various dimensions of economic development at the local and regional scales. Before commencing his doctoral studies in city and regional planning at the University of California at Berkeley, he worked in the Economic Development Unit of the Durban Metropolitan Council. This experience led to his doctoral and subsequent research examining the connections between shipping and logistics chains, transport sector employment and the development of port cities.

Prof Yehuda Hayuth is Head of the Wydra Shipping and Aviation Research Institute at the University of Haifa. During the years 1993-2004 he served as the President of the University of Haifa and in 2004-2005 he was Vice President for planning, development and strategy for Zim Integrated Shipping Services LTD. He studied toward his PhD at the University of Washington in Seattle, were he is also an Affiliate Professor. Yehuda Hayuth worked in the UN planning team in Thailand and served as a chairman of Arebee star shipping agency in Mumbai, India. He is an author of *Intermodality-Concept and Practice*, published by Lloyds of London Press and has published many articles in professional journals.

Dr Peter W. de Langen has worked for over nine years as a transport, port and regional economist at Erasmus University Rotterdam. He is active in teaching, contract research and academic research. He specialises in port economics, policy and management. He has participated in numerous research projects, e.g. on change processes in the port of Rotterdam, international policies related to seaports, clustering in maritime industries, governance in port clusters, entrepreneurship in seaports and innovation in ship design. He has project management experience from a substantial number of projects over the last three years. He has finished a PhD-thesis on the performance of seaport clusters and published a number of articles on various port related topics in international scientific journals.

Dr Robert McCalla is Professor of Geography at Saint Mary's University in Halifax, Canada. His research and teaching interests are in maritime transportation. He has published in journals such as *Journal of Transport Geography, Canadian Geographer, Maritime Policy and Management, Geoforum*, and *Tijdscrift voor Economische en Sociale Geografie*. He is the author of *Water Transportation in Canada* (Formac, 1994). Currently, he is an External Examiner of the World Maritime University (Malmo, Sweden) and Shanghai Maritime University. His BA degree is from the University of Western Ontario; his PhD is from the University of Hull, England where he was a Commonwealth Scholar.

Dr Enrico Musso is full professor in Applied Economics at the University of Genoa, where he is involved in research and teaching activities in Transport Economics and Urban and Regional Planning. He is Director of the PhD programme in *Transportation and Logistics* of the University of Genoa and Lecturer in the Master programme in *Transport and Maritime Management and Transport and Maritime Economics* at the University of Antwerp. He is Former visiting professor in many universities in Italy and abroad and Director of international research programs financed by the European Union and other private and public institutions concerning ports, maritime transport and urban mobility. Musso is author, co-author or editor of more than 100 scientific publications and is Director of the international centre of research *Go UP – Governance of Urban Policies* and the Master Science in *Governance of territorial economic policies* at the University of Genoa. He is Co-founder of *Transportnet*, a research network of 8 European universities, and of the Italian Centre of Excellence for Integrated Logistics. He is a member of the scientific board of the *Maritime Transport and Ports Group* at the *World Conference on Transport Research Society*, and editor of the reviews *Maritime Economics and Logistics* (Palgrave-Macmillan) and *European Transports*.

Dr Photis M. Panayides is Associate Professor, Chair of Marketing and Shipping Management at the CIIM Business School in Cyprus. Previously he was Assistant Professor of Shipping Strategy and Marketing at The Hong Kong Polytechnic University. He has also been a Lecturer at the University of Plymouth, UK. He is the MPA Visiting Associate Professor at the National University of Singapore and a Visiting Associate Professor on the MBA Shipping programme at ALBA Graduate Business School in Greece and held visiting appointments at the Copenhagen Business School, Denmark and, Northern Jia Tong (Beijing), Qingdao and Nankai (Tianjin) Universities in China. He has authored three books and over 50 journal and conference papers.

Dr Francesco Parola started his studies in maritime and transport economics at the University of Genoa (Italy), where he got his bachelor degree cum laude in early-2001. During his Ph.D. studies he has been visiting researcher at the Center for Maritime Economics & Logistics of the Erasmus University in Rotterdam. He successfully defended a doctoral thesis about the strategies of transnational container terminal operators in the port reform era. His favourite research topics are liner shipping and port economics. Currently he is lecturer at the Faculty of Economics in Genoa and researcher at the Italian Centre of Excellence for Integrated Logistics. He is (co-)author of papers in peer-reviewed international journals and conference proceedings.

Mr Glen Robbins is a part-time Research Fellow at the School of Development Studies, University of KwaZulu-Natal (Durban), and is a graduate of the Institute of Development Studies at the University of Sussex. He also works as a consultant to a number of multi-lateral organizations specializing in regional and local economic development with a focus on city strategies, infrastructure planning and financing and industrial policy. Until recently he headed up the Economic Development and City Enterprises functions in the eThekwini Municipality (Durban).

Dr Jean-Paul Rodrigue is an Associate Professor at the Department of Economics and Geography at Hofstra University, New York. His research covers the fields of economic, transport and urban geography with regional interests in East and Southeast Asia and North America, notably concerning transportation, distribution and trade issues. In such a setting, the emergence of global production and distribution networks and their impacts on freight distribution have been the object of Dr. Rodrigue's recent work. This work is particularly concerned with transport corridors, intermodal terminals and the logistics of maritime and inland transport systems.

Dr Martin Soppé graduated his PhD in *Transport Economics and Land Planning* from Le Havre University (France) in 2001, with doctoral thesis dealing with the role of freight load centres in reconnecting western and eastern European economies past

1989. He was Senior Lecturer at that university (2002–2006), involved in research and lecturing related to transportation and land planning. He seconded to INRETS (The French National Institute for Transport and Safety Research) in 2006 and currently works as Full Time Researcher. His current research activity specialises in freight transportation issues, both inland and maritime, focusing inland transportation chains, shippers' strategies, as well as performance and sustainability of transport chains. His previous research work includes container shipping lines strategies, maritime networks and hinterland connexions of maritime ports in the context of globalization and consolidation trends. In collaboration with the University of Genoa (Italy) he investigated the forms of vertical integration/coordination between the shipping and the handling industries. In the frame of various research projects he was also involved in the research on port governance and maritime pollution.

Chapter 1

Introduction

James Wang, Daniel Olivier, Theo Notteboom and Brian Slack

Global trends in policy and technology related fields are rapidly reshaping the port industry worldwide. Port cities are confronted with changing economic and logistics environments. The global market place, with powerful and relatively footloose players, extensive business networks and complex logistics networks, has a dramatic impact on port-cities. Port-cities have had to assimilate and accommodate advances in logistics to sustain their competitive status as key interfaces in the building of smooth global trade flows. The logistics environment creates a high degree of uncertainty and leaves port managers and city officials with the question how to respond effectively to market dynamics.

Transformations in the past decade have also largely outpaced scholars and policymakers' capacity to survey, conceptualise and interpret change. Meanwhile, As port/terminal management is increasingly engaging with supply chain management practices, ports are increasingly recognised as core constitutive elements of emerging global supply chains. Thus, both industry and research are at an exciting frontier, in clear need of new paradigms.

Recent research stresses how spatially variegated port-cities have become: at one extreme young and dynamic port-cities are emerging 'out of nowhere', notably in Asia (e.g. Shenzhen in China, Pelepas in Malaysia), while at the other extreme established port-cities are looking for ways to revitalise their participation in the global 'buzz' that has become logistics. Operational, structural and technological change incurred by logistical advances is giving way to a new generation of port-cities endowed with increasingly sophisticated logistical spaces. At the same time, the drive towards value adding port activities seems well under way: how have global port-cities accommodated such activities, what are the lessons learnt and what is the way forward?

All of these become new challenges to the development of port cities themselves, since they are forced or seduced to adopt new ways to facilitate, accommodate, and regulate the physical movements that use them as critical interface or gateway. What can be done and should be done to insert these port cities along the global supply chains thus become an imperative area for research. Realizing this need, we held an International Workshop of Port Cities and Global Supply Chains in December 2005 in Hong Kong. Scholars from North America, Europe, and Asia with different disciplinary backgrounds discussed and debated intensively on the challenging issues. In order to share our views, approaches, analysis, methodologies, and understanding of these issues with more people, we decided from the preparation stage of the Workshop to get our research papers selectively collected into this book.

This book aims to provide multidisciplinary insights on the role port cities adopt in dealing with global supply chains. Throughout the book, concepts of strategic management, supply chain management, port and transport economics as well as economic/transport geography are applied to offer an in-depth understanding of the processes underlying global supply chains and associated spatial and functional dynamics in port-cities. The book also discusses policy outcomes and implications relevant to port-cities positioned in different segments of global supply chains.

The first part entitled *Conceptualization of Port-cities and Global Supply Chains* provides a background to some of the main themes of this book. Two chapters deal with supply chains (SC), their nature and impacts. The principal objective of these two chapters is to assess the importance for ports of being integrated in SCs. The other two chapters examine the evolving character of contemporary ports, their internal changes and external links.

Valentina Carbone and Elisabeth Gouvernal provide definitions of several of the key concepts involving supply chains (SC). They demonstrate that while 'supply chains' are receiving a great deal of attention in the professional and academic literature, there is no single definition that has universal support. The lack of agreement over terminology extends to many of the concepts that have been developed such as 'supply chain management' and 'supply chain integration'. They suggest that the lack of agreement over definitions is the outcome of the field attracting the attention of many diverse disciplines with different approaches and focuses. The second part of the chapter reports on their questionnaire survey of a sample of maritime experts, many of whom are authors of chapters in this book. The experts were presented with a range of definitions of SC terminology and asked which best met their understanding of the terms. They were then asked to suggest likely trends and to identify how supply chains might impact on port competitiveness. It is not surprising that there was little unanimity over the terms, although respondents indicated that information technology integration was a major challenge for SC and that port reliability was a critical factor in measuring port performance. The chapter concludes by providing a set of questions raised by the survey as well as an agenda for further maritime research incorporating SC.

The issue of supply chain integration is revisited in the following chapter. Photis Panayides returns to the diversity of definitions, only this time the survey is administered to port authorities, with the goal of determining the extent to which SC integration is a factor in port competition, as perceived by the professional managers. Again the survey is based on factors identified in the literature: use of technology for data sharing, relationships with shipping lines, value added services, transport mode integration, relationships with inland transport providers, and channel integration practices and performance. Results of the multiple regression analysis reveal the key importance of value added services in inserting ports in SCs. Furthermore, the link between technology adoption and high quality of the services offered by the port was identified, confirming a result of the Carbone and Gouvernal survey. Responsiveness and reliability are suggested as port performance measures that in the context of SCs are superior to port throughput data. Finally, the establishment of client relationships by ports has a beneficial effect on the port's function of fulfilling its modern role in the era of logistics and supply chain management.

Brian Slack continues the focus on ports. His chapter suggests that the nature of container ports has changed, which requires a very different approach by researchers and policy makers. Today the modern container port is a collection of separate terminals, each with different clients, distinctive handling methods, and managed by different companies with divergent policy objectives. So to continue to treat the port as a whole entity is misleading. He provides examples of how the traffic growth at different terminals in the same port is unequal, and of how the strategies of terminal operators in the same port differ. He suggests that while the terminalisation of the port may facilitate its integration into SCs, it will further the divorce between maritime activities and the port-city.

The final chapter in this part continues the focus on the contemporary port, but examines the changing port hinterland relationships. Theo Notteboom and Jean-Paul Rodrigue stress the importance of global commodity chains (GCC), and argue that the landward extensions of these chains from port gateways are restructuring physical and organisational relationships and are redefining port hinterlands. They suggest that contemporary hinterlands possess macro-economic, physical and logistical dimensions. They indicate that all three are interrelated, and together give rise to complex spatial structures. They point out that these dimensions involve different agencies and stakeholders that may be in conflict, and because they may have different response times to the challenges, major time lags may arise over the provision of infrastructures. As examples, they demonstrate the long lead times necessary to conceive, plan, obtain approval, and build major new port facilities. They conclude by suggesting that a new spatial structure is being established in the port hinterland, a process they refer to as port regionalisation, where inland freight distribution centres which are physically and logistically linked to ports have been established in response to GCCs.

Part 2 of this book is entitled *Shipping Networks and Port Development*. The logistics needs of global supply chains in terms of reliability, lead times and costs have forced liner service networks to become more complex and agile. Shippers take the global coverage of liner services for granted. Port terminals had to adapt to the imperatives of the new liner service configurations and scale increases in vessel and call size. Following these developments, transhipment hubs emerged at locations along the east-west main shipping lanes. The new hubs rely heavily on traffic flows that are distantly generated by the interaction of widely separated places and stimulated by the port's intermediacy.

Chapter 6 by Alfred Baird addresses the development of transhipment hubs. Dr Baird points out that cityports have had to adapt their often-inadequate harbours at enormous cost in order to cope with traffic growth. Environmental legislation and social concerns impose further constraints on the ability of cityports to cater for such changes, both now and in future. One way to help reduce pressure on congested and physically constrained cityports is the recent shift towards transhipment-oriented terminals combined with logistics free-trade zones. Sea-sea transhipment is the fastest growing segment of the container port market. The author underlines the importance of trade intercepted, associated employment impacts, and enhanced competitiveness generated through development of a transhipment terminal.

The second contribution in this part zooms in on the role of Mediterranean ports in the global network. Enrico Musso and Francesco Parola start from the observation that since the 1990s the Mediterranean ports have been offered the opportunity of capturing a growing amount of cargo on the Europe-Far East trade. This has resulted in the development of transhipment hubs, close to the trunk routes and located outside the congested old port cities. Their maritime tradition and expertise combined with strategic position increased the competitiveness of Mediterranean ports compared with Northern Europe port range. Nonetheless, their growth is now facing major structural bottlenecks: scarcity of space in the gateway or spoke ports, inadequate road and rail networks, no barge transport, and geographical barriers. Growth is also hindered by the relative eccentricity from major EU final markets. On the macroeconomic side, the risk of 'demaritimisation' of old port cities cannot be avoided through quantitative growth, which combines a decreasing demand of labour, increasing land consumption and environmental effects. This raises the question of the sustainability of growing throughputs in the long term. The paper outlines some weaknesses and strengths of Mediterranean ports and some possible strategies for their sustainable development, based on value added activities, co-operation between hubs and spoke ports of the 'Latin Arc' and opening to emerging markets in the Mediterranean. These strategies aim at decoupling the growth of value added from the growth of throughput and outline possible growth paths for old port cities in post-industrialised countries.

Shifting the regional focus in this part further north is a chapter by Antoine Frémont and Martin Soppé who examine shipping line concentration and the port hierarchy in the Northern European Range from Le Havre to Hamburg. They use the empirical Weekly Containerized Transport Capacities data to measure the degree of concentration of container traffic. They suggest that a concentration of shipping line services is leading the forwarding agencies and cargo handlers to follow. They call this a process of *actor concentration*, due to the imitation or modification of strategies by the other actors in the chains. At the same time, they notice that the port hierarchy has been stable even with the number of dedicated hubs increasing due to variety of reasons, many on the landside.

The importance of landside accessibility is examined further by Robert McCalla in the last chapter of this part, using two Canadian ports – Halifax and Vancouver as examples. The cases are simple but convincing in demonstrating that the efficient operation of intermodal chains follows Oram's (1968) First Law of Mechanisation: *If you improve a stage in the process of cargo handling you will immediately have to improve the stage before and after that one*. His analysis points out that when sea shipping and port capacities are no longer the constraints, the port cities may face land access constraints, which may probably lead to more stakeholders with vested interests. Therefore, a successful outcome of cooperation through the entire intermodal chains would be critical for port development.

Part 3, *Inserting Port-cities into Global Supply Chains*, focuses on how port-cities are actually inserting into the global supply chains. At the international level, most countries have themselves more closely linked up with other economies as their seaport cities become components of world production and consumption due to better and cheaper shipping. But for one reason or another, the land connections of these cities to their hinterland vary significantly. At the national and regional level, port-cities compete for hub positions and higher share of shipping volumes, as ports are key place for the value-added logistics in global supply chains. When examining individual port cities, we then see the real competition between the global supply chains. It is this competition that involves the cities and ports. We want to know, who are the stakeholders in this interplay? How is the game played? Who gains? And what are the impacts to the cities involved?

Yehuda Hayuth provides a general evaluation of the impacts that globalisation has on port-urban interface. Since the 1970s, containcrisation and intermodality were the two major phases of changes in technology and institutions. In the past few years, particularly since China has become a major producer of containerised cargo, seaports and port-cities have been confronted with a more mature globalisation process. This third and present phase of the port-city interface is characterised by an unprecedented volume of trade and container throughput, record-size container vessels, the dominant position of a relatively new component of the globalisation process – the global port operator – and finally, the intensification of the globalisation process of logistics, distribution, and supply-chain management. He examines the ongoing trends that relate to this round of port-city dynamics, and argues that the most important challenge for seaports and port-cities is to respond to the great opportunities that are currently presented to them.

In the next chapter, César Ducruet provides an empirical attempt to identify the nature and regional dimension of port-city relationships on a world scale. Although general processes can be identified in the literature, regional variations are still not well understood. An analysis of a world sample is undertaken using parameters including geographical coordinates, urban population, logistics activities, port infrastructures, maritime traffic and transport connections. Factors of port hierarchy, land/sea, port/city, and logistics/inter-modal oppositions are extracted revealing north-south and east-west patterns. This chapter serves as an experimental complement to the study of world regionalisation and global-local processes.

Following this meta-geography of 330 port cities is a case study of China by James Wang and Daniel Olivier. They apply and convert Gereffi *et al.*'s global value chain models to examine Chinese port cities and conclude that these cities are dialectically shaped by different functional needs of global supply chains under forces from both the market and the government. The market forces show the different needs of global supply chains (GSC), and the State, particularly the local governments, have put in place sophisticated enabling policy frameworks to accommodate the specific needs of GSCs. Since buyer-driven GSCs differ significantly from supplier-driven GSCs for semi-final products, and only large hub-port cities are able to create 'enclaves' for international articulations, the second-tier port-cities focus themselves by providing subsidies to attract port-related industries. Many empirical details here provide a good support of the arguments suggested by Hayuth earlier.

Chapter 13 by Peter de Langen explores the methodological improvement for better analysing the economic performance of seaport regions, using the United States as an example. His research has produced a number of interesting points. First, there is a negative relationship between a specialisation of an area in port activities and the average personal income in this area. The interpretation of these results is not straightforward but the results provide evidence to seriously question the widely-made claim that seaports enhance regional economic development. Second, the growth of throughput volumes is not related to the economic development of the port region. Third, counties specialised in seaports have underperformed in the last 20 years compared to the average performance of counties in the US. Finally, it turns out that the personal income levels of specialised port counties are related to the education level in these counties. These conclusions provide a basis for a further analysis of the economic performance of seaport regions.

A fourth and final part deals with *Corporate Perspectives on the Insertion of Ports in Global Supply Chains*. The 1990s and early 2000s have been marked by successive waves of corporate consolidation on both supply and demand sides of port services. On the supply side, profound institutional changes since the early 1990s in favour or liberalisation of port industries worldwide have been followed by the emergence of powerful transnational terminal operators. On the demand side, alliances and mergers & acquisitions among mega-carriers have further consolidated the industry as well as port service demand, thereby putting additional competitive pressure on ports. As leading agents of change in the industry, both ocean carriers and international terminal operators' corporate strategies command greater research and scrutiny. This part provides a wide range of views on how such actors carrying ports into the supply chain management (SCM) era.

The chapter by Daniel Olivier and Francesco Parola makes a strong case for private terminal operating firms as spearheading the insertion process of ports into global supply chains through their active engagement with state-of-the-art technologies. Following large scale deregulation of port industries worldwide, the port industry is witnessing the emergence of transnational port operators. The strength of Asian global operators is becoming particularly obvious. The authors argue that impacts of various technologies on micro-managerial responses in container terminal operations have been empirically neglected. They seek to redress this gap by demonstrating that: (1) information technology (IT) an essential and *sine qua non* condition for inserting ports into complex global supply chains and is profoundly redefining the logistics environment; (2) managerial responses to IT is a core component of global operators' internationalisation strategy; and therefore (3) since terminals operators have taken the lead in adoption of SCM IT, the true locus of insertion of ports into supply chains is the individual terminal. This last point echoes arguments made by Brian Slack in Chapter 4 of this book. Their illustrated analysis of inter-corporate arrangements in the way operators engage with modern SCM technologies is particularly insightful.

In the following chapter by Peter V. Hall and Glen Robbins, the corporate perspective on supply chains and ports is shifted from terminal operators to automobile assemblers. They adopt an original scalar lens to the challenges of port insertion into global supply chains. The authors also provide a useful distinction between logistics chains and value chains, the latter being more encompassing since characterised by complex inter-firm arrangements. They use the case of Durban, with a particular focus on Toyota MC, to illustrate the scalar relations at play between local ports, municipal and national governments, global supply chains and transnational firms converging to create a globally competitive automotive value chain. The process is not without challenges, however. Their analysis reveals there exists sources of 'contests' between multiple stakeholders in precisely defining a strategy for inserting local actors into global chains: the port being a major locus of such 'contests'. The case study is an excellent illustration of how power imbalances among players populating value chains of global outreach are actually played out locally.

The chapter by Claude Comtois and Brian Slack offers a very timely overview of how maritime firms are confronting the challenges of sustainable development and changing environmental legislation proper the industry. They begin by examining current international environmental legislation governing the industry. They then conduct an extensive survey of environmental statements of 800 ports and 120 carriers to provide an accurate picture of corporate practices regarding environmental issues. Interestingly, it is found that ocean carriers have been faster than ports at adopting environmental monitoring systems. Notably, Japanese and European carriers have led change. It is found that in the context of global strategies maritime firms are increasingly adopting sustainability as a competitive asset. There are increasingly strong market-based rationales for environmentally-sound practices and the industry is progressively realizing the benefits of best practices to maintain its long term competitiveness.

Overall, the book aims to advance research in the fields of the interaction between cities and ports in a logistics-restructured environment, the spatial, economic and functional dynamics in port-cities in response to global supply chains and the outcomes on and implications for port governance structures and policy makers.

This book fills a gap in existing literature. On the one hand, existing literature on the relationships between cities and ports primarily focuses on spatial issues (including the spatial development of seaports and land use in the framework of waterfront redevelopment) and related governance structures. This literature lacks a supply chain dimension. On the other hand, there is a wide literature available on global supply chains and the associated reconfiguration of logistics networks. Supply chains are being redesigned to respond to varying customer and product service level requirements. Logistics service providers have developed powerful tools to assist shippers in selecting an appropriate network configuration and in site selection. While setting up logistics platforms, logistics service providers favor locations that combine a central location (*i.e.* proximity to the consumers market) with an intermodal gateway function. While a lot of seaports typically meet these requirements, mainstream supply chain literature only vaguely discusses the role seaports have to play as nodal points in global supply chains.

As contributors to this book are from different parts of the world and with different disciplinary backgrounds, we sincerely hope the book will be able to provide our readers with multiple perspectives and fresh ideas for this area of research. At the same time, we are also aware of the fact that this area is also highly policy sensitive. Any impact of this book towards a sustainable globalizing future will be seen as a reward to our collective efforts.

Finally, we would like to express our acknowledgements to Hui Oi Chow Trust Fund, Provisional Contemporary China Studies Council and School of Geography of the University of Hong Kong for their sponsorships to make the conference and this book possible. Thanks go also to the Series Editor Dr Richard Knowles and an anonymous reviewer for their supportive and constructive comments, and Miss Pekoe Ng for her warm-hearted and careful editing assistance.

PART 1
Conceptualization of Port-Cities
and Global Supply Chains

Chapter 2

Supply Chain and Supply Chain Management: Appropriate Concepts for Maritime Studies

Valentina Carbone and Elisabeth Gouvernal

Introduction

Effective management of a supply chain has been increasingly recognised as a key factor in differentiating product and service offerings and gaining competitive advantage for firms (Christopher 1998). However, Supply Chain Management (SCM) as a multidisciplinary concept needs to be defined and 'placed' in the right context before using it as an analytical tool: it is widely used in logistics and strategic management literature, i.e. at a micro-level, as a new managerial approach presumed to better cope with increased competition at global level. Even if it has traditionally been employed for the analysis of industrial and retail companies, in the shipping and port economics literature some authors make use of this concept for the analysis of the new competitive factors for ports and maritime services (Bichou and Gray 2004; De Martino and Morvillo 2005). These authors argue that 'it is somewhat disturbing that a clear definition of SCM and a major SCM role model are lacking' (Kuipers 2005).

Our contribution searches for common ground over the definitions, methodologies and the usefulness of research results of Supply Chain (SC) analysis. More specifically, it seeks to identify research problems that represent gaps in the literature, concerning the effects of the widespread adoption of the SCM approach on transportation providers' behaviour. The final aim is to develop a new research agenda for maritime studies, according to a SCM perspective.

From a methodological point of view, the study is based on a questionnaire survey to an international panel of 25 selected experts, drawn largely from the maritime field. The methodological approach aims at applying the scientific knowledge derived from SCM literature to the maritime business.

In the following section the literature on SC and SCM is reviewed in order to identify key concepts and apply them in the survey instrument. In the second section, the results of the survey are presented. The final section proposes a research agenda for SCM applied to maritime studies.

Literature review

Definitions

SCM is a popular topic, and many disciplines claim it as part of their core competencies (e.g. logistics, marketing, operations management and strategy). The concept can be studied from different perspectives, such as system engineering, economics and sociology. First and foremost, SCM is identified as a management discipline, as indicated by a very large number of international conferences, books and articles in journals on this topic (Halldorsson *et al.* 2003).

As the SCM literature grows both in terms of number of publications and disciplines using SCM concepts, efforts to rationalise the plethora of works have also increased. Numerous taxonomies (Ganeshan *et al.* 1999), critical literature reviews (Croom *et al.* 2000), definitions (Mentzer *et al.* 2001) and research agendas (Cox 1999) have been produced during the last decade.

Supply Chain Definitions: Different Meanings for Different Purposes

SCM literature offers many variations in defining a supply chain. The most common definition (see for example, Jones and Riley 1984; and Lamming 1996) is a system of suppliers, manufacturers, distributors, retailers, and customers where materials flow downstream from suppliers to customers and information flows in both directions.

A more precise definition of a supply chain is from Stevens (1989) who defines it as: 'a connected series of activities which is concerned with planning, coordinating and controlling materials, parts, and finished goods from supplier to customer. It is concerned with two distinct flows (material and information) through the organization.' This definition emphasises the system integration, not only the interface, as the key element in a supply chain.

Most of the definitions tend to include the main suppliers, the manufacturers, the retailers and the customers in order to justify the existence of a supply chain. Other researchers also include the carriers and the logistics service providers in the supply chain (Gentry 1995), even if most of the SCM models still fail to include these providers (Fabbe-Costes 2002). Still others (O'Brien and Head 1995) include governments, both central and local, since managing the supply chain would also include all of the issues associated with government regulations and customs. Due to the very high number of actors comprising the SC, some authors prefer to use the term 'network', which better describes the complex system of relationships between the actors at each level of the chain.

Such a broad definition of SC is useful when a seaport is included as one of the elements of the chain. In such a case, the extended definition of SC mirrors the labelling of ports as clusters (De Langen 2001), where the port cluster includes business units in cargo handling, transport, logistics, production and trade systems. Other maritime authors have proposed a definition for a supply chain centred on shipping companies: 'maritime supply chain is [...] the management by shipping companies of the supply-side of supply chains to exercise control over the entire chain in pursuance of the lowest cost and efficiency gains' (Van Niekerk and Fourie

2002). However, in this chapter, we adopt the general definition for SC, which does not refer to shipping companies as focal firms.

Supply Chain Management: Origins and Fundamentals

The definition of 'supply chain' is more widely accepted than the definition of SCM. Mentzer *et al.* (2001) argue that 'it is important to realize that implicit within these definitions [of SCM] is the fact that supply chains exist whether they are managed or not'. They draw a definite distinction between supply chains as phenomena that exist in business and the management of those supply chains. The former is simply something that exists, while the latter requires overt management efforts by the organisations within the supply chain.

A joint effort to effectively manage the supply chain is needed in order to produce higher value for the final customer. According to Porter (1985), competitive advantage, derives primarily from the value created by a firm. At the SC level, it is proposed that the implementation of an integrated management of the whole chain makes value creation easier and leads to higher customer satisfaction. Value creation entails a higher and stable competitive advantage [as well as a major profitability] both for each actor and for the chain as a whole (LaLonde 1997). However, not all the members of the supply chain play the same role. Some carrying out activities with higher added value (primary members) directly affect the final delivered value to a specific customer or market (Davenport 1993).

The origins of the SCM concept are unclear, but its initial development was in the field of physical distribution and transport, using the techniques of industrial dynamics derived from the work of Forrester (1961). His contribution demonstrated that focusing on a single element does not ensure the effectiveness of the entire system (supply chain). The importance of an integrated approach is most crucial in dispersed organisations, where the effort to integrate processes and flows stands as a challenge for SC managers. In the literature, integration is the core concept of the Global Supply Chain Forum SCM definition: 'the integration of key business processes from end user through original suppliers that provide products, services, and information that add value for customers and other stakeholders.' This definition, extensively used by academics, clearly points out that SCM is based on management by processes and it stresses the importance of the integration of these processes in the supply chain.

The integration issue often relates to Information Technology (IT) development and to the coordination of the information flows between customers and suppliers. The effects of IT on logistics and SCM have been explored in detail (Introna 1993; Hammant 1995).

The term SCM has been used not only with regard to the optimisation of physical and informational flows inside the company and between the actors of the chain (transport and logistics approach), but also as a management philosophy (Mentzer *et al.* 2001) based on cooperation and coordinated efforts to enhance customer service and economic value. In this case, SCM is a holistic managerial concept and relates to the business level and the strategic orientation of the company.

For some authors, SCM is referred to as an alternative organisational form to the vertically integrated firm (Ellram 1991). Even if most authors do not agree with this, the inter-organisational stream of SCM literature is more developed than the intra-organisational one (Cox 1997). Subsequently, a considerable field of interest (Håkansson and Snehota 1995) concerns the identification and the description of the relationships between the actors belonging to the same network, through the analysis of the different coordination mechanisms: power, trust, contract, etc. (Cox *et al.* 2002). In maritime studies, some of these concepts have already been used; Robinson (2002) emphasises the power exercised by dominant firms in logistics to control assets, technology and markets; Bergantino and Veestra (2001) focus on the coordination of activities in liner shipping, through the concept of 'interconnectivity', which leads to integration of companies and networks in liner shipping.

Trends and Challenges for Global Supply Chains and the Transport Sector

Managing supply chains in today's competitive world is increasingly challenging due to high uncertainties in supply and demand, globalisation of markets, shorter and shorter product and technology life cycles (Christopher and Lee 2001). Accordingly, new management models, such as time based production systems and increasing outsourcing, are changing the importance of the critical success factors in transport and logistics within global supply chains. 'Just-in-time' philosophy forces companies to produce and deliver in response to demand, with the aim of reducing stocks and, hence, lead time along the entire logistics chain. To this end, the time factor is crucial and, consequently, so is transport (de Langen 1999).

The outsourcing of an increasing number of activities perceived by manufacturers as not being strategic is occurring at the same time as the general trend of focusing on core business (Hamel and Prahalad 1990). This phenomenon is particularly intense for transport and logistics activities. Due to their essential spatial dimension, provision and control of transport and logistics by the single enterprise is unlikely (Heaver 2001). Time-based competition, increasing outsourcing and other structural changes in the production systems (relocation strategies) are affecting the critical success factors and the performance criteria in transport and logistics, both for individual logistics service providers, such as logistics specialists, freight forwarders and carriers (Shirokawa 2000), and for clusters of organisations, such as maritime ports:

> Not only are providers' capabilities changing but so, too, are their organization structures: a multi-activity group, with some dominant specializations seems to be the common configuration for large providers. Within the same organization different competencies and methods coexist, at both the operational and the analytical levels (Carbone and Stone 2005).

Concerning ports, their complex organisational structure has always been a central issue in port management, and probably constitutes the major obstacle to the development of a comprehensive framework for port logistics management (Bichou and Gray 2004) and a set of integrated performance indicators. Port critical success factors rely on the ability to create synergies, as well as converging interests between the players of the port community (as well as the other actors of the SC) in order to guarantee reliability, continuous service and a high level of productivity. Reliability and productivity depend on a multiplicity of factors, such as physical accessibility and effective information flow management. These are decisive factors for customers regarding the choice of a seaport (Herfort *et al.* 2001). In order to increase the attractiveness of a port, some authors suggest an orientation towards agility, to move cargo quickly and smoothly through ports, delivering a service in alignment with market demand while eliminating waste (Marlow and Paixão 2003a). An 'agility' orientation needs, in turn, a business process reengineering, which is at the basis of SCM.

Actors' Strategies for Supply Chain Integration

Within the network of organisations which form a supply chain, the manufacturing firm has been considered as the key player in most of the SCM literature. Its development strategies, relationship attitude, logistics choices have been observed and analysed in detail. Likewise, the issue of the supply chain integration has interested many authors (Reck and Long 1988). Even if the literature has focused mainly on the supply chain integration process of manufacturing and retailing companies, it has been acknowledged that the widespread adoption of the SCM approach by manufacturers and retailers is forcing transportation providers to rethink their business processes to better satisfy customer needs (Heaver 1996; Slack *et al.* 1996).

A common conclusion of these studies is that the international market for transportation services is becoming larger and more complex. Growth and diversification present opportunities and challenges for companies. Therefore, it is useful to examine the strategic behaviour of leading carriers and other transportation providers to identify recent trends of the industry, relating to the development of SCM (Carbone and Stone 2005).

In the case of liner shipping, two variables have been put forward to assess the degree of SC integration: the level of logistical integration and the level of organisational integration (Evangelista and Morvillo, 2000). The vertical (logistical) integration objectives can be achieved directly through vertical (organisational) mergers and acquisitions, and indirectly through horizontal mergers, which lead to the creation of bigger organisations with more bargaining power and financial resources which facilitate entry into inland markets (Panaydes 2001). The consequence of this evolution is greater market power for large shipping companies *vis-à-vis* other service providers, such as port authorities and goods-handlers (Meersman *et al.* 2005).

The other market players in the logistics chain are responding quickly and effectively through similar initiatives. For example, the emergence of terminal companies whose portfolios include operations in ports around the world has become a driving force shaping the contemporary port scene. In Chapter 4 Slack raises the question about the possible shift in maritime academic research, from port to terminal, in terms of the unit of observation for the analysis of port competition, regional impacts and port functions.

Above and beyond the integration strategies pursued by each of the maritime actors, cooperation strategies, both horizontal and vertical, are being developed. Thus, an alternative strategy in liner shipping to gain control over the entire supply chain, is cooperation, which leads to the set up of strategic alliances with other liner companies as well as with other land, rail ports, inland hubs, and freight forwarding companies (Frankel 1999). Dedicated terminals can be generally considered as a development of vertical agreement between lines and ports (Musso *et al.* 2001). With regard to Port Authorities, cooperation and networking are still in their infancy (Blomme 2005).

Expert-Study Results

The questionnaire used to carry out our survey was structured into three sections: the first section sought to obtain the maritime experts' understanding of the SCM terminology drawn from the literature review; the second identified the experts' opinions concerning the main trends and challenges facing the maritime and port industry; and, the third part focused on actors' behaviours and on industry evolution, in terms of the competitive environment.

Definitions

Several alternative definitions of 'Supply Chain' and 'Supply Chain Management' were presented to the experts who were asked to choose those which best met their understanding of the terms. The lack agreement around SCM concepts is evident from the results. This mirrors the divergence in the traditional SCM literature, where different streams adopt different definitions centred around different units of analysis (actors vs. flows, vs. infrastructure).

Regarding the 'Supply Chain' concept, two definitions each drew 35 per cent of the responses. The first focuses on the 'network of "organizations" involved in upstream and downstream linkages' (Christopher 1998). This definition of SC is one of the most widely used in current SCM studies, especially in some streams of the literature, such as Relationship/Partnership (relationship development, contract view, supplier involvement, etc.), Strategic Management (Strategic networks, make or buy decisions, strategic alliances, etc.), Organisational Behaviour (Communication, power in relationships, organisational culture and learning, etc.) and Marketing (relationship marketing, Internet Supply Chains, customer service management, etc.).

The second definition, which specifies that 'SC is concerned with two distinct flows (material and information) through the organizations' (Stevens 1989), stresses the role of flow and process integration. It is mainly used in the literature when referring to Best Practices based on IT development (JIT, MRP, EDI) and to the analysis of physical efficiency vs. market oriented supply chains (Fisher 1997).

A third definition received 17 per cent of the responses: 'a supply chain is a network of facilities and distribution options that performs the functions of procurement of materials; transformation of these materials into intermediate and finished products;

and distribution of these finished products to customers' (Ganeshan and Harrison 1995). Such a definition pertains to the logistics and transport stream of literature (just in time, cross docking, logistics postponement, etc.), which also embraces the issue of intermodal transportation. In maritime intermodal studies (Slack *et al.* 2002a; Notteboom 2002; Gouvernal and Daydou 2005), ports are defined as 'fourmodal nodes where ocean ships, short-sea/river ships, road and rail modes converge and where a complementarity between waterborne and land modes must exist' (Charlier and Ridolfi 1994). Within this context, it was also argued that, when analyzing which activities are included in the port (cluster), analyzing the supply chains of different commodities is a good starting point (Teurelincx 2000).

Regarding the SCM concept, 39 per cent of respondents agreed with La Londe (1997), who suggests that the integration and the synchronisation of flows between the actors of the chain is at the core of SCM. Shipping and port economics researchers suggest the importance of IT integration within the port community as a tool to increase flexibility and to smooth flow management (Evangelista 2002). Twenty-six per cent of respondents agreed with the statement that 'the management of multiple relationships across the supply chain is referred to as supply chain management' (Christopher 1998). This definition is complementary to the definition of Supply Chain as a network of organisations and is, as well, very frequent in marketing and inter-organisational literature.

Twenty-two per cent of the answers chose the Council of Logistics Management (CLML 1986) definition : '[SCM] … the process of planning, implementing, and controlling the efficient, cost-effective flow and storage of raw materials, in-process inventory, finished goods, and related information flow from point-of-origin to point-of-consumption for the purpose of conforming to customer requirements.' The concepts of efficiency and cost-effectiveness make this definition useful for the analysis of physically efficient vs. market oriented supply chains (Fisher 1997) and for the analysis of port performance within a given supply chain, in terms of costs and lead-times.

The most surprising results regarding SCM understanding by maritime experts is the high score received by 'the management of multiple relationships across the SC,' which puts to the fore organisational issues at the expense of the physical and infrastructural ones in the management of the SC. This indicates that within the maritime field a certain sensibility for a business and organisational approach is being developed.

Trends and Challenges

The key questions asked in this section of the questionnaire related to the 'global trends' and to the 'demand requirements' which are likely to have the greatest impact on maritime supply chains. These questions also tried to identify key factors for port competitiveness and key performance indicators (KPI).

Global trends

Even if within the maritime field, there is a lot of discussion about the increasing control of ports by International Terminal Operators (ITOs) (the second best score in our survey), and increasing ship size (the third best score), the trend which was perceived as having the highest impact on SC is the development of EDI, Tracking and Tracing Systems, SCE, etc. (it is indicated as the most important one in 48 per cent of the cases. See Table 2.1).

Regarding the increasing ship size, some interviewees argued: 'The introduction of 10,000 TEU vessels (and above...) in a near future will put pressure on port facilities and landside infrastructure. This will imply an overall logistic and SC "rethinking".'[1]

'If ports cannot handle the increasing ship sizes then shipping lines will go to those ports that can.'

Table 2.1 Global trends on maritime SC

	I*	II	III
Development of EDI, Tracking & Tracing systems, SCE systems	48%	13%	13%
Increasing control of ports by ITOs[a]	26%	13%	13%
Increasing ship size	13%	13%	17%
Security legislation	9%	9%	17%
Coastal zone planning legislation	4%	9%	4%
Rail Reforms	0%	9%	22%
Truck congestion	0%	17%	9%
Landside hardware technological improvements	0%	17%	4%
Increasing air and water quality environmental legislation	0%	0%	0%
Total per column	100%	100%	100%

* Note: I: the most important; II: the second most important; III: the third most important.
[a] The increasing role of ITOs will be discussed in the section Actors' Strategies.

In addition, security legislation is a source of costs and increases the need of information and flow management. 'It may have serious consequences on SCM

---

1   In this section, quotations refer to comments received by the maritime experts comprising the panel of the survey.

by creating possible checkpoints along the chain, adding financial and operation burdens, and constantly requiring change in operational standards.'

Surprisingly 'increasing air and water quality environmental legislation' was not considered as a significant factor affecting SC, while there was agreement that 'inland port access problems (congestion) are a powerful force shaping maritime SC.' Moreover, 'given the dependence of ports on trucking services and the problems of providing those services in a timely manner (especially on the West Coast of North America) it may be that ports that can handle big ships (ship size increase) won't be able to deal with the increased demand for land access required by trucking companies.'

Two general remarks about the results may be drawn. First, there is considerable variation in the responses and there is little convergence towards a common perception of the main factors affecting the evolution of the maritime industry. Second, there were no significant differences noted in the replies based on regions of origin of the experts, since North American, European and Asian respondents presented equally varied opinions.

Demand Requirements

Regarding the main demand factors, global sourcing and distribution were selected by 39 per cent of the respondents as the first factor (see Table 2.2). 'Transport intensive production systems maintain a steadily increasing demand for maritime transport services. This is supported particularly by global sourcing because knowing 90 per cent of trade volumes circulate via maritime, the expansion of the geographical scope of production creates a growth environment for ports and shipping.'

Table 2.2 Demand requirements

	I	II	III
Global sourcing and distribution	39%	22%	13%
Increasing Outsourcing of T&L and greater reliance on fewer suppliers	17%	9%	22%
Growth of international trade with China	17%	9%	22%
Attention to cost reduction throughout the entire supply chain	9%	39%	13%
Reduced cycle times and enhanced inventory management	9%	13%	17%
Need for information sharing and transparency (tracking and tracing)	9%	9%	13%
Total per column	100%	100%	100%

Global sourcing and consumer markets call for global management of the SC and for cost reductions. This leads to increasing outsourcing of logistics and transport (17 per cent of the first choices), which in turn leads to different chain configurations with considerable consequences for ports.

Globalisation of supply and demand radically changed the former market environment. In particular, China, thanks to the lower labour costs, has become the most important manufacturing centre. 'The 'China effect' has been very strong on freight distribution, simply looking at the imbalance in containerised trade across the Pacific (and with Europe),' However, some argue that 'the role of China should not be overstated as the global economy is entering a recession which will substantially impact trade.'

Port Competitiveness and KPI

Against such global trends and demand requirements, interviewees were questioned about the new critical success factors for ports and the relating key performance indicators.

Table 2.3 shows that the two factors that are mentioned frequently in the literature on port competitivity: availability of efficient port-infrastructure and efficient hinterland connections drew 26 per cent and 22 per cent of first choices respectively. These are perceived as preconditions necessary to favour competitive advantage for a port and to allow the development of traffic flows.

Table 2.3 Port competitiveness factors

	I*	II	III	IV
Stable relationships with the other actors in the SC	30%	4%	9%	14%
The availability of efficient port-infrastructure	26%	26%	5%	14%
Proximity to major sourcing and final markets	22%	0%	14%	9%
Efficient Road Network	4%	26%	9%	9%
Transit time	4%	9%	14%	14%
Number of direct connections to overseas destinations	4%	9%	9%	5%
Efficient Rail Network	4%	4%	23%	18%
Extent of feedering services	4%	4%	0%	5%
Good labour climate	0%	9%	9%	9%
Efficient Inland Water Ways connections	0%	9%	9%	5%

*From I to IV: from the most to the least important factor.

However, what is striking is that the very highest score (30 per cent of the first answers) is attained by 'stable relationships with the other actors in the

SC.' This confirms the increasing awareness of the role of effective relationship management for the success of a port (see section about SCM definition). It means that the competitive position of a port is not only determined by its internal strengths (efficient cargo handling) but it is also affected by its links in a given supply chain. In other words port competitiveness is becoming increasingly dependent on external coordination and control of the whole supply chain (Huybrechts *et al.* 2002). It is worth mentioning that the relationship issue is a critical one in maritime studies, as bargaining power can vary a lot between the different actors involved in a transport chain, thus leading to a high degree of dynamism in the network of suppliers of the main firms concerned with a port (see Carbone and de Martino 2003).

In contrast to the divergence of opinions regarding the previous questions, there was considerable agreement over port KPI measures (see Table 2.4). Port reliability seems to be the critical KPI (70 per cent of first choices), followed by transit time (which can be a crucial factor for ports in satisfying port users) and frequency of services. The other factors scored poorly.

Table 2.4 Port KPI

	I	II	III
Reliability	70%	13%	9%
Transit time in ports	17%	39%	17%
Frequency of services	13%	39%	22%
Security	0%	4%	22%
Leanness	0%	0%	22%
Availability of information	0%	4%	9%
Total per column	100%	100%	100%

*From I to III: from the most to the least important KPI.

Actors' Strategies

The recent evolution of the maritime industry is marked by a significantly greater market power for the large shipping companies (see the section *Actors' strategies for Supply Chain Integration*). The questions in this section aimed at ranking new trends which might affect international port competition, and identifying the most relevant strategies pursued by shipping lines.

With regard to the main trends for port competition (Table 2.5), the increasing role of ITOs has been indicated as the most important trend (74 per cent of respondents consider it important). The phenomenon of dedicated terminals also received a high score, even if some respondents did not consider it a lasting one. In contrast, the experts do not expect Port Authorities to launch new initiatives in the short run to revitalise their role in the SC.

Table 2.5 Main trends in port competition

	Very Important	Important +	Important -	Not Important
Increasing power of international terminal operators	52%	22%	17%	4%
The increasing phenomenon of 'dedicated terminals'	30%	39%	13%	17%
The acquisition of financial stakes in terminal by some shipping groups	13%	26%	52%	9%
Increasing number of 'new initiatives' by Public (Port) Authorities.	4%	13%	17%	70%

Referring to the behaviour of shipping lines, the responses regarding their strategies (see Table 2.6) highlighted the increasing role of shipping lines as integrated logistics service providers (45 per cent of respondents consider it as the main strategy). This new positioning is often pursued via vertical integration (32 per cent of the first answers). Most respondents indicated Maersk as the typical company pursuing such a strategy. However, these strategies are not exclusive, as becoming a niche operator and offering low cost transportation seem to be other strategies that are employed by some shipping lines. A dramatic diversification into non complementary services is not seen as a possible trend.

Table 2.6 Global shipping lines' main strategies

	I	II
Acting as 'integrated logistics service providers' (3PL)	45%	5%
Pursuing vertical integration	32%	40%
Surviving by emphasizing low-cost transportation services	14%	5%
Becoming a niche market operator (ex: region specialisation)	5%	40%
Seeking to achieve market leadership through innovation	5%	10%
Diversifying into non complementary activities	0%	0%

In order to achieve a higher degree of supply chain integration, shipping lines have to undertake different tactical decisions (Table 2.7). The respondents considered that setting up of privileged relationships with selected logistics service providers (48 per cent of the first answers) and the IT integration with the other actors of the SC (13 per cent), are needed to consolidate shipping lines within the chain. However, possible conflicts may arise between the shipping lines and the traditional logistics service providers when the former broaden their range of logistics services.

Table 2.7 Shipping lines' tactical decisions

	I	II	III
Select the key logistics service providers	48%	30%	13%
Establish long-term relationships with customers (bypassing intermediaries)	17%	22%	9%
Standardise procedures and methods	17%	4%	13%
Integrate the supply chain via IT	13%	22%	35%
Broaden the range of supplied services (value-added logistics services…)	4%	22%	30%

The coexistence of different types of transport and logistics providers within the SC requires a better understanding of the contribution to the value creation of each actor. In this study, some respondents argue that the actors who will deliver higher value are those able to offer a door-to-door service. In most cases these actors are the logistics divisions of shipping lines or the large freight forwarders. Likewise, in terms of bargaining power, 42 per cent of the responses indicate that shipping lines have the highest power in the supply chain, while 28 per cent indicate freight forwarders. New service providers which may enter the SC in the future could be 4PL (i.e. non-asset-based logistics service providers), Distribution Centres, IT providers and E-Market players.

Terminology Assessment and Research Agenda

Despite some data limitations, a number of generalisable results concerning the relationship between SCM and maritime research stand out. First, the joint results of the literature analysis and the maritime experts' contributions make it possible to propose a first assessment of terminology, according to different disciplinary contexts and thematic issues. Then, a research agenda is proposed, combining experts' opinions with gaps in the literature.

Terminology Assessment

The SC and SCM definitions which gather the highest agreement among the panellists revolve around the terms of 'actors' or 'organisations'. These are definitions drawn from inter-organisational studies, and are used for the analysis of relationships structure and dynamics between the different actors of the SC. Accordingly, in maritime studies, these definitions are suitable for dealing with similar issues, such as relationship among the actors of the 'port community' and between the 'port community' and the other actors (shipper, recipient, service providers, etc.) along the SC. It is worth highlighting, however, that even if the 'organisational' definition of SCM seems to be widely recognised and accepted by maritime academics, rarely are their analytical tools and methods inspired by the theoretical approaches behind such definitions. More research drawing upon principles derived from Relationship/ Partnership, Strategic Management, Organisational Behaviour and Marketing theories could be beneficial for an enhanced understanding of the SC.

SC definitions referring to facilities and distribution options are consistent with the SCM definition based on flow integration and synchronisation. These definitions are mostly used by maritime researchers interested in themes such as hinterland connections, infrastructure development and land use, and port performance analysis. Maritime contributions pertaining to these streams are inclined to make use of several concepts stemming from the SCM 'operational' research, even if they also adopt some of the previously mentioned 'organisational' concepts. In this way they manage to take into account, in an integrated way, both the technical and the organisational issues of 'intermodalism' in a port context. It is in this field that some synergies could be generated between SCM approaches and maritime-specific themes.

Port Competitiveness and KPI

There seems to be a certain agreement over the two elements which one has to take into account when dealing with a SCM approach in the context of ports. These concepts are hinterland connections (or intermodalism, according to Bichou and Gray 2004) and attention to relationship management along the SC. The following research questions should be addressed:

• Which framework for process integration in intermodalism?
• How to coordinate activities in a port and to implement integrated performance indicators?
• What performance indicators for what kind of performance (physical, economic, financial, etc.)?

In order to formulate possible responses to these research questions, maritime specialists could refer to the SCM literature on performance measures and models, as some of the issues faced by industrialists and retailers (for whom these models have been conceived) could be comparable. On the other side, there is a need to integrate ports in the existing performance measurement models for effective SCM (see Chapter 3).

Actors

Concerning actors' strategies, the following research questions are proposed in order to improve understanding of the network structure of the SC and the role played by each actor of the SC:

- What is the role and contribution to value creation of each actor?
- What are the relationships between the different organisations constituting a port?
- How to optimise shipping lines' diversified portfolio of activities?
- Which portfolio of activities for which strategy (niche, low cost, differentiation)?
- When is it best to establish a separate logistics service organisation within a shipping group? And, which organisational configuration is appropriate for a logistics unit retained by a carrier?
- What will be the consequences of extensive cooperative agreements and take-overs on goods handling?
- How will collaboration and networking between Port Authorities evolve?

As Cox (1999) has proposed 'for supply chain thinking', a key for future research, may be the development of a proper understanding of the structural properties of (maritime) supply chains.

Conclusions

One common paradigm could not be identified to apply SCM concepts to maritime research, because practices vary on a number of levels regarding research objectives and methods. This is confirmed by the high variability of responses. In spite of this, some maritime research areas have been addressed as being potentially concerned with a SCM approach (Table 2.8), such as the identification of new strategic directions for a port within the competitive arena, intermodal transportation trends and the issue of power (within the larger context of relationship management), among others.

The fact that we took into account only the views of academics on maritime research sets certain limitations on these findings. Further studies should address practitioners and should aim at defining a 'business oriented' research agenda. Also it should be noted that SCM (applied to maritime studies) is a relatively young construct and is fragmented. Thus, the results may merely reflect a snapshot of the main issues and methodological options during this early and turbulent period.

Table 2.8 Research context

	I	II	III
Identification of new strategic directions for a port	30%	9%	22%
Analysis of competition between two or more ports	26%	9%	17%
Intermodal transportation	17%	22%	26%
Hinterland analysis	17%	17%	13%
Relationships and 'power'	9%	30%	22%
Policy analysis	0%	4%	0%
Pricing	0%	9%	0%
Total per column	100%	100%	100%

Chapter 3

Global Supply Chain Integration and Competitiveness of Port Terminals

Photis M. Panayides

Introduction

The importance of seaports for national economies is well established in the literature. It has been held that an efficient port raises the productivity of prime factors of production (labour and capital) and profitability of the producing units thereby permitting higher levels of output, income, and employment (Walter 1975; Talley 1988).

Ports have been recognised as the springboards for economic development of the hinterland. On this basis much of the research and developmental emphasis has been on the ability of ports to carry out their functions of accommodating ships and other modes of transport effectively and efficiently. Contemporary developments in transportation however, dictate that emphasis should be placed on the ability of ports to fulfil a new role in the logistics era in the context of operating as parts of integrated global supply chain systems.

This chapter aims to identify the parameters of port supply chain integration, develop measures for assessing the extent of seaport (container terminal) integration in global supply chains and investigate the relationship between port supply chain orientation and port competitiveness. It begins with reviewing the relevant literature including supply chain integration and the integration of ports and terminals in supply chains. The literature review will assist in the development of the conceptual model in the following section by identifying the parameters of port/terminal integration in supply chains, and the impact of port/terminal integration in the supply chain on port competitiveness. The interrelationships are empirically examined via a survey involving a global sample of container terminals. The results are presented and the implications of the study for theory, practice and further research are discussed.

Literature Review

Supply Chain Integration

As discussed in Chapter 2 supply chain management is defined as the systemic, strategic coordination of the traditional business functions and tactics across these business functions within a particular organisation and across businesses within the supply chain for the purposes of improving the long-term performance of the individual organisations and the supply chain as a whole (CLM 2000). The definition recognises the strategic nature of coordination between trading partners and explains the dual purpose of supply chain management to improve organisational and supply chain performance.

The literature acknowledges that the higher the degree of integration across the supply chain the better a firm performs (Narasimhan and Jayaram 1998; Johnson 1999; Frohlich and Westbrook 2001) whereas there are dangers if suppliers and customers are not fully integrated in terms of their business processes (Armistead and Mapes 1993; Frohlich and Westbrook 2001). The findings together with the inherent strategic nature of coordination render supply chain integration a concept of overriding importance in supply chain management.

Recent studies have conceptualised and tested measures of supply chain integration. Vickery et al. (2003) emphasise the existence of integrative information technologies and secondly the existence of practices that strengthen linkages between companies occupying different positions in the supply chain (vertical linkages as in supplier partnering and closer customer relationships and horizontal linkages as in forming intra-firm linkages using cross-functional teams).

Narasimhan and Kim (2002) used three levels of integration, viz. a company's integration with suppliers (measured using six items adopted from Stevens 1989; Narasimhan and Carter 1998; Tan, Kannan and Handfield 1998; Carr and Pearson 1999), internal integration across the supply chain (measured using eight items from Stevens 1989, Narasimhan and Carter 1998; Wisner and Stanley 1999) and integration with customers (measured using seven items from Stevens 1989; Zaheer, McEvily and Perrone 1998; Tan, Kannan and Handfield 1998; Wisner and Stanley 1999).

A key characteristic of supply chain integration is the presence of integrative information technologies that increase the flow of relevant information amongst process participants to facilitate the integration of processes that transcend functional and firm boundaries (Bowersox and Daugherty 1995; Lewis and Talalayevsky 1997).

Customer and supplier relationships also seem to be central in the context of supply chain integration. Supplier partnering treats the supplier as a strategic collaborator manifested by supplier involvement in product design or acquiring access to superior supplier technological capabilities (Narasimhan and Das 1999). Closer customer relationships involve proactively acquiring information from downstream customers about their needs and becoming responsive in serving them.

Seaports and Supply Chains

Traditionally port authorities played the role of facilitator, focusing on the provision of superstructure and infrastructure for ship operations, loading/unloading, temporary storage and intra-port operations. On this basis the bulk of research in the area has been on the efficiency and performance of seaports and container terminals (e.g. Cullinane *et al.* 2002; Tongzon and Heng 2005).

Ports nowadays play an important role as members of a supply chain. In this role, the port is considered as part of a cluster of organisations in which different logistics and transport operators are involved in bringing value to the final consumers. In order to be successful, such channels need to achieve a higher degree of coordination and cooperation (DeSouza *et al*. 2003). The determination of the parameters that encompass the extent of integration of ports/terminals in global supply chains has, therefore, become of great importance for ports.

Scholarly work on the integration of ports/terminals in the supply chain has been limited. Carbone and De Martino (2003) identified the most suitable variables as 'relationships between the port operators and the focal firm', 'supplied services that add value', 'information and communication technologies', and 'performance measurement indicators common to supply chain partners'. The recognition that ports are increasingly integrated in supply chains is illustrated in the papers by Paixao and Marlow (2003), Marlow and Paixao (2003b) and Bichou and Gray (2004). Paixao and Marlow (2003) and Marlow and Paixao (2003b) introduce the logistics concepts of 'lean' and 'agile' operations as key factors in the measurement of port performance. This implies, therefore, that port performance depends to a large extent on logistics measures of cost and responsiveness. Bichou and Gray (2004) indicate that adopting a logistics approach to the measurement of port performance is beneficial to port efficiency because it directs port strategy towards relevant value-added logistics activities.

Conceptual Model and Hypotheses

Six parameters have been extracted from the literature review to make up the concept of port integration in supply chains: 'use of technology for data sharing', 'relationships with shipping lines', 'value-added services', 'relationships with inland transport providers', 'transport mode integration' and 'channel integration practices and performance'.

1. Use of technology for data sharing Establishing electronic links with suppliers and customers enables companies to transmit and receive orders, invoices and shipping notifications with much shorter lead times, which give the potential to speed up the entire shipping transaction (Stefansson 2002). The sharing of information among supply chain partners is viewed as a building block that characterises a solid supply chain relationship (Lalonde 1998). Authors have suggested that the key to the seamless supply chain is making available undistorted and updated information at every node within the supply chain (Towill 1997) and by taking the data available and sharing them with other parties within the supply chain, information can be used as a source of competitive advantage (Novack *et al*. 1995). Information sharing to be effective requires accuracy, timeliness, adequacy and credibility (Monczka et al. 1998). This means that integrated information technology should be central in facilitating the exchange of information among supply chain partners and between ports and their downstream and upstream partners.

2. Relationship with shipping lines In discussing the importance of integration in supply chains it has been stated that a supply chain based on relationships has the greatest potential to result in unique solutions that are simultaneously effective, efficient and relevant (Bowersox *et al.* 2000). The importance of creating long-term relationships in supply chains has also been made explicit by Kalwani and Narayandas (1995) who state that supplier firms in long-term relationships with select customers are able to retain or even improve their profitability levels more than firms which employ a transactional approach. To achieve intermodal operational synchronisation it is essential to have an appropriate governance structure in the relationship between ports and shipping lines (Panayides 2002). Ports that build long-term cooperative relationships will be deemed to have higher levels of integration in the supply chain.

3. Value-added services This variable entails the ability of the port to add value to the services that it provides in the context of facilitating further the objectives of the supply chain system. For instance, Robinson (2002) suggests that ports form part of a value-driven chain and as such they can add value to the goods passing through them. Carbone and De Martino (2003) indicate that procurement and pre-assembly stages are becoming of considerable significance and may well shape the future development of ports.

Paixao and Marlow (2003) put forward a framework that can be adopted for adding value in a port environment. This involves adding value in the context of the different operations, services and capabilities that take place in a port environment. These include the capacity to provide hinterland and foreland for road/rail access; the ability to launch new tailored services and to handle different types of cargo; the speed at which the port can take decisions on altering schedules, amend orders and changing design processes to meet customers' demands; the ability to offer a variety of services in intermodal operations; the capacity to convey cargo through the most diversified routes/modes at the least possible time to end-users' premises; and, the capacity to deliver tailored services to different market segments and to act as collaborative intermodal hub networks.

4. Transport mode integration Ports are bi-directional logistics systems in which they receive goods from ships to be distributed to land (road/rail) and inland waterway modes that perform the remaining legs of the transport systems, whereas at the same time ports receive cargoes arriving by road/rail and inland waterway and deliver them to ships for the sea-leg. This bi-directional logistics system requires a high level of coordination and interconnectivity capabilities within the port system.

Robinson (2002) suggests that ports are part of a value-driven chain system competing with other value-driven chain systems. Cargo flows will seek for routes that offer the lowest cost, ports offering efficient hinterland accessibility due to productivity, efficiency and reliability in intermodal transport connectivity and inter-operability adding value to shippers and consignees in the supply chain.

5. Relationships with inland transport providers Supply chain relationships entail customer as well as supplier relationships. In the same way that ports formulate and engage in relationships with shipping lines, they should also initiate, develop and foster relationships with inland transport providers and operators. As indicated by Notteboom and Rodrigue (2005), regional port authorities and market participants can engage in coordination that can substantially improve inland freight distribution like for instance streamlining container flows and reducing empty hauls. Various methods of networking strategies may be used from informal programs of coordination to advanced forms of strategic partnerships. Central to all forms of coordination is communication and the characteristics of the relationship among the participants.

6. Channel integration practices and performance Bichou and Gray (2004) indicate that port and terminal integration may involve the extent to which the port plans and organises activities, processes and procedures beyond its boundaries and monitors performance in such activities. Their findings, however, were discouraging in that most respondents in the particular survey did not seem to understand/appreciate the issue of port integration in the supply chain channel. Notteboom and Rodrigue (2005) indicate that such practices may include involvement in the introduction of new shuttle train service to the hinterland, together with the respective national railway companies, rail operators, terminal operators, shipping companies and/or large shippers. In addition, it includes the extent to which port management collaborates with other members of the supply chain in order to identify cost-effective and supply chain performance enhancing solutions for the goods passing through the system.

As revealed in this literature survey, integration of contemporary terminals in global supply chains is essential and such integration should lead to performance improvements and to competitive advantages for the port (terminal) that fulfils its modern role in the logistics era. Port integration in the supply chain is suggested to impact port performance. This follows logically the understanding that the role of modern seaports involves integration in the supply chain and fulfilling this role means greater ability of the port to satisfy customers and achieve its objectives. On this basis, it is hypothesised that specific measures of integration in the supply chain will be positively related to specific measures of port performance and competitiveness – the measures themselves reflecting contemporary logistics goals and not merely traditional efficiency measures.

Methodology

Measure Development

The first step in this study was to develop a survey instrument in order to collect data on the parameters that measure port integration in the supply chain as well as the terminal competitiveness performance.

The very basic requirement for a good measure is content validity, which means that the measurement items in an instrument should cover the major content of a construct (Churchill 1979). Content validity is usually achieved through a comprehensive literature review and interviews with practitioners and academicians.

The items for port integration in the supply chain were generated based on the literature reviewed above.

In order for ports to fulfil their performance goals as well as those of the supply chain, they must be capable of attaining objectives of the supply chain and not merely objectives of efficiency. The items conceptualised to be critical to terminal competitiveness in the supply chain era include issues of cost advantage (price), quality, reliability, customisation and responsiveness to customer's needs. Such items are increasingly regarded as critical in the measurement of contemporary container terminal performance and those that clients will be looking at, whereas traditional measures of efficiency (i.e. how quickly and efficiently containers are loaded/ unloaded and passed through the port as quantified by throughput) have passed into the zone of expectation for customers. The performance measures for each item were derived from the literature and can be seen in Table 3.1 in the Appendix.

Sampling and survey

A survey questionnaire was developed to measure the six key variables identified through the review. In addition data were collected on the competitiveness factors for ports and terminals, such as 'price', 'quality', 'reliability', 'customisation' and 'responsiveness'. The measures can be seen in Table 3.1 in the Appendix.

The questionnaire was submitted to managers of 300 ports and container terminals worldwide. Seventy-six useable questionnaires were returned after three mailings, representing a response rate of 25.3 per cent, considered acceptable for surveys of this nature. The survey was specifically addressed to those individuals that were responsible for strategy at the port/terminal. The respondents were asked to indicate the degree to which they agreed/disagreed with the series of questions based on the above-mentioned parameters using a Likert-scale ranging from 1: strongly disagree to 7: strongly agree.

Response bias was minimised by providing assurances of confidentiality and anonymity as well as offering incentives in the form of a management report of the results once the study was completed. Non-response bias was tested by assessing the differences on a sample of variables between early and late respondents (Armstrong and Overton 1977). No statistically significant differences were identified indicating the absence of non-response bias.

Data Analysis

Descriptive Statistics

Tables 3.2 and 3.3 show the descriptive statistics (means and standard deviations) for the variables as well as the reliability statistics (Cronbach alpha values).

Table 3.2 Descriptive statistics and reliability values for port integration items

Variable	Mean	St. Dev.
Use of technology (cronbach a=0.86)	5.2	1.8
Information sharing (cronbach a=0.88)	4.9	1.5
Relationship with shipping lines (cronbach a=0.81)	5.4	1.4
Value-added service (cronbach a=0.88)	5.2	1.5
Integration of transport modes (cronbach a=0.87)	5.1	1.6
Channel integration practices and performance (cronbach a=0.90)	5.1	1.5
Relationship with inland transport operators (cronbach a=0.89)	4.6	1.8

Table 3.3 Descriptive statistics and reliability for competitiveness variables

Variable	Mean	St. Dev.
Price (cronbach a=0.86)	5.2	1.6
Quality (cronbach a=0.88)	5.9	1.1
Reliability (cronbach a=0.86)	5.9	1.0
Customisation (cronbach a=0.81)	5.8	1.0
Responsiveness (cronbach a=0.88)	4.8	1.3

The Cronbach alpha values are indicative of the high reliability of the scales employed as all measures exceed the 0.7 threshold that is commonly applied.

Multiple Regression Analysis

Multiple regression analysis was adopted to test the hypothesised interrelationship between the dependent performance variables and the independent variables that relate to the integration of container terminals in the supply chain. Five equations were built; one each with price (cost) Y1, quality Y2, reliability Y3, responsiveness Y4 and customisation Y5, and with each equation including all the independent variables.

The regression models were as follows:

$$Y_1 = \alpha + \beta_1 \chi_1 + \beta_2 \chi_2 + \dots \beta_n \chi_n + \varepsilon_1$$
$$Y_2 = \alpha + \beta_1 \chi_1 + \beta_2 \chi_2 + \dots \beta_n \chi_n + \varepsilon_2$$
$$Y_3 = \alpha + \beta_1 \chi_1 + \beta_2 \chi_2 + \dots \beta_n \chi_n + \varepsilon_3$$
$$Y_4 = \alpha + \beta_1 \chi_1 + \beta_2 \chi_2 + \dots \beta_n \chi_n + \varepsilon_4$$
$$Y_5 = \alpha + \beta_1 \chi_1 + \beta_2 \chi_2 + \dots \beta_n \chi_n + \varepsilon_5$$

All variables were metric satisfying the conditions for multiple regression analysis. The stepwise method was used with settings at 0.05 α levels. *t*-tests were conducted on each independent variable and *F*-tests for the overall regression. As no multi-collinearity was detected among the explanatory variables, all variables were included in the analysis. Examination of pair-wise correlations indicates correlations below the 0.8 point that may suggest a potentially problematic degree of multi-collinearity. Further examination of tolerance and variance inflation factor (VIF) statistics did not reveal any multi-collinearity concerns. All variables in the model demonstrated normal distribution following a test for univariate normality by applying the Kolmogorov-Smirnov test and low skewness and kurtosis statistics. The threat of heteroscedasticity was checked by examining the residual plots of the actual residual values of the dependent variables against the predicted residual values. The examination did not show any pattern of increasing or decreasing residuals, hence confirming the assumption of homoscedasticity. The plots also indicated linearity. The significant results of the regression analysis are shown in Table 3.4.

Table 3.4 Results of multiple regression analysis

Independent variables	Port terminal competitive performance measures				
	Cost	Quality	Reliability	Responsiveness	Customisation
Use of technology	ns	0.272** (1.975)	ns	ns	ns
Relationship with shipping line	ns	Ns	0.375** (2.073)	0.382* (2.212)	ns
Value-added service	0.326* (2.351)	ns	ns	ns	0.393** (2.966)
F-Statistic	3.251**	3.365**	3.503**	4.713***	5.745***
Adjusted R2	0.132	0.138	0.203	0.274	0.235

***p<0.001, **p<0.01, *p<0.05, ns=not significant, t-values in brackets

The regression analysis suggests the existence of the following relationships:

1. Value-added services and price (cost) in the port
2. Value-added services in the port and the ability of customisation by the port
3. Use of technology and the quality of the port's services
4. The relationship with the shipping line and the port's reliability and responsiveness.

Discussion and Implications

Theoretical Implications

The positive relationship between value-added services provided by the port and the prices that the port charges for use of its services and facilities suggests that provision of value-added services justifies the higher charges. Because the port is perceived to be offering prices that are competitive since it is offering services that add value to the users, unlike competitors who may charge less but not offer the same added-value. It follows that a high price will not necessarily render a port uncompetitive as long as the port offers services that users perceive to be adding value to their business, which includes customisation of port services.

The results indicate a positive association between technology adoption and high quality of the services offered by the port. This association is supported by previous empirical evidence in other contexts, which indicates a strong positive association between technology adoption and quality (Prajogo and Sohal 2006). It seems that the investment in technology is merited by the resulting higher performance (in terms of service quality) which is an important parameter for the selection as well as evaluation of the services of the port.

Another important theoretical implication from the results of the study is the association between the relationship port terminals have with the shipping lines and the beneficial effects this has on the performance of the port terminal. It is interesting to note that the performance measures used relate to responsiveness and reliability and not the traditional performance measures of throughput. Responsiveness and reliability are performance measures utilised in the context of logistics, and the establishment of client relationships by ports has a beneficial effect in the port's function of fulfilling its modern role in the era of logistics and supply chain management. The finding is in line with previous research by Durvasula, Lysonski and Mehta (2002) that identify a positive association between the relationship with the shipping lines and performance effects in the supply chain.

Other theoretical implications which can be extracted from the results are the possible need for a re-conceptualisation of what constitutes port performance and how port performance should be evaluated and assessed. This arises from the fact that there is a positive relationship between input factors into port productivity such as investment in technology or in extending port services and output factors such as higher quality, value-added services, customisation, responsiveness etc.; factors which have not been previously treated as potential parameters for evaluating port performance (and port competitiveness) by traditional efficiency-related measures and techniques. It can be stated that throughput as a proxy for terminal efficiency may not be sufficient to measure aspects relevant to port performance in the global supply chain era. The results also indicate that orientation towards supply chain management has positive effects on the competitiveness of container terminals.

Implications for Ports, Shipping Lines and Logistics Providers

Competition between ports, particularly those in the same geographical range has intensified. Port competitiveness nowadays depends to a large extent on the ability of ports to integrate in global supply chains. This study crystallises parameters that contribute to port/terminal integration in supply chains. The identification of the parameters enables port operators to establish strategies to increase integration and achieve competitive advantage. The results suggest that the identified variables of technology, value-added services, relationship with clients and liner operators, facilitation of intermodal transport and channel integration practices are critical for port integration in supply chains. To achieve competitive advantage port operators must implement strategies that involve the above-mentioned parameters, suggesting that they must look beyond the narrow geographical limits of the port in attempting to achieve competitiveness. By benchmarking their own port's performance on the above-mentioned variables, port operators are also able to determine the degree of integration of their port/terminal in the supply chain and decide on strategies to enhance such performance.

Evaluation of the extent of port/terminal integration in the supply chain can also be useful to shipping lines, logistics service providers and inland transport operators. It has been established that the interest of these stakeholders, being part of the supply chain, is direct as the integration of ports and terminals in supply chains has an impact on their operations and the satisfaction of their customers. In liner shipping, more economical ships and alliance cooperation have lowered the costs associated with the sea-leg and ship operation. At the same time, intermodal costs account for an increasing part of the total cost. The portion of inland costs in the total costs of container shipping can range from 40 per cent to 80 per cent (Notteboom and Rodrigue 2005). This suggests that liner shipping companies have a direct interest in working with ports (and other stakeholders) in an attempt to reduce the costs associated with port and inland handling and transport operations in a door-to-door context. Port integration in the supply chain as hereby conceptualised can certainly assist in this direction.

Implications for Research

The results of the study contribute to the quest for integrating logistics and supply chain management concepts in port research, in line with the integration that has been taking place at physical and management level between port terminals and port users, and the integration of the port into the logistics and value chain. The study identifies certain parameters instrumental in the integration of ports in global supply chains. Further research is required to develop a measurement instrument for assessing port/ terminal integration in global supply chains. The lack of an appropriate measurement instrument has hindered research in the area. Without a valid and reliable instrument measuring port integration in supply chains, generalisable implications and strategies cannot be accomplished.

In addition, this study examines and identifies a positive relationship between terminal integration in the supply chain and terminal performance. It is important for this association to be replicated empirically using different ports and different contexts and performance measures. It is important for measures of competitiveness to be also incorporated in the measurement of port performance. The privatisation of ports and terminals, together with the quest for competitiveness means that traditional performance measures such as market share, sales growth and even profitability become legitimate performance measures for ports. A container terminal with high efficiency indicators may not be necessarily competitive due to the higher cost involved in becoming more efficient.

Conclusion

This chapter has dealt with an area that is highly topical and relevant to developments taking place in maritime logistics, transportation and port development. Port authorities have traditionally played the role of facilitator, focusing on the provision of superstructure and infrastructure for berthing and loading/unloading operations. As such, research has focused on efficiency and performance within ports. Contemporary developments in maritime transport and logistics indicate that ports should play a strategic role as a member of a supply chain that involves sea and inland transportation. The paper puts forward six parameters to account for most of the variations in the degree of seaport integration in logistics and supply chain management. They include adoption of information and communication technologies, relationships with shipping lines, value-added services, interconnectivity/inter-operability with inland modes of transport, relationships with inland transport operators and channel integration practices and performance. In addition, the chapter investigates and identifies a positive relationship between certain parameters of supply chain integration (e.g. use of technology, value-added, user relationships) and parameters of port competitiveness such as cost, quality, reliability, responsiveness and customisation. The findings form a basis for further research on what really can contribute to port competitiveness in the supply chain and how such competitiveness can be achieved and assessed.

Appendix 1

Table 3.1 Measures of terminal supply chain integration

Construct	Measures
Use of Information and Communication Technology	1. We use integrated electronic data interchange to communicate with shipping lines 2. We use integrated information systems to share data/information with shipping lines 3. We adopt computerised port service systems for our operations with shipping lines
Relationship with Shipping Line	1. The shipping line is viewed as a strategic partner in mutually designing the flow of goods and information 2. The relationship with the shipping line is more based on mutual trust rather than on contractual obligations 3. We work together with the shipping line to ensure higher quality of service 4. We work together with the shipping line to reduce costs
Value-Added Service	1. We have adequate facilities for adding value to cargoes (e.g. pre-assembly, manufacturing, packaging) 2. We have the capacity to provide the widest possible hinterland and foreland for road/rail access 3. We have the capacity to launch new tailored services should the need arise 4. We have the capacity to handle different types of cargo 5. We are quick on taking decisions regarding altering schedules, amending orders and changing design processes to meet customers' demand 6. We have a variety of services to handle the transferring of cargo from one mode to another 7. We have the capacity to convey cargo through the most diversified routes/modes at the least possible time to end-users premises 8. We have the capacity to deliver even more tailored services to different market segments
Integration of Transport Modes	1. The port has adequate connectivity/operability for the ship/rail interface 2. The port has adequate connectivity/operability for the ship/road interface 3. The port has adequate connectivity/operability for the ship/inland waterway interface (if applicable)

Relationship with Inland Transport Operators	1. We use integrated electronic data interchange to communicate with inland transport operators
	2. We use integrated information systems to share data/information with inland transport operators
	3. We adopt computerised port service systems for inland transport operations
	4. We study how road/rail transport operators use the port facilities
	5. We listen to inland transport operators in developing/upgrading our port facilities
	6. We meet with inland transport operators to discuss issues of mutual interest
Channel Integration Practices and Performance	1. We constantly evaluate the performance of the transport modes available for linking our port/terminal to its hinterland destinations
	2. We evaluate alternative routes for more efficient transportation of cargoes via our port/terminal
	3. We collaborate with other channel members (e.g. shipping lines, shippers etc) to plan for greater channel optimisation
	4. We seek to identify other competing channels for cargoes that might flow through our port
	5. We benchmark the logistics/supply chain options available for cargoes that will flow through our port *vis-à-vis* alternative routes via competing ports
	6. We seek to identify least cost options for the transport of cargoes to hinterland destinations
Cost	1. We offer competitive prices
	2. We are able to offer prices as low or lower than our competitors
	3. We can offer lower service charges than competitors
	4. The cargo handling services at our port are cheaper than competitors
Quality	1. We are able to compete based on quality of services
	2. We offer port services of high quality to our customers
	3. Our port service performance creates higher value for customers
Reliability	1. Our port services are highly reliable
	2. We deliver the kind of port services needed
	3. We deliver services on time (minimise delays)
	4. We provide dependable service delivery
Customisation	1. We provide customised port services to our customers
	2. We alter our service offerings to meet client needs
	3. We respond well to customer demand for 'new' service features or specific performance
Responsiveness	1. We have fast new service development
	2. We deliver new services to the market quickly
	3. We are first in the market in introducing new services
	4. We have time to market lower than industry average

Chapter 4

The Terminalisation of Seaports

Brian Slack

Introduction

Because they are points of interchange in shipping networks, ports have been a major focus of academic research in marine transportation. A rich literature has evolved drawing on the expertise of economists, engineers, geographers, political scientists, sociologists, historians and architects. Much port research treats the port as a unity, as for example studies of administrative reforms, port impacts, inter-port competition, and port functions. The port-centric character of research may be explained by the fact that ports occupy specific sites, they possess a precise legal-jurisdictional status, and they perform particular functions dealing with the transfers between vessels and the shore.

Such port-focused research has always presented a number of difficulties. A long standing problem has been the fact that traffic is made up of different commodities, and standard measures of weight and value are difficult to compare and combine. Because bulk cargoes are inevitably weighty, terminals specialised in such cargoes will inevitably record higher throughputs measured in tons than others more specialised in general cargoes. The difficulty of comparing traffic totals of different commodities has led to attempts to 'weight' cargoes based upon some indications of the value added they contribute to the terminal. One of the most famous is the so-called 'Bremen rule'. This was developed in 1982 by the port of Bremen and was based on a survey of the labour cost incurred in the handling of one ton of different cargoes. The results found that handling one ton of general cargo equals three tons of dry bulk and 12 tons of liquid bulk. Although this is the most widely used method, other 'rules' have been developed by individual ports, such as Rotterdam, and more recently by the port of Antwerp. The 'Antwerp rule' indicates that the cargo with the highest value added is fruit. Using this as a benchmark, forest products handling requires 3.0 tons to provide the same value added as fruit, cars 1.5 tons, containers 7 tons, cereals 12 tons, and crude oil 47 tons (Haezendonck 2001).

The problem of comparing different commodities has been somewhat relieved by the introduction of containerisation, with its standard unit of measurement, but whose contents may be made up of many diverse cargoes. As more and more cargoes became containerised, so commodity-handling became more standardised. The importance of container traffic over the last 40 years inevitably drew the attention of academic researchers. However, this interest has taken place in an unparalleled fashion, to the degree that research on non-containerised traffic has greatly diminished. Containerisation and the issues around intermodality are now dominant in the academic discourse. This has tended to reinforce the already strong port-centric orientation of marine studies. Most academic studies of container trade treat the handling ports as a unit, in which the flows on both land and sea are routed from a common transfer point.

Containerisation itself is changing, however, and a new set of research questions are being confronted. One of the major developments has been the growing concentration in the shipping industry, with 65 per cent of capacity in 2004 being controlled by just 20 shipping lines. This is having an impact on ports, because there are fewer carriers and they are wielding greater influence and market power. In addition the terminal handling business is being transformed. From the inception of containerisation terminal handling tended to be carried out by local private firms or by public port authorities themselves. Over the last several years the situation has been transformed by the entry of international terminal operators (ITOs). In 2005 the top ten ITOs controlled 40.7 per cent of container handling in ports (Drewry 2006). At the same time shipping lines have extended their presence on terminal handling. In 2005 the top ten carriers controlled 24.3 per cent of terminal handling of ports.

The changes in the organisation of container handling are mirrored by the transformations that have taken place in port governance. Over the last decade there has been a global shift towards liberalisation and privatisation of ports. This trend has been a factor in the transformations in terminal handling, because liberalisation provided opportunities for entry by the private international terminal operators and the shipping lines. The changes in governance were more than an opportunity for certain international industry players, however. They represent a fundamental shift in the concept of a port, from one whose operations are coordinated and controlled by a public agency whose actions are shaped by local and regional interests, to one that is made up of independent terminals whose activities are determined by the commercial interests of its transnational owners/long term lessors.

The trends briefly sketched above have led some researchers to query the concept of a port. They suggest that because ports are made up of discrete terminals, each with their own operators, with different operating strategies, the terminals should be the objects of study. For example, Heaver (1995, 126) has written:

> Terminals are the main focus of competitive strategy, not ports. (…) the most important element in the port industry is the terminal, treatment of the topic as one of 'ports' may have some unintended adverse consequences.

In a similar vein, Slack and Wang in their study of peripheral ports (2002, 166) suggest that 'The "port" may not be the most useful entity in looking at how containerised traffic is organised spatially'. They conclude that 'a new geography of terminals needs to be fashioned' (Slack and Wang 2002, 166). It is somewhat paradoxical that containerisation, which led to the reinforcement of the port as the focus of study, should now be a driver for the consideration of the terminal as the prime unit of observation and analysis.

How valid is a shift in focus of maritime research from the port to the individual terminal? What can such an approach provide? Will a terminal focus contribute new insights? What are the impacts for port cities and supply chains? These are the questions explored in this chapter.

Terminal Entry

Many researchers are already pursuing a terminal-based approach. Several teams are actively exploring the causes and consequences of the entry of different actors in terminal handling (Peters 2001; Ferrari and Benacchio 2000). The research is beginning to show that the dichotomy between the horizontally integrated international terminal operators and the vertically integrated shipping line terminal operators is more complex than considered at first glance. The shipping lines in particular, exhibit a range of responses and have adopted various strategies in terminal management. While many lines lease dedicated terminals, in some cases terminal operations are sub-contracted to terminal operating companies, so that the carriers are not directly involved in terminal handling activities. There are other cases where the carriers conduct terminal operations themselves. Some carriers, such as Maersk Line, have established stand-alone terminal operating companies that manage facilities that may or may not include the parent shipping line as customers. Thus A.P. Moeller Terminals operates the major terminal in Kingston, Jamaica, a hub for several other lines, and until recently not for Maersk Line. While the international terminal operators are seemingly in opposition to the carrier in developing and operating terminals, some new terminals are now being developed cooperatively, as for example the Gamma terminal in the port of Busan which is being developed by three Korean carriers (Global Enterprises, Hanjin, and Korea Express) and by HPH, and even PSA in Singapore, which had hitherto forth resisted shipping line involvement in terminal operations, has entered in a JV with COSCO (Olivier 2005).

The entry of the different international actors has been seen as a process (Peters 2001). While the major developments have been shown to have taken place over the last decade, it has been demonstrated that carrier involvement goes back to the very origins of containerisation, with the establishment of dedicated terminals on the West Coast of the US and Japan from the early 1970s. A recent paper has sought to place the evolution in terms of a stage model, comprising several waves of development (Midoro *et al.* 2005). A wider range of models of terminal handling developments is explored in the paper by Olivier *et al.* (2005). There both 'push' and 'pull' factors are considered, with developments being seen as a 'push' response by certain private sector actors seeking to enhance revenues or to reduce costs (see below), and the 'pull' attraction generated by the liberalisation and privatisation processes that have reshaped port governance around the world.

Governance has been an issue explored widely in maritime studies. Earlier port-focused approaches to governance were based largely on the institutional relationships between public authorities (Stevens 1999). But with the massive entry of private actors into port operations coupled with the reduction in influence of public port authorities, the focus has shifted to consider the role of private stakeholders and the power relationships and dependencies between them. Firm and inter-firm linkages become critical, which draws attention to commercial and social environment as well as the institutional setting.

One of the most interesting approaches to terminal governance is followed by researchers in Hong Kong. Wang and his co-researchers explore the cultural dimensions of the process of terminalisation (Wang, Ng and Olivier 2004; Wang and Slack 2004; Olivier 2005). They bring to light the extremely important commercial linkages and associations that are culturally-based. These cultural relationships are shown to be critical in understanding the process of expansion of the portfolios of many of the largest Asian terminal operating companies that are often shaped by the culture of corporate organisation such as the Japanese *keiretsu*, the Korean *chaebol* or the ethnic Chinese conglomerate. The interest and success of HPH and PSA, two Chinese corporations, in the China market is particularly evident. At the same time cultural difference are accounting for some difficulties encountered between some of the new Asian operators and European port authorities, as for example in Genoa and Antwerp.

Coming out of these studies is the recognition that the financial linkages between the partners in terminal development are extremely complex. Investment in terminals involves more than the participation of the direct operators. In Asia a range of equity, non-operating corporations have entered the market, producing highly complex patterns of ownership. Olivier (2005) has painstakingly shown that the Japanese carrier NYK alone controls no less than 329 subsidiaries, of which ten are terminal operation/stevedore subsidiaries operating across the globe under various banners.

The rescaling of the port towards a terminal focus engenders potentially fertile linkages with the broader economic literature on the firm. The transnational character of terminal operating firms clearly places them alongside corporations in other sectors with a global reach. The literature on the behavior and performance of Transnational Corporations (TNCs) is very rich, and can serve transport researchers with established theories and methodologies that may be applicable to the business of terminal operations. For example, Olivier *et al.* (forthcoming) have suggested how leapfrogging, a process recognised by some researchers of Asian service firms (Li 2003), has been particularly evident in the expansion of Asian terminal operators. This link with the literature is by no means one sided however (Olivier and Slack 2006). Maritime research is beginning to produce many insights into the strategic decisions of companies seeking to expand globally that are spreading their operations internationally. The lean structure of HPH has been demonstrated as a model for rapid response to market opportunities for example (Airriess 2001b; Olivier 2005). These firm-based studies are contributing to the understanding of corporations with global operations.

Terminal Operations

There are several operational distinctions that arise out of the entry of international corporations in terminal handling. As a number of researchers have noted, the transnational terminal operators are taking up leases or ownerships of terminals for different reasons than the shipping lines. A range of factors have been put forward, including the opportunities to apply their expertise, to broaden the base of operations having reached the limits of possible expansion in their home countries, and to spread the risks among a portfolio of operations. At the heart of the reasons, however, are the opportunities to achieve high profits from terminal handling. For these companies the objective is to maximise throughput, since revenues are based on traffic volumes. To realise this requires maximizing berth occupancy and crane utilisation. This is best attained by operating as multi-user facilities in which many shipping line clients are served. Down time is kept to a minimum.

For the shipping lines entering terminal handling, the objective is to reduce costs. With the deployment of the new generation of expensive and high capacity post and super-panamax vessels the need to reduce waiting times for ships and to avoid port delays is imperative. Terminal operations are therefore undertaken for the benefit of the carrier-operator, and are dedicated to the line to ensure that equipment, berths and terminal space are available to meet the convenience of ship arrivals and departures. This is becoming an important consideration in many markets where port capacity is becoming increasingly scarce. Terminal operations become integral to the logistics chain. Even if other carriers are served at the terminal, their needs are secondary to the prime operator and simply reflect additional sources of revenue.

These contrasting approaches to terminal operations have produced a good deal of academic interest. Some see the dichotomy in terms of multiple user facilities versus dedicated terminals (Slack and Fremont 2004). Which is the most efficient form of operation – multi-user or dedicated? There is no widely accepted answer. Some theoretical research suggests that in terms of throughputs, multi-user terminals achieve the highest volumes, because they can make better utilisation of cranes and space by serving many clients. This is confirmed by empirical evidence provided by Turner (2000) who suggests that the port of Seattle could expand capacity with no additional space provision by 17 per cent if the existing dedicated terminals became multi-user. On the other hand, Haralambides *et al.* (2002) have produced theoretical conditions where a dedicated facility is optimal. Drewry (2003) has produced a table of terminal utilisation rates for 2002 which indicated that three of the four terminal operators achieving utilisation rates in excess of 90 per cent were shipping lines. The consultants go on to say: '..... carriers can also plan schedules to ensure a more even pattern of vessel arrivals to reduce the likelihood of unacceptable queuing' (Drewry 2003, 184). Drewry also points out that multi-user terminals have less control over vessel arrivals of their various customers. This point has been made by Midoro *et al.* (2005) who provides an example of problems of scheduling in multi-user facilities.

Olivier (2005), however, urges caution, because he claims that in fact truly dedicated terminals are comparatively rare. This may be true in the absolute sense; many 'dedicated' terminals may have several customers. But most of the so-called shared terminals operated by a carrier are organised with the primary goal of serving the schedule of ship rotations of the carrier-operator. The other users are incidental, having to fit in their ships at the convenience of the primary carrier.

Ports, Cities, and Global Supply Chains

Port and Terminal Competition

A great deal of port research is occupied with questions concerned with competition (Haezendonck 2001). Competition is frequently expressed in terms of traffic totals and rates of traffic growth. Inevitably such totals disguise important differences between the terminals. Table 4.1 compares the traffic evolution of a sample of ports over three years with the traffic of their component terminals over the same period.

Table 4.1 Port and terminal traffic in selected ports

Port	Terminal	Year 1	Year 3	% change
Hong Kong		**14,567,231**	**16,210,792**	11.28
	CT3	1,038,038	1,071,376	3.21
	CT8	1,271,887	1,220,001	-4.08
	4/6/7/9	5,087,286	5,236,594	2.93
Busan		**9,453,356**	**11,430,000**	20.91
	Han	506,000	548,074	8.32
	JCT	1,534,586	1,825,523	18.96
	ShCT	1,547,599	1,963,304	26.86
	SGCT	481,182	976,321	102.90
	UaCT	510,632	549,872	7.68
Gwangyang		**1,080,333**	**1,321,865**	22.36
	DGCT	65,101	126,729	94.67
	GGCT	116,237	224,244	92.92
	HGCT	295,446	270,386	-8.48
	KE	397,550	396,211	-0.34
Osaka		**1,723,630**	**1,609,631**	-6.61
	OT	200,911	381,699	89.98
	C1	183,507	109,517	-40.32
	C2	109,358	119,456	9.23
	C3	322,802	136,582	-57.69
	C4	157,535	146,475	-7.02
	C6/7	394,255	290,955	-26.20
	C8	252,072	101,413	-59.77
	C9	112,011	172,143	53.68
Genoa		**1,500,632**	**1,531,254**	2.04
	MCT	289,937	259,466	-10.51
	SECT	320,000	213,460	-33.29
	VCT	743,910	875,574	17.70

Note: base years are not the same.
Source: Containerisation International Yearbooks.

There is no relationship between the terminals and the ports to which they belong. Furthermore, there is considerable variance between the terminals, so that conclusions drawn from port total traffic hide important features that a terminal-based approach would illuminate. Terminals have different physical characteristics and they are managed by different companies with different management strategies and goals. Comparing port traffic in order to explain competition is too crude, therefore. This is the distinction that Heaver (1995) was referring to in the quotation cited above.

A glimpse into the different strategies of container terminal operators is provided by the work of de Langen (2004). He sought to assess the degree of internal competition in the container handling cluster in Rotterdam, and identified different strategies among the four terminal operating companies. For ECT, the major player, its strategy is based in achieving high throughputs and stressing reliability. In the case of RST, a niche market focus on the North Sea, its commercial strategy is based on specialisation. For Hanno the focus is on flexibility, while for Uniport the major issue is price competitiveness. These differences manifest themselves in many ways, from the kinds of customers sought, the equipment deployed, the way operations are carried out, and on the markets served. These distinctions are masked in the typical port-centric analyses that have sought to place the port in the context of competition on the Northern Range (Kreukels and Wever 1998).

An opportunity offered by a terminal approach is that similarities and differences between diverse functional elements in the port may be brought into closer focus. Port-based studies have become overwhelmingly commodified and specialised, in which research has become concerned almost exclusively with particular traffic components, most typically containers. Other traffic, especially bulk, has been largely ignored. Yet bulk traffic is handled at specialised terminals that share space with the container facilities. Many bulk terminals are owned or leased by private operators. They have been shaped by scale economies for many more years than container facilities. They too are linked into logistics chains. Without denying the fundamental differences between the trades, a terminal focus may provide an opportunity to integrate further the different functional structures into a broader understanding of terminals of all types and the markets and customers they serve.

Spatial Relationships

Slack and Wang (2002) expressed dissatisfaction with a port-based approach on the issue of peripheral ports. In a landmark paper Hayuth (1981) had suggested that congestion in major ports led to the emergence of peripheral ports that would compete with the established centres. Slack and Wang (2002) apply this model to explore the developments taking place at the end of the 1990s in Asia and find it wanting in two regards. First, there was limited evidence of congestion being the driver of development of neither Tanjung Pelepas nor Shenzhen. The other was a spatial problem. Maasvlakte is further from the older container terminals in Rotterdam than Shenzhen is from Hong Kong, yet because they belong to different jurisdictions the later can be considered a peripheral port, the former not. That example is compounded by the fact that a similar set of actors are involved in terminal management. Decisions to develop Yantian, Shekou or Tanjung Pelepas are made by corporations for internal strategic reasons. For example, James Tsien, Executive Director, Hutchison Port Holdings said:

> We have now drawn these [South China] facilities together into what we call our South China Hub Port, which our customers can treat as one single port of call. (…) The globalised economy calls for a change in the concept of 'port' from a single facility in a single location to multiple services across multiple locations. The kind of global service network is exactly what HPH is in the process of creating. (Quoted in Olivier and Slack 2006)

A port approach leads to a particular conclusion, while a terminal approach provides another context and explanation.

A terminal approach may lead to new insights into the spatial structure of maritime networks. The idea of cooperation between ports has been mooted in several studies (Song 2003; Comtois *et al.* 1997; Slack and Comtois 2004). The idea of a regional association of ports has been put forward as a means of rationalising investments and integrating operations. The links between the port of Rotterdam, Flushing and Moerdijk have been cited as examples. The evidence, however, is extremely limited. Port authorities have not exhibited a great willingness to work together, except in very general ways such as information sharing and joint publicity. Furthermore, significant questions would be raised if ports began to cooperate on rates, since that would be considered as price fixing by the regulatory agencies.

Multi-terminal linkages and associations are at the heart of the developments in terminal handling. Distinct spatial groupings are evident, the PSA network and the HPH portfolio for example; these are the modern Hanseatic League equivalents. But the spatial dimensions are likely to be intensified through closer cooperation between terminal operators and shipping lines. Terminal operators are beginning to tie down there carrier clients through preferential rates and treatment, so that carrier x who calls at terminal is induced to call at other terminals operated by that terminal operator in other parts of the world. This has been made explicit by COSCO president Captain Wei Jiafu who at the time of the formation of the joint venture with PSA was quoted as saying: 'COSCO planned to encourage its ships to use those ports managed by PSA worldwide. These would include ports in Belgium, Italy, India, South Korea and China' (*PortView* 2003, 20).

Global shipping networks appear to becoming shaped by corporate linkages that are terminal-based.

Terminals and Supply Chains

In recent years there have been a number of studies that have examined how ports should become more integrated into supply and logistics chains (Heaver *et al.* 2002; Robinson 2002; Notteboom and Rodrigue 2005). Although there have been several examples where port authorities have developed projects to better integrate the port with markets, such as the Port Authority of New York-New Jersey's sponsorship of a barging network, or the port of Barcelona's involvement in the dry port at Zaragossa, the opportunities for most public authorities is limited. Few port authorities have the means or opportunities themselves to directly shape logistics chains. This is particularly evident as an increasing number have become landlord ports or privatised.

On the other hand, private terminal operators have greater opportunities to engage in logistics chains. As more and more of the traffic of their clients is being organised this way there are incentives for them to integrate themselves in these chains. At the same time logistics is seen as an important source of additional revenue, since profit margins from logistics operations are often higher than from shipping.

The entry of the new private terminal operators may be seen itself a product of chain extension, whether the horizontal expansion of terminal operating companies or the vertical integration of the shipping lines. These actors have already sought to extend their operations geographically as well as functionally. As mentioned above, their networks already provide an architecture along which the supply chains are channeled. However, it must be recognised that there is a great variability in the degree of involvement of individual firms in logistics and in the forms of participation. In the case of the shipping lines some carriers, such as Maersk, provide a wide range of logistics services to customers, maintain inland terminals, and operate rail and barge services to inland destinations. Others, such as CP Ships (prior to its take-over by Hapag-Lloyd), remained focused on their core competencies: the transportation of containers by ship. A similar range of strategies is evident among private terminal handling companies, with some, such as Eurogate, being deeply interested in providing logistics services beyond the port and operate rail services, while others remain focused on terminal handling. These few well-known examples hint at large inter-firm differences which may account for many of the distinctions between ports and may help explain differences in the spatial extent of hinterlands, and may not reflect the policy intentions of port authorities. Much more research is required in this area is called for.

Port-city – Terminal Relations

Port and port-city relationships have been a fertile research area, as demonstrated by other chapters in this book. The dynamic nature of the economic linkages between ports and cities are extensive and diverse (Musso *et al.* 2000; Davies 1983). Ports are seen as a factor in industrial and commercial location and the performance of port clusters is seen to help shape port competition (de Langen 2004). The urban land use impacts of ports have been explored from a number of perspectives, including waterfront redevelopment (Hoyle *et al.* 1988), site constraints (McCalla 1999) and negative externalities (Fawcett and Marcus 1991).

The nature of the linkages between port and city is unlikely to be changed by a terminal-focused, instead of port-based approach. Employment, traffic generation, and congestion will be generated by the cargo handling activities regardless. The growing terminalisation will affect how these relationships are managed, however. The terminal operators are almost certainly further removed from the city than the port authority. The goals and interests of the former have a global focus, while the concerns of the municipal authorities are local. While there may be strong governance ties between the city and the port authorities, with therefore an opportunity to influence the affairs of each other, the terminal operators have no political affinities or responsibilities with the municipalities. Instead, urban issues will be negotiated through the port authority, which may have limited powers to influence the actions of the terminal operators. The divorce between cities and seaports is likely to widen further as a result of terminalisation.

Conclusion

A greater terminal orientation in maritime studies does not constitute a paradigm shift, but rather a redirection following the commercialisation of port operations. Terminals are now increasingly controlled by multinational corporations that differ in their management and operating philosophies, and have varied strategic interests. The outcomes of their activities are diverse as a result. This diversity represents a challenge both for the academic researchers who investigate these issues and for the port-cities that have to adjust to the new commercial and governance environments.

It must not be overlooked that there are still important port-level responsibilities. Dredging, navigation aids and pilotage, and, in many ports, working conditions and labour costs are port-based. Long-term infrastructure planning, environmental regulations and community relations are issues addressed by the port and not by individual terminals. However, commercial activities, cargo handling and network links are shaped by actors who operate at the level of the terminal. This new focus represents a fundamental shift in maritime transport and is helping transform the supply chains of the early twenty-first century.

Chapter 5

Re-assessing Port-hinterland Relationships in the Context of Global Commodity Chains

Theo Notteboom and Jean-Paul Rodrigue

Introduction

Given the tremendous changes in logistics, ports are coping with a very flexible environment. This has brought several major challenges in contemporary maritime transportation, particularly over the hinterland which has received renewed attention in recent years. The maritime component of the global freight transportation system has become very dynamic and efficient. As large segments of freight distribution systems are becoming more closely integrated, port-hinterland relationships have become a fundamental component of freight distribution. It may even been argued, and as paradoxically as it sounds, that contemporary improvements in maritime shipping are mainly derived from improvements in inland transport systems. The current technological and commercial context indicates important changes in the conceptualisation of hinterlands. Among the most significant forces that are shaping hinterlands, the fragmentation of Global Commodity Chains (GCC) can be considered as particularly relevant.

The setting of GCC leans on using the comparative advantage of space, namely to insure a better access to markets, labour, parts and resources, through a spatial fragmentation of production and consumption and this while maintaining the integrity of the commodity chain in terms of frequency and level of service. A complementarity between the actors of a commodity chain is established. Through the *principle of location* each actor seeks to find cost- and/or income-effective locations based on respective comparative advantages. Spatially fragmented commodity chains are emerging as the outcome of such a strategy. The function of distribution may also be expanded to cope with this geographical specialisation, with a wide variety of physical flows.

Port hinterlands have become a key component for linking more efficiently elements of the supply chain, namely to insure that the needs of consignees are closely met by the suppliers in terms of costs, availability and time in freight distribution (Notteboom and Winkelmans 2001; Robinson 2002). Through a set of supply/demand relationships involving physical flows, efficiencies, and thus economies, are achieved through the *principle of flow* (Hesse and Rodrigue 2004). In this flow-based system, demand is synchronised more closely with supply, imposing a reorganisation of freight distribution. The complementarities in terms of origin/ destination and supply/demand are thus impacting port hinterlands.

This chapter will assess the main driving forces impacting on port hinterlands and how they are coping with the substantial changes brought by the setting of global commodity chains. Doing so requires a reconsideration of the concept of hinterland itself as a dynamic space where macroeconomic, physical and logistical factors are at play. Each represents a layer of intervention. It is thus argued that there is a *macro-economic*, a *physical* and a *logistical hinterland*. These processes are not without tensions between the major actors involved, such as port authorities, maritime shippers, logistics service providers and inland transport operators.

Types of Hinterlands

As early as in 1941 Van Cleef argued that geographers have not agreed upon the definition of hinterland or even upon its meaning, though it is a word of long standing (Van Cleef 1941). One element all traditional definitions of the hinterland have in common is their spatial focus. It is widely acknowledged that a hinterland is the area over which a port draws the majority of its business. At the end of the 1980s, research on the issue of hinterlands waned. This development was caused by a number of factors. First of all, the static conceptualisation of the term hinterland was increasingly difficult to reconcile with the dynamic nature of maritime shipping, particularly containerisation. Secondly, and probably more importantly, logistics market developments and the discontinuous nature of complex logistics networks have permitted the emergence of a discontinuous and clustered hinterland. Conventional perspectives based on distance-decay are thus ill-fitted to address this new reality. It requires a more functional approach to the concept of hinterlands, particularly its integration with issues pertaining to logistics and commodity chains.

To understand the spatial and functional nexus that hinterlands have become, three basic sub-components can be applied: the macro-economic, the physical and the logistical hinterland. The *macro-economic hinterland* tries to identify which factors are shaping transport demand, particularly in a global setting. The *physical hinterland* considers the nature and extent of the transport supply, both from a modal and intermodal perspective. Finally, the *logistical hinterland* is concerned by the organisation of flows as they reconcile transport demand and supply. Although the rationale behind these components appears simple, the shape they take is subject to complex spatial and functional structures.

The macro-economic hinterland

The macro-economic hinterland is a matter of transport demand in terms of origins, destinations, but also the whole transactional setting in which the actors generating this demand evolve. The simplest way it can be represented is by a set of *logistical sites* with some focusing on production and others on consumption; commonly distribution centres. It is uncommon that activities generating cargo or the final consumers are directly linked with the port, instead distribution centres act as intermediaries, particularly for consumption. The exception is bulk cargo which is often directly linked with ports, but the concerned commodity chains are simpler and involving fewer actors. Logistical sites tend to be clustered often as an outcome of economies of agglomeration and regional specialisation, underlining the discontinuity of most port hinterlands.

The macro-economic hinterland now goes beyond the consideration of the clients of the port, either existing or potential, within a regional setting. Globalisation has insured that additional macroeconomic issues have to be considered since they play a fundamental part in the generation of maritime freight traffic. They include interest rates, exchange rates, prices, savings, productive capacities and debt, factors deep within the realms of economic and financial geography. This environment is continuously changing, which increases the volatility of freight markets. Economic integration and globalisation go on par with the level of political integration with initiatives such as NAFTA and the EU Single Market at the regional level, and at the global level, supported by the continuing evolution of the WTO.

Macroeconomic conditions have often been considered in the concept of port forelands and hinterlands, but always as exogenous forces. In the current context, the structure of international trade has become fundamental to port-hinterland relationships. Since international trade is rarely a balanced account, trade imbalances, especially at the regional level, have a significant impact on port hinterlands since they impose a general direction in traffic flows completely outside the level of intervention of ports.

The physical hinterland

The physical hinterland is a matter of transport supply, both from a modal and intermodal perspective. It considers the network of transport infrastructure, modes and terminals connecting the port to its hinterland; the means to achieve regional accessibility in freight distribution. Intermodal transportation has become of particular relevance to improve the efficiency and accessibility of hinterlands as it links the global access of the port (through its intermodal facilities) with regional customers (ECMT 2001). Already, significant variations in the structure of hinterlands are being observed, mainly because of differences in the capacity and efficiency of inland transport infrastructures (Figure 5.1). For instance the remarkable level of containerised port activity along the Chinese coast is linked with very small hinterlands. This is partly the outcome of China's export-oriented strategy where manufacturing activities are located at sites in close proximity to a port, in addition to the general limited capacity of inland distribution (Wang and Oliver 2006). On the opposite the hinterland of North American and European ports, particularly large gateways, is extensive as it is shaped along long distance inland corridors.

Efficient Inland Freight Distribution   **Inefficient Inland Freight Distribution**

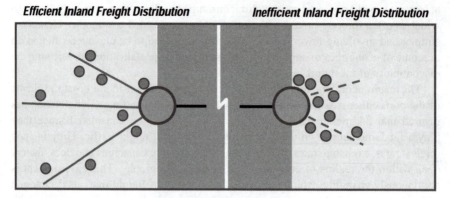

Figure 5.1 Gateways, accessibility and hinterland effect

The logistical hinterland

The logistical hinterland is a matter of flows, how they are organised and how they are taking place considering the existing macroeconomic and physical settings. Main issues involve modal choice and the sequencing/synchronisation of maritime and inland freight distribution.

The competitiveness of global commodity chains is to a large part determined by the performance of the logistics networks as they link production, distribution and consumption (Hesse and Rodrigue 2004). These logistics networks are highly dynamic and flexible as a result of mass customisation in response to product and market segmentation, lean manufacturing practices and associated shifts in costs. Two main developments concern the decoupling of order and delivery and the transition from chains to networks (see Figure 5.2). Distributions systems have to adapt to the new requirements brought by logistics.

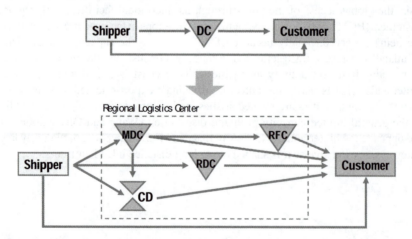

Figure 5.2 Reconfiguration of logistics networks: from chains to networks

Logistics networks serving global commodity chains are being redesigned to respond to varying customer and product service level requirements. The variables which affect site selection are numerous and quite diverse and can be of a quantitative or qualitative nature, *cf.* centrality, accessibility, size of the market, track record regarding reputation/experience, land and its attributes, labour costs, quality and productivity, capital (investment climate, bank environment), government policy and planning (subsidies, taxes) and personal factors, and amenities. Many products need to be made country- or customer-specific (labelling, kitting, adding manuals in local languages, *etc.*) before they can be delivered to the customer. Historically these country or customer specific activities were mostly done in the factory, and this led to high inventory levels. Due to the increasing variety of products and shorter product life cycles, many companies have chosen to move their country- and customer-specific kitting or assembly operations as close to the customer as possible. This implied that the traditional storage and distribution functions of many distribution centres are supplemented by semi-industrial activities such the customizing and localizing of products, adding components or manuals, product testing, quality control or even final assembly. These activities are referred to as value-added logistics services (VAL). While setting up their logistics platforms, logistics service providers favour locations that combine a central location (i.e. proximity to the consumers market) with a gateway function. Seaports and sites along hinterland corridors typically meet these requirements.

Global commodity chains have made many manufacturers contemplate global logistics strategies rather than simply relying on conventional shipping or forwarding activities. Most actors in the transport chain have responded by providing new value-added services in an integrated package, through freight integration along the supply chain. Thus, it has become widely acknowledged that the functional integration of global commodity chains goes beyond the function of manufacturing, but also includes governance and transportation (Gereffi and Korzeniewicz 1994; Gereffi 2001; Chopra and Meindl 2001; Appelbaum 2004). Carriers are becoming increasingly active in the management of hinterland flows in many ports (see e.g. Cariou 2001; Frémont 2006; Heaver 2002), namely through alliances and contracts with rail and road transport companies. For many global maritime operators the control of maritime distribution networks as well as port access (some have become terminal operators as well) has been firmly established. The matter has become to synchronise more efficiently inland distribution capacities with port/maritime distribution capacities while coping with congestion and the costs associated with a high throughput maritime/land interface. A shift to other modes (or other distribution channels) appears to be a suitable alternative to increase port hinterland efficiency.

Elements and attributes of the three types of hinterlands

The concepts, elements and attributes of each of the types of hinterland are summarised in Table 5.1. The three types are highly interrelated: changes in one of the attributes will have a ripple effect on the macro-economic, physical and logistical hinterlands. For instance, exchange rate mechanisms can result in shifts in the trade balance between nations. Shipping lines might react by adjusting freight rates on both legs of the trade route, while logistics service providers might take decisions ranging from simple routing actions up to the complete reconfiguration of logistics networks. The changing trade balance might also have an impact on the capacity utilisation of terminals, corridor infrastructures and physical assets.

Table 5.1 Types of port hinterlands

	Macro-economic	Physical	Logistical
Concept	Transport demand	Transport supply	Flows
Element	Logistical sites (production and consumption) as part of GCCs	Transport links and terminals	Mode, Timing, punctuality and frequency of services
Attributes	Interest rates, exchange rates, prices, savings, production, debt	Capacity, corridors, terminals, Physical assets (fixed and mobile)	Added value, tons-km, TEU, Value of time, ICT
Challenge	International division of production and consumption	Additional capacity (modal and intermodal)	Supply chain management

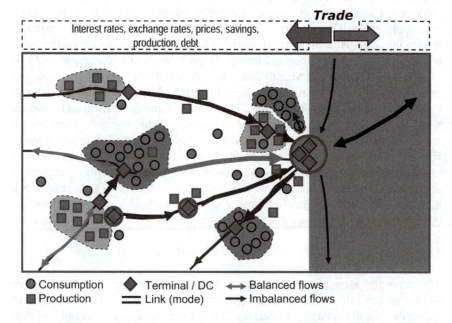

Figure 5.3 Gateways and the new port hinterlands: the 'regionalised port'

An overlay of these three hinterlands reveals a complex spatial structure where logistical sites are often *functionally clustered* (Figure 5.3). In this particular case, imbalances that are normally occurring in the macro-economic hinterland because of clusters and their functional differences (production and consumption) are exacerbated by macroeconomic conditions linked with trade imbalances. The major challenges of the contemporary hinterlands are thus linked with the international division of production and consumption for the macro-economic hinterland. Many supply chains have been extended and spatially dislocated, putting some pressures on the physical hinterland to provide additional modal and intermodal capacity. All these flows have underlined the need for supply chain management in the logistical hinterland.

Processes and Tensions within Hinterlands

The dynamics in contemporary port-hinterland relationships is not taking place in a vacuum, but is articulated by the strategic and operational decisions of the stakeholders involved. These stakeholders approach hinterland issues from their respective viewpoints and objectives. Governments typically tend to follow macroeconomic objectives and are deploying physical infrastructure as a prime planning tool in this context. Port authorities are a salient example of this process. Logistics providers see physical infrastructure more as a constant, because their range of objectives relate more to the operational level, i.e. managing flows that emanate from macroeconomic balances. (Landlord) port authorities develop physical infrastructure (including land) to respond to and in some cases to anticipate the perceived microeconomic strategies of the port users. This section unravels some of the main tensions and issues connected to the types of hinterlands identified in the previous section.

Adaptability/responsiveness of the physical hinterland

The first major tension lies in the limited adaptability/responsiveness of the physical hinterland to changes in transport demand and associated flows. Since ports are the nexus of maritime and inland transport systems, port hinterlands are strongly shaped by port dynamics, particularly over four interrelated layers ranging from a spatial to a functional perspective:

- The *locational layer* relates to the geographical location of a port *vis-à-vis* the central places in the economic space and forms a basic element for the intrinsic accessibility of a seaport. The concept of centrality and intermediacy fits well within this maritime locational perspective (Fleming and Hayuth 1994). A good intermediate location can imply a location near the main maritime routes such as offshore hubs (e.g. Singapore, Mediterranean load centre ports such as Marsaxlokk and Gioia Tauro) and/or near production and consumption centres such as gateway ports (e.g. Rotterdam, New York, Santos) (World Bank 1992). For gateway ports, a good location is a necessary condition for attaining a high intrinsic accessibility to a vast hinterland, which often builds upon the centrality of the port region. It becomes a sufficient condition when the favorable geographical location is valorised by means of the provision of efficient infrastructures and transport services.

- The *infrastructural layer* involves the provision and exploitation of basic infrastructure for both links and nodes in the transport system. Containerisation and intermodal transportation, particularly the transhipment infrastructures they rely on, have contributed to a significant accumulation of infrastructures in a number of ports. This is where the intrinsic accessibility is valorised since a port site has little meaning unless capital investment is provided.
- The *transport layer* involves the operation of transport services on links and corridors between the port and other nodes within the multimodal transport system and the transhipment operations in the nodes of the system. It is a matter of volume and capacity.
- The *logistical layer* involves the organisation of transport chains and their integration in logistical chains. This layer is mostly managerial with a decision making process in terms of the allocation of modes and the booking of transhipment facilities.

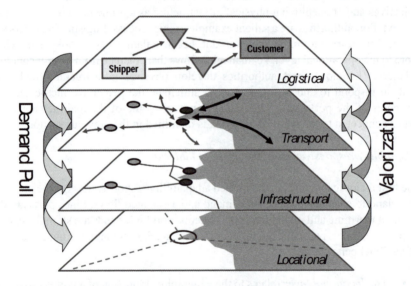

Figure 5.4 A multi-layer approach to port dynamics

The upward arrow in Figure 5.4 depicts that each layer valorises the lower layers. The downward arrow represents the demand pull exerted from the higher levels towards more fundamental layers. In a demand-driven market environment the infrastructural layer serves the transport and logistical layers. The more fundamental the layer is, the lower the adaptability (expressed in time) in facing market changes. For instance, the planning and construction of major port and inland infrastructures (infrastructural level) typically takes many years. The duration of the planning and implementation of shuttle trains on specific railway corridors (transport level) usually varies between a few months up to one year. At the logistical level, freight forwarders and multimodal transport operators (MTOs) are able to respond almost instantly to variations in the market by modifying the commodity chain design, i.e. the routing of the goods through the transport system. As adaptable as they may be, they are still dependant on the existing capacity, but their decisions are often indications of the inefficiencies of the other layers and potential adjustments to be made.

The differences in responsiveness on the proposed levels leads to considerable time lags between proposed structural changes on the logistical and the transport levels and the necessary infrastructural adaptations needed to meet these changes adequately. This issue becomes particularly acute when a paradigm shift towards supply chains takes place (see e.g. Robinson 2002). This observation partly explains both the existing undercapacity (congestion) and/or overcapacity situations in hinterland networks and port systems around the world. It is becoming increasingly common to see transport operators taking control of the valorisation process by positioning themselves through the logistical, transport, infrastructure and locational layers. Global port holdings, such as PSA, Hutchison Port Holding, APM Terminals and DP World, are a salient example of this strategy as they select relevant locations (valorising intermediacy and centrality); invest in the development of infrastructures, including hinterland access; have intricate linkages with (maritime) transport companies and are a crucial element of global commodity chains.

The tensions between the infrastructural layer and the transport and logistics layers can be illustrated by analyzing the development of terminal capacity in European ports. Table 5.2 points to considerable delays in the planned opening of terminals and the actual opening of the container handling facilities. The delays are a mixed result of:

- Time-consuming planning processes involving a large number of stakeholders (market players, community groups, environmental organisations, *etc.*). Unfortunately, quite a number of stakeholders take seaports for granted and are ignorant on how ports operate or in what ways they contribute to the economy as a whole and our wellbeing in particular (Notteboom and Winkelmans 2003; Dooms and Verbeke 2006). Ports are considered by many as nodes that are abundantly available and as tools in satisfying the hunger for consumption of globally produced products.
- Complex environmental legislations which do not always guarantee legal certainty to port/terminal developers. The application of the Bird and Habitat Directives of the European Commission serves as a good example (Van Hooydonk 2006). Additionally, nimbyism has become a significant force sidetracking many large infrastructure projects, ports being no exception.
- Legal complications with financial institutions or building contractors, which can result in a construction halt that can last for months.
- The political aspect related to the provision of most basic port infrastructures further complicates and lengthens the decision-making process.

Because of the above factors, seaports are on the verge of becoming scarce goods. Port congestion along the US West Coast and in many European ports, such as in the summer of 2004, demonstrated how scarcity of port facilities and intermodal throughput capacity can impact a broader economic system. Scarcity in markets can lead to more efficient use of resources, which is on the long run positive. But accepting a continuous high level of scarcity as the new normal might in the longer term have adverse effects on the whole logistics system and eventually also on global production and consumption networks. Therefore, it is a joint responsibility of port managers, policy makers and other stakeholders to foster seaports and the broader networks of which they are part, to look after their well-being and to safeguard their future development potential.

Table 5.2 Delays in the planning process – some cases from northwest Europe

	Development of initial plans	Proposed date for start operations (first phase)	Actual or earliest date for start terminal operations
Le Havre 'Port 2000' – France	1994	2003	2006
Antwerp – Deurganck Dock - Belgium	1995	2001	2005
Rotterdam – Euromax Terminal – the Netherlands	2000	2004	2008
Rotterdam – Maasvlakte II – the Netherlands	1991	2002	2013/2014
Deepening Westerscheldt* – the Netherlands/Belgium	1998	2003	2008 ?
Wilhelmshaven/JadeWeserPort - Germany	n.a.	2006	2010
Cuxhaven – Germany	n.a.	2006	Never
Dibden Bay – UK	n.a.	2000	Never
London Gateway – UK	n.a.	2006	2009
Bathside Bay – UK	n.a.	2004	2008
Felixstowe South – UK	n.a.	2006	2007
Hull Quay 2000/2005	n.a.	2000	2007

* Nautical access to the port of Antwerp.

The limited and slow adaptability of the physical hinterland to changes in transport demand and associated flows is equally felt in inland infrastructures. The implementation of modal shift policies of governments at the local, regional, national and supranational levels are often hampered by the existence of infrastructural bottlenecks and a low interoperability and interconnectivity between modal transport systems (both point and line infrastructures).

As the dynamics in the macro-economic and logistical hinterland is high, long delays in the realisation of physical infrastructures could ultimately lead to a misallocation of resources. Hence, the market conditions might change considerably in the time-span between the planning phase and the actual realisation of an infrastructure. So, an infrastructure investment which at the time of its conception seemed feasible and market-driven, could end up as an investment in the wrong place, at the wrong time, for the wrong market and using the wrong technology. Such missteps can have serious impacts on markets in terms of rates, user costs and competition levels.

The logistical hinterland and a broader functional focus on ports: Port regionalisation

In addition to ports facing a restructuring of their facilities, mainly due to external pressures, their hinterlands are also subject to considerable changes, particularly in the context of the emergence of global commodity chains. It is now widely acknowledged that port forelands and hinterlands are part of the same continuum and that they are closely bound together in a symbiotic relationship. Robinson stressed the need for an integral approach of the triptych foreland-port-hinterland by stating that the separation of foreland and hinterland relationships of a port into two neatly labelled packages represents a false dichotomy. The flow of commodities from foreland to hinterland might better be viewed as a continuum (Robinson 1970). However, this continuum has become increasingly blurred even if at the start they were never considered to be well defined spaces of interaction. This is more so with forelands with for instance pendulum services where ports have become a sequence of calls that can be modified quite rapidly. Since hinterlands are at priori serviced by inland transport systems, and thus more bound to the friction of distance, they have a more cohesive spatial structure.

Changing port-hinterland relations have a clear impact on port development patterns. The performance of seaports is strongly entwined with the development and performance of associated inland networks that give access to cargo bases in the hinterland. Load centres are only as competitive as the inland and relay links that connect to it. To reflect changes in port-hinterland dynamics, Notteboom and Rodrigue (2005) introduced a regionalisation phase in port and port system development by extending existing spatial models of Taaffe *et al.* (1963), Hayuth (1981) and Barke (1986). Regionalisation expands the hinterland reach of the port through a number of strategies linking it more closely to inland freight distribution centres. The phase of regionalisation brings the perspective of port development to a higher geographical scale, i.e. beyond the port perimeter. The port regionalisation phase is characterised by a strong functional interdependency and even joint development of a specific load centre and (selected) multimodal logistics platforms in its hinterland, ultimately leading to the formation of a regional load centre network or logistics pole (Figure 5.5). The port system consequently adapts to the imperatives of distribution systems as supply chain management strategies finally permeate to less dynamic layers (transport, infrastructure and even locational).

An important driver for the creation of regional load centre networks and logistics poles relates to the requirements imposed by global production and consumption networks. No single locality can service efficiently the distribution requirements of a complex web of activities. Port regionalisation permits the development of a distribution network that corresponds more closely to fragmented production and consumption systems.

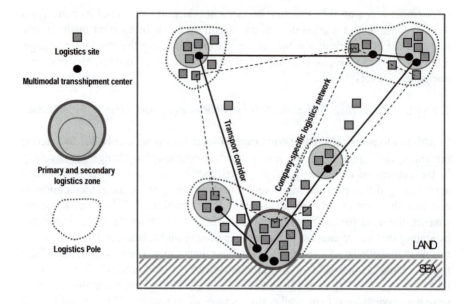

Figure 5.5 Port regionalisation and the development of logistics poles

The transition towards the port regionalisation phase is a gradual and market-driven process that mirrors the increased focus of market players on logistics integration. In the regionalisation phase it is increasingly being acknowledged that land transport forms an important target for reducing logistics costs. The responses to these challenges go beyond the traditional perspectives centred on the port itself. Regionalisation as such provides a strategic answer to the imperatives of the inland distribution segment of the supply chain in terms of improving its efficiency, enhancing logistics integration and reducing distribution costs.

Another factor having a major impact on port development dynamics are local constraints. Ports, especially large gateways, are facing a wide array of local constraints that impair their growth and efficiency. The lack of available land for expansion is among one of the most acute problems, an issue exacerbated by the deepwater requirements for handling larger ships. Increased port traffic may also lead to diseconomies as local road and rail systems are heavily burdened. Environmental constraints and local opposition to port development are also of significance. Port regionalisation thus enables to partially circumscribe local constraints by externalising them.

Many ports around the world are reaching a stage of regionalisation in which market forces gradually shape regional load centre networks with varying degrees of formal linkages between the nodes of the observed networks.

One of the problems port authorities are facing relates to the infrastructural part of the port regionalisation phase. Port authorities try to enhance the intermodal capacity of the port with a heavy reliance on the performance of infrastructures and transport services. However, the manoeuvrability offered to port authorities seems to be restricted. First of all, the hinterland infrastructure level is dominated by public authorities who have to take into account social and political aspects and financial limitations in the decision making process. Secondly, the logistical hinterland is dominated by market players, which under normal circumstances do not have to give account to the port authority.

Landlord port authorities are very dependent on the government for guaranteeing the maritime access and land access to the port. The dispersion of responsibilities among several government departments and ministries makes it very difficult to develop an integrated intermodal transport policy and obliges the port authorities to design their lobbying strategies accordingly, involving a large number of departments of the local, regional, national and supranational government agencies. The situation becomes even more complicated when considering the involvement of local and regional governments in the development of logistics zones and inland terminals. In summary, the powers of port authorities in developing hinterland infrastructure are limited. In most cases, the role of the port authority is restricted to initiator and facilitator of the necessary infrastructures that should guarantee a maximum of land accessibility in relation to the logistics pole.

The logistical hinterland facing the macroeconomic reality: the repositioning of containers

Port hinterlands around the world have been shaped by powerful macroeconomic forces. With global trade imbalances, the logistical hinterland has been facing acute pressures to cope with disequilibrium in transport flows. For example, the US-Asia imbalance in container flows is particularly revealing; containerised exports have simply not kept pace with imports. In recent years containerised freight flows between Asia and Europe have become three times as voluminous as containerised flows between Europe and the United States. For the United States, this implied an imbalance of about 11.1 million TEU with Asia and Europe in 2005, which has grown substantially in the last 10 years. The outcome are rate imbalances across the Pacific as it costs more per TEU for westbound flows than for eastbound flows, making freight planning a complex task for container shipping companies. About 70 per cent of the slots of containerships leaving the United States were empty in 2005 (Boile 2006). Thus, production and trade imbalances in the global economy are clearly reflected in physical flows and transport rates. The impacts on the geography of maritime transportation are major, requiring a reassessment of their strategies in terms of port calls and hinterland transportation.

As such, the repositioning of empty containers is one of the most complex problem concerning global freight distribution, an issue being underlined by the fact that the equivalent of about 2.5 million TEU of containers (USA) are being stored empty, waiting to be used. The major causes of this problem include:

- *Trade imbalances.* They are probably the most important source in the accumulation of empty containers in the global economy. A country/region that imports more than it exports will face the systematic accumulation of empty containers, while a country/region that imports more than it exports will face a shortage of containers. If this situation endures, a repositioning of large amounts of containers will be required between the two trade partners, involving higher transportation costs and tying up existing distribution capacities.

- *Repositioning costs.* They include a combination of inland transport and international transport costs. If they are low enough, a trade imbalance could endure without much of an impact as containers get repositioned. Repositioning costs can also get lower if imbalances are acute as carriers (and possibly terminal operators) will offer discounts for flows in the opposite direction of dominant flows.
- *Manufacturing and leasing costs.* If the costs of manufacturing new containers or leasing existing units are cheaper than repositioning them, which is particularly possible over long distances, then an accumulation can happen. Inversely, higher manufacturing or leasing costs may favour the repositioning of empty containers.
- *Usage preferences.* A large number of shipping lines use containers as a way of branding the company name. This observation combined with the reluctance of shipping lines to share market information on container positions and quantities, makes it very difficult to establish container pools or to widely introduce the grey box concept.

The repositioning of empty containers is becoming a logistical challenge, particularly in North America where imbalances are taking dramatic proportions. At start, the causes are linked with the macro-economic hinterland where acute trade imbalances are forcing an accumulation of empty containers in the United States at the rate of 150,000 TEU per week. The problem is also exacerbated in recent years by the comparative costs of long distance repositioning versus container manufacturing costs. The manufacturing alternative has often been made more attractive than repositioning, particularly in the case of China. Container repositioning is itself a multi-scale problem. The lower the repositioning scale the more sustainable container repositioning is. Three scales can be considered:

- *Local repositioning* occurs regularly as containers are reshuffled between locations where they are emptied to those where they are filled. It is of short duration with limited use of storages facilities since containers are simply in queue at the consignee or the consigner, especially if they are managed by the same freight distributor. Massive local repositioning is very common in gateway regions with multiple load centres. For instance, the container exchanges between Antwerp and Rotterdam, both located in the Rhine-Scheldt Delta and only 100 km apart, amounted to some 1 million TEU in 2004. About 30 per cent of these flows involved the repositioning of empties, as Rotterdam is a major import port and Antwerp is more export-driven.
- *Regional repositioning* involves industrial and consumption regions where there are imbalances, often the outcome of economic specialisation. For instance, a metropolitan area having a marked service function may be a net importer of containers while nearby area may have a specialisation in

manufacturing, implying a status of net exporter. The matter then becomes the repositioning of the surplus containers from one part of the region to the other. This may involve a longer time period, due to the scale and scope of repositioning and often requires the usage of specialised short duration storage facilities. This scale offers opportunities for freight forwarders to establish strategies such as dedicated empty container flows and storage depots at suitable locations. Sometimes very simple coordination actions can substantially improve inland freight distribution, with benefits for all parties involved. In the Netherlands, for instance, the Rotterdam port authority, regional authorities and market parties worked out a better streamlining of container flows by barge. Import-dominated locations in the hinterland were linked to export-dominated locations by barge, creating a loop system resulting in shorter distances and considerable savings in costs due to the reduction of empty hauls (Figure 5.6).

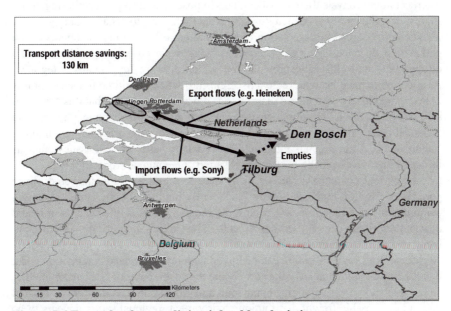

Figure 5.6 Example of streamlining inland box logistics

- *Global repositioning* is the outcome of systematic macroeconomic imbalances between trade partners, as exemplified by China and the United States. Such a repositioning scale is obviously the most costly and time consuming as it ties up substantial storage capacity, in proportion to the trade imbalance. Significant inland freight distribution capacities are also wasted since long distance trade, especially concerning manufactured products, tend to involve a wide arrays of destinations in a national economy. This is paradoxical as maritime container shipping capacity will be readily available for global repositioning, but high inland freight transport costs could limit the amount of empty containers reaching the vicinity of a container port. It may even force an over supply of containers as the trade partner having a net deficit of containers (exporter) may find it more convenient to manufacture new containers than to reposition existing units, which disrupts the container leasing market. In the United States particularly, the macroeconomic imbalances forbid any short term solutions to this problem. In fact, those imbalances are exacerbating repositioning costs.

Conclusions

This chapter underlines the need to reassess port-hinterland relationships. The conventional spatial representation of hinterlands is being challenged by new functional realities notably with the emergence of global commodity chains. Given this paradigm shift, port-hinterlands can be represented within three dimensions: macroeconomic, physical and logistical. This imposes a broader perspective regarding supply, demand and their related flows. Stakeholders have to act accordingly.

The conventional representation of a hinterland, often linking the clients of the port with a distance decay perspective, is being replaced with one where spatial discontinuity and clustering prevails, but which is more functionally integrated. As such, ports have become regionalised entities, where maritime transportation is linked more closely with inland distribution. It was demonstrated that this paradigm shift has given rise to mounting tensions between the macroeconomic, physical and logistical layers, inviting port authorities, market players and other port community stakeholders to develop an integrated approach towards critical issues such as infrastructure development, port regionalisation and container repositioning.

The current context also leaves many questions and issues unanswered. Since port regionalisation involves a more functionally integrated hinterland, substantial commitments in terms of access need to be secured, such as investments in inland distribution (load centres) or agreements with inland freight forwarders (rail, barge and truck operators). The outcome is commonly the setting of high capacity corridors. Thus, regionalisation can be linked with less hinterland competition and a more secure customer base for the port. While the development of global commodity chains, global maritime shipping companies and global port operators are associated with a very flexible freight distribution environment, regionalisation appears to be a strategy where ports are coping through spatial fixity. The role of port authorities remains to be seen in such a setting which goes beyond what they would conventionally consider as their jurisdiction, both from a geographical and functional perspective. At an even wider scale, to what extent global maritime transport companies and port operators will be able to control segments of the commodity chains, particularly over port hinterlands?

PART 2
Shipping Networks and Port Development

Chapter 6

The Development of Global Container Transhipment Terminals

Alfred J. Baird

Introduction

The rapid increase in world container port traffic has led to ongoing demands for additional container port capacity. This analysis evaluates development of world container port traffic by country and region over the last ten years or so. All major world container ports are considered, highlighting the growing incidence of transhipment. A survey of these ports undertaken by the author further emphasises the impact this has had on the need for new port capacity geared towards serving transhipment markets.

Development of new types of specialised container transhipment ports has been an important feature of the container port market over the last ten years. This analysis assesses important ratios in relation to TEU-per-capita and container trade (value)-per-capita for the world's major economies. This permits evaluation of differences at national, as well as at port level, highlighting the importance of container transhipment ports in this respect.

The analysis illustrates the emerging significance of transhipment ports compared with what might be regarded as traditional city ports in terms of trade and logistics capability. It further signals the significant evolving role of transhipment ports in relation to the movement of global trade flows, as well as the advantages that national governments derive through promotion of container transhipment activity on their territory.

World Container Port Traffic

For this study container traffic data was obtained for 60 countries for the years 1995 and 2003. In 1995, these 60 countries together accounted for 96.5 per cent of world container traffic, totalling 137.2 million TEU.[1] By 2003, world container traffic rose by 121 per cent to reach 303.1 million TEU, with these same 60 countries accounting for 97.4 per cent of the market.

Countries experiencing the most significant percentage growth rates between 1995 and 2003 were Oman (+2250.1 per cent) and Bahamas (+957.9 per cent), coincidentally both reflecting the opening of new bespoke transhipment ports at

---

1 TEU = twenty-foot container equivalent.

Salalah and Freeport respectively. Other significant growth rates were experienced in Vietnam (+778.4 per cent), Colombia (+563.5 per cent), Iran (+560.4 per cent), Bangladesh (+525.2 per cent), and Russia (+466.5 per cent), although in volume terms many of these are from a low base.

The largest volume increase was experienced by China, where ports saw an increase from 17.2 million TEU to 61.6 million TEU, a rise of 257.6 per cent. This made Chinese port volumes almost double that of second placed country, the USA. It also meant that Chinese ports accounted for 20.3 per cent of world port container traffic in 2003. Average growth over the 1995–2003 period across all 60 countries was 234.3 per cent.

A number of more mature economies, by comparison, experienced moderate growth rates between 1995–2003, for example, USA (+70.9 per cent), Japan (+37.4 per cent), Netherlands (+48.2 per cent), and UK (+51 per cent). Singapore's low growth rate of 55.7 per cent during 1995–2003 illustrates difficulties in expanding further from a high base.

More rapid growth rates were experienced by countries like South Korea (+188.6 per cent), Germany (+136 per cent), Malaysia (385.3 per cent), Italy (183.2 per cent), Spain (+132.7 per cent), Belgium (+129 per cent), Brazil (+206.4 per cent), and India (+187.9 per cent). Other notable increases were recorded by Turkey, Saudi Arabia, Greece, Mexico, Panama, Canary Islands, Malta, Jamaica, and Mauritius. Countries experiencing higher growth rates tend not unexpectedly to be the same locations where most new container terminal capacity has been provided over the past decade or so.

Combined volumes for the top-20 countries totalled some 242.3 million TEU in 2003, equivalent to 80 per cent of total world container port traffic. This represented little difference in the share held by these same 20 countries since 1995, at that time equivalent to 81 per cent (i.e.110.6m TEU).

Table 6.1 indicates the regional split of global container port activity for the years 1997 until 2003. The main trend here is the ongoing increase in the share of the Far East, particularly China, from 27.8 per cent in 1997 to 34.3 per cent in 2003. Taking all Asia together (i.e. Far East, South and South East Asia) this region as a whole accounted for almost 51 per cent of total world container port traffic in 2003, compared with 45.1 per cent in 1997.

North America and West Europe have both lost share, though South Europe appears to have maintained a better position primarily due to the development there of several new transhipment terminals. This is reflected in relatively higher country growth rates experienced by Italy, Spain and Malta in particular.

Essentially, one half of world container port traffic is concentrated in Asia, with almost one third in North America and West Europe, and the remainder split between other regions. Between 1997 and 2003, the share in other regions has tended to increase in the Mid-East and Eastern Europe, the latter from a very low base, whilst being relatively stable in Latin America, Oceania and Africa.

**Table 6.1 Regional share of global container activity, 1997–2003
(TEU port handling moves, including empties and transhipment)**

	1997	1998	1999	2000	2001	2002	2003
North America	14.2%	13.9%	13.6%	13.1%	12.6%	12.4%	11.8%
West Europe	22.8%	23.3%	22.5%	22.0%	21.3%	20.8%	19.8%
North Europe	*14.6%*	*14.3%*	*14.0%*	*13.5%*	*12.9%*	*12.5%*	*11.8%*
South Europe	*8.2%*	*9.0%*	*8.5%*	*8.5%*	*8.4%*	*8.3%*	*8.0%*
Far East	27.8%	27.4%	28.9%	30.2%	30.4%	31.7%	34.3%
South East Asia	14.8%	14.7%	14.4%	14.6%	14.9%	14.9%	14.3%
Mid-East	4.6%	4.6%	4.8%	4.7%	5.0%	4.9%	5.1%
Latin America	7.4%	7.9%	7.7%	7.6%	7.6%	7.0%	6.7%
Caribbean/C.America	*3.9%*	*4.3%*	*4.3%*	*4.2%*	*4.2%*	*3.8%*	*3.6%*
South America	*3.5%*	*3.6%*	*3.4%*	*3.3%*	*3.4%*	*3.2%*	*3.1%*
Oceania	2.2%	2.2%	2.2%	2.1%	2.1%	2.2%	2.0%
South Asia	2.5%	2.4%	2.4%	2.3%	2.4%	2.4%	2.2%
Africa	3.2%	3.0%	3.0%	3.0%	3.1%	3.1%	3.1%
Eastern Europe	0.5%	0.5%	0.5%	0.5%	0.6%	0.6%	0.7%
World	100%	100%	100%	100%	100%	100%	100%

Source: Drewry Container Market Quarterly, June 2004.

Major World Container Ports

Traffic at the top-100 container ports increased from 112.1 million TEU in 1995 to 289.9 million TEU in 2004, a rise of 159 per cent. The total world container port market in 2004 was 354.5 million TEU, which implies that the top-100 container ports accounted for an estimated 82-per-cent share of the global market. Some 76 of the top-100 container ports each handled in excess of 1.0 million TEU in 2004, compared to just 32 ports handling over 1.0 million TEU in 1995.

Shanghai recorded the biggest increase of any port over the 1995–2004 period, with throughput rising 853 per cent from 1.5 million TEU to 14.6 million TEU, propelling that port from 19th to 3rd place in the world. Given continuation of such high growth rates, added to the development of the new offshore port near Shanghai at Yangshan Island, as well as more moderate growth rates experienced at Hong Kong and Singapore, it would seem very likely that Shanghai will become the world's number one container port very soon, probably before 2010. The port with the second fastest growth rate over this period was Xiamen, also in China, the latter recording a rise of 773 per cent to 2.9 million TEU.

In North America, ports experiencing good growth rates over the 1995–2004 period included Los Angeles (+191 per cent) and Vancouver (+235 per cent). Highest growth ports in the Mid-East were Dubai (+210 per cent), Jeddah (+205 per cent), Bandar Abbas (+584 per cent), and Port Said (+769 per cent). In Latin America high growth ports included Panama (+398 per cent), Kingston (204 per cent), Buenos Aires (+303 per cent), Callao (+550 per cent), and Limon-Moin (+233 per cent). In Europe the highest growth ports were Valencia (+218 per cent), Malta (+199 per cent), Las Palmas (+294 per cent), Ambarli (+320 per cent), and St. Petersburg (+749 per cent). Elsewhere, in Asia, the highest growth ports included Port Klang (+359 per cent), Tianjin (+443 per cent), Laem Chabang (+585 per cent), Jawaharlal Nehru (+358 per cent), Surabaya (+497 per cent), Incheon (+835 per cent), and Fuzhou (+280 per cent).

In 2004 there were six Chinese ports within the top-20 container ports – Hong Kong, Shanghai, Shenzhen, Qingdao, Ningbo, and Tianjin – which together accounted for over 60.0 million TEU. Given anticipated continued high growth rates, these ports will probably be joined in the top-20 by two more Chinese ports – Guangzhou and Xiamen – within the next couple of years, giving China eight ports in the top-20.

Fourteen brand new major ports have opened for business since 1995, all of which have developed sufficiently rapidly to propel them into the top-100 port rankings. Indeed, from a zero start, the rapid growth rate of these ports has been staggering. This is notwithstanding the ongoing development of new terminals within existing ports or port areas. Nevertheless, the creation and rapid development of entirely new major seaports merits separate analysis.

The leading new port in this category is Shenzhen (port area), which in 2004 recorded a throughput of 13.7 million TEU, making it the 4th largest container port in the world. Within the top-20 there are three new ports that have been developed since 1995, all of which are in China – Shenzhen, Qingdao, and Ningbo – reflecting the very significant growth in trade experienced by that country. A 4th new Chinese port, Guangzhou, lies just outside the top-20 at number 22.

Aside from the new Chinese gateway[2] ports, a common factor associated with most of the other new ports created since 1995 is that they tend to have a primary focus on transhipment markets. For example, new ports with a very high container transhipment incidence (shown in brackets) are – Tanjung Pelepas (96 per cent), Gioia Tauro (95 per cent), Salalah (95 per cent), Freeport (98 per cent), and Taranto (86 per cent). Further new transhipment ports have opened since 2004, including Cauceda in the Dominican Republic, and Suez Canal Container terminal (SCCT) at Port Said East, with work now starting on a new terminal in Tangier, at the point where the Atlantic Ocean meets the Mediterranean Sea.

Other major new transhipment hubs are being proposed. State-owned China Shipping Group is currently evaluating a project to develop a new container transhipment terminal on the Greek island of Crete (Lowry 2005). This followed visits by China Shipping to a number of European locations to review potential locations for container transhipment. According to China Shipping, the geographical location of Crete makes it an ideal choice to develop a transhipment centre there to serve the East Mediterranean, the Black Sea and the Adriatic Sea. The main focus

---

2   In this regard, a gateway port implies a port serving a large hinterland mostly via land transport and also perhaps to some extent by inland navigation, with feeders used to a lesser extent.

is on the port of Timbaki on Crete's south coast, which apparently has the essential features for a successful transhipment terminal, including natural deep water and minimal ship deviation time.

In northern Europe, there is a proposal for a major new container transhipment terminal at Scapa Flow in the Orkney Islands, at the very point where the North Sea meets the Atlantic Ocean (Pentland Firth), already a long-established location for ship-to-ship oil tanker transhipment (Orkney Islands Council 2005). The terminal proposed by Orkney Harbour Authority, within the vast natural deep-water sheltered anchorage of Scapa Flow, is intended to target existing northern European transhipment markets, which include the Baltic Sea area, Scandinavia, Iceland/ Faeroe, UK and Ireland. Current feeder/transhipment markets in northern Europe already account for approximately one third of total container traffic in the Le Havre-Hamburg range ports, amounting to nearly 10 million TEU in 2005, demonstrating an already strong and fast growing transhipment market in the region. Scapa Flow is aimed at securing some of this existing transhipment traffic, as well as attracting new traffic.

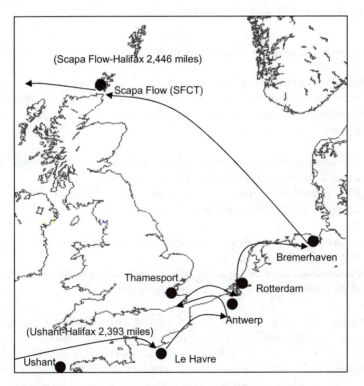

Figure 6.1 North European port rotation with call at Scapa Flow Container Terminal

The competitiveness of transhipment ports such as Scapa Flow are primarily based on their potential to reduce average feeder distance/cost as well as mainline ship deviation time/cost, particularly for end-to-end Transatlantic, Asia-Europe-US East Coast pendulum, and Round-The-World services. Liner shipping operating cost savings (via a hub such as Scapa Flow) compared with current transhipment options at traditional cityports in the Le Havre-Hamburg range are estimated to be as high as 20 per cent across a wide range of spoke ports, with port productivity benefits additional to this (Baird 2006). It is anticipated that the terminal at Scapa Flow will have a transhipment incidence of at least 95 per cent. Deep-sea vessels would be able to use Scapa Flow with minimal deviation time, as either first port inbound to northern Europe, or as last port outbound, maintaining existing port call rotations as they are more or less at present (Figure 6.1).

Thus, on the one hand developments include major brand new gateway ports created to serve the fast growing Chinese market, plus new terminals built within traditional ports elsewhere. On the other hand we see the development of almost pure regional transhipment hubs positioned at strategic locations/intersections along the main east-west trade corridors, the latter fulfilling very much a hub and spoke transhipment function and consequently involving minimal land transport requirement or conflict with urban area priorities.

Development of Container Transhipment Ports

According to Ocean Shipping Consultants (2003), the outlook for global transhipment demand is very positive, comprising as it does both hub-and-spoke and relay movements. In reality there are at least four different types of container transhipment:

- *Hub and spoke transhipment,* where containers are exchanged between connecting deep-sea and feeder vessels at hub ports;
- *Relay transhipment,* where containers are exchanged between deep-sea vessels deployed in different long-haul routes;
- *Interlining transhipment,* which involves the exchange of containers between connecting deep-sea vessels deployed in parallel strings but with different port rotations; and
- *Feeder-to-feeder transhipment,* where containers transfer from one feeder ship to another feeder ship (i.e. intra-regional traffic).

Not only has there been increased demand for new types of pure transhipment hubs, the overall transhipment incidence at many major ports has continued to increase, and this has been evident since the beginning of containerisation. Table 6.2 shows that, between 1980 and 2005, total world container port traffic rose ten-fold, from 38.8 million TEU to an estimated 394.9 million TEU. However, when this traffic is broken down into its component parts we see a quite different position. Whereas total port-to-port traffic has increased eight-fold, from 34.5 million TEU in 1980 to 282.0 million TEU in 2005, transhipment has actually risen by over twenty-six times from 4.3 million TEU in 1980 to an estimated 112.9 million TEU in 2005. Essentially, transhipment has been growing more than three times as fast as the port-to-port segment, making transhipment the fastest growing segment of the container port market.

This reflects a highly positive trend in relation to the incidence of transhipment, which refers to the average proportion of transhipment units measured across all ports. It is important to note, however, that while some ports will have a high transhipment incidence, others may have a more moderate incidence, and indeed at some ports there may be a negligible transhipment incidence. While the transhipment incidence across all ports in 1980 was just 11.1 per cent, by 1990 this had increased to 18.1 per cent, and by 2000 to 26.4 per cent. This implies that, by 2000, transhipment moves accounted for over one quarter of all world container port activity, at that time involving some 62.2 million TEU in transhipment traffic alone. Based on estimates for 2005, transhipment volumes are expected to have almost doubled over the five years since 2000, to 112.9 million TEU, effectively giving transhipment an even higher global incidence of 28.6 per cent.

The average transhipment incidence for the top-10 container ports is 40.2 per cent. For all ports in the top-30 rankings the transhipment incidence is 32.5 per cent. Across all top-100 ports the average transhipment incidence in 2004 was estimated at 24.1 per cent, equivalent to 94.6 million TEU. This compares with Drewry Shipping Consultants estimate of a world transhipment market size (i.e. for all ports) of 99.9 million TEU in 2004 (Hailey 2005).

This data is partly based on established sources, supplemented by a survey of the top-100 container ports undertaken by the author. The survey sought to establish for top-100 container ports their transhipment incidence in 2004. There were 20 responses to the survey giving a response rate of 20 per cent. In support of this data, additional information on transhipment incidence for ports not responding to the survey was derived from three other sources, namely:

- Cargo Systems Top-100 Container Ports (2004).
- Ocean Shipping Consultants World Container Port Outlook to 2015 (2003).
- Drewry Container Market Quarterly (2004).

These sources provided data on transhipment incidence for a further 24 ports in the top-100 rankings. Estimates were then made for transhipment incidences at the remaining 56 ports: as most of these ports primarily function as gateway ports, they were assumed to have a relatively low transhipment incidence.

According to Ocean Shipping Consultants (2003), since 1980, transhipment volumes have been expanding at an annual rate of 18 per cent, which is almost double the rate of growth for port-to-port traffic (the latter 10 per cent). This growth has slowed slightly over recent years to between 13–15 per cent, although this is still far higher than port-to-port growth. Plans for a rapid increase in transhipment port capacity over the next several years reflect an expectation that transhipment growth will continue to outpace port-to-port traffic growth.

Table 6.2 Estimated world container traffic and transhipment incidence, 1980–2005

	(Million TEU)			
Year	Total Port Handling	Port to Port	Transhipment	Transhipment Incidence
1980	38.8	34.5	4.3	11.1%
1985	57.4	49.4	8.0	13.9%
1990	87.9	72.0	15.9	18.1%
1995	145.2	112.9	32.3	22.2%
2000	235.4	173.2	62.2	26.4%
2001	247.4	181.3	66.1	26.7%
2002	275.8	200.4	75.4	27.3%
2003	316.7	230.2	86.5	27.3%
2004	354.5	254.6	99.9	28.2%
2005 (est)	394.9	282.0	112.9	28.6%
Increase (80/05)	10.2	8.2	26.3	

Note: includes empty units Estimates for 2005 are based on Drewry's 11.4% growth forecast (see Hailey, 2005).
Source: Derived from Drewry Container Market Quarterly, June 2003 and June 2004.

Figure 6.2 helps explain the important relationship between world economic or GDP growth, container port growth, and transhipment growth. For example, between 1993 and 2004 world economic growth consistently ran at between 2–4 per cent per annum, while container port growth over this period was between 8–13 per cent per annum, and in more recent years between 9–11 per cent. Growth in transhipment traffic, however, runs even higher, typically between 12–16 per cent per annum.

This confirms that transhipment is the fastest growing segment of the container port market. It also helps explain the recent trend towards development of pure transhipment hubs at strategic locations around the world. New transhipment-dedicated port capacity introduced to the market has helped maintain this growth trend.

According to the World Bank, world trade (including oil) expanded dramatically in 2004, increasing by some 10.3 per cent (World Bank 2005). China's integration into the global marketplace continued, with exports and imports increasing by some 30 per cent, and the effect of this is easily seen in the rapid rise in container volumes there, as noted elsewhere in this paper. The pace of trade expansion elsewhere in the developing world was more moderate (12.3 per cent) but nevertheless much higher than the 8.5 per cent expansion registered by high-income countries, the latter also exhibiting rather more moderate increases (relative to China) in container volumes.

World GDP is estimated to have increased by 3.8 per cent in 2004, supported by the impressive 10.3 per cent increase in total trade volumes.

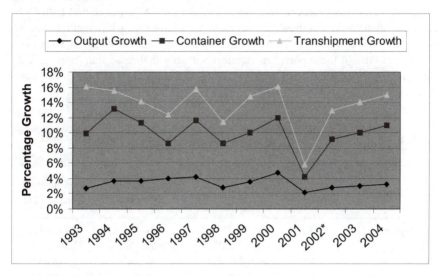

Figure 6.2 World Economic, container and transhipment growth, 1991-2004

Prior to 1995 the only major ports in the world recording what might be considered a particularly high transhipment incidence (e.g. above 80 per cent) were Singapore and Algeciras, and to a lesser extent Colombo (about 70 per cent). These transhipment ports tended to be the exception rather than the rule. Rapidly increasing trade flows is driving the demand for new port capacity in China, but what is driving the momentum for new, virtually 'pure' transhipment ports in other regions?

According to Ocean Shipping Consultants (2003), as ship sizes continue to increase and shipping line mergers and alliances lead to greater industry concentration, the economic advantage of reducing the number of port calls per string has become more pronounced. As a result, major lines are expected to continue to serve regions by as few direct port calls as possible, which suggests the role of hub-and-spoke container distribution will continue to strengthen, leading to further growth in the transhipment sector.

The rather more recent trend in the relay sector is driven by different factors, although, from a port perspective, the requirement to move containers between vessels is the same as transhipment. The aim of relay transhipment is to extend service coverage and flexibility by linking two or more mainline services – typically east-west services with north-south services – thus enabling carriers to extend the number of revenue earning legs on their larger vessels. It is also believed that relay transhipment could become more common in areas where it is currently unusual, thereby helping to grow the transhipment market even more.

Table 6.3 presents traffic flow data for ports that have a transhipment incidence of 50 per cent and above, or, in other words, ports at which the main activity is in fact transhipment. There are 21 ports in this category, all of which except one are within the top-100 world container ports group. The average transhipment incidence across all 21 of these transhipment ports is 78.1 per cent, with the highest incidence being 98 per cent at Freeport (Bahamas), and the lowest 50 per cent at both Dubai and Port Klang. Seven of these transhipment ports have a transhipment incidence of 90 per cent or above, while 13 ports have a transhipment incidence of 80 per cent or above. Many of these ports are therefore virtually dedicated transhipment hubs. Thus, today, about one fifth of the world's top-100 container ports are in fact major container transhipment ports.

Table 6.3 Ports with 50 per cent and above transhipment incidence, 2004

Port	World Ports Ranking	Total Throughput TEU	Transhipment Incidence	Transhipment Volume TEU
Singapore	2	21,329,100	91.0%	19,409,481
Kaohsiung	6	9,710,000	54.6%	5,301,660
Dubai	10	6,428,884	50.0%	3,214,442
Port Klang	13	5,200,000	50.0%	2,600,000
Tanjung Pelepas	20	3,480,000	96.0%	3,340,800
Gioia Tauro	23	3,260,000	95.0%	3,097,000
Algeciras	25	2,937,381	85.0%	2,496,774
Jeddah	30	2,425,930	59.0%	1,431,299
Panama	31	2,406,741	81.0%	1,949,460
Salalah	34	2,228,546	95.0%	2,117,119
Colombo	36	2,200,000	72.0%	1,584,000
Sharjah	43	2,003,000	70.0%	1,402,100
Piraeus	56	1,541,563	57.0%	878,691
Malta	57	1,541,563	89.9%	1,385,557
Kingston	65	1,200,000	86.0%	1,032,000
Damietta	68	1,150,000	87.1%	1,001,650
Las Palmas	70	1,105,438	56.8%	627,889
Freeport	72	1,052,000	98.0%	1,030,960
Taranto	88	763,318	86.0%	656,453
Port Said East		750,000	90.0%	675,000
Cagliari		494,766	90.0%	445,289
Average		3,486,106	78.1%	2,651,315
Average (excl Singapore)		2,593,957	77.4%	1,813,407

Sources: Derived from survey data plus Cargo Systems (2004), Ocean Shipping Consultants (2003), and Drewry Container Market Quarterly (2004).

The largest container transhipment port in the world is Singapore, the latter handling 19.4 million TEU of transhipment traffic in 2004, giving it a transhipment incidence of 91.0 per cent. Based on total port throughput, Singapore has the highest TEU-per-capita figure in the world at 4.16. Collectively, the 21 ports shown in Table 6.3 handled 55.7 million TEU in transhipment traffic during 2004, generating over half (55.7 per cent) of the entire world transhipment market for that year. As some 36 of the top-100 ports each have a transhipment incidence of 25 per cent or above, this implies that transhipment represents an important or very important part of activity for more than one third of all ports in the top-100.

A key feature of the transhipment port market is the ongoing development of new ports with a specific focus on transhipment markets. No less than nine of the 21 transhipment ports shown in Table 6.3 have been developed since 1995. What is also noticeable is the fact that these ports have been able to attract significant traffic volumes very quickly. For example, Tanjung Pelepas only opened in 1999, yet by 2004 was handling 3.4 million TEU, while Suez Canal Container Terminal (Port Said East) handled 750,000 TEU in its first year of operations (2004–2005), and is planning to achieve double that volume in year 2.

It seems no coincidence that the last 10 years have also witnessed the rapid emergence of port-operating transnational corporations (TNC). These are firms, according to Olivier (2005), that operate a global portfolio of terminals across various ports, regions and countries (e.g. Hutchison, P&O Ports, PSA, Dubai World Ports etc.). Olivier goes on to argue that the emergence of such TNC's requires a fundamental reconceptualisation of the conventional port as a fixed spatial entity, towards a global network of terminals operating under corporate logic. Increasingly, nowadays, that corporate logic extends to certain leading global carriers (e.g. AP Moller/Maersk, Evergreen, CMA-CGM, MSC, China Shipping, NYK etc.), many of the latter now in the process of developing a global network of container terminals, a number of which have a dominant focus on transhipment.

These new types of specialised, or what might be termed 'offshore', transhipment ports stress a number of advantages that make them ideal for handling transhipment traffic, including:

- Outstanding strategic location providing major network advantages to ocean carriers, leading to reduced mainline ship costs
- Reduced distance and transit times to major local markets, saving on feeder costs
- Commitment to high service standards, plus state of the art equipment and IT/EDI
- Simplification of tariff and local procedures
- Local government backing in developing the region and promoting employment
- Built in capacity expansion options
- Local Free Trade Zone to help expand local cargo content
- Low terminal construction capital costs due to natural physical advantages such as:

a. Terminal built on low cost land well away from more expensive cityport urban locations;
b. Direct access to deep-water avoiding high dredging costs;
c. Very limited need for expensive landside road/rail infrastructure as vast majority of traffic arrives and departs by ship;
d. Easier/faster planning processes due to local support (instead of opposition) towards development.

(*Source*: Derived and adapted from Suez Canal Container Terminal website http://www.scctportsaid.com/)

In seeking to propose a new mega-container transhipment terminal at Vizhinjam in India, Paul (2005) considers the Malaysian port of Tanjung Pelepas as a valid role model, and highlights the main attributes (of the latter) as being a favourable geographic location, natural depth of water, green field site, and the absence of a regulatory and bureaucratic regime. Tongzon (2005), a long-standing analyst on the role of transhipment ports, identified the following six key factors as being responsible for the success of the port of Singapore as a transhipment port:

• Strategic location
• High level of port efficiency
• High port connectivity
• Adequate infrastructure
• Adequate info structure
• A wide range of port services

Apart from its strategic location, Tongzon asserted that Singapore did not become a successful transhipment hub through luck or coincidence. Rather, this was the result of proactive government intervention and the effective implementation of appropriate seaport policies and investments, which has in turn allowed the container transhipment port to develop into what it is today, one of the world's foremost global logistics hubs.

Transhipment business tends to be priced by ports at somewhat lower levels than direct import-export traffic. Thus, a more expensive to build cityport is not necessarily the most optimal place to handle lower margin transhipment traffic anyway, especially when the cityport may already be struggling to cope with handling increasing import-export traffic for its natural hinterland. When gateway ports have to make a choice between handling direct import/export traffic or transhipment traffic, usually as a result of capacity constraints, they will therefore tend to adopt a preference for the former.

A necessary emphasis on feeder ships as well as mainline ships is a feature of transhipment ports, whereas gateway cityports tend to focus attention on mainline ships and road/rail access for containers, with feeder vessel berthing requirements and hence transhipment cargo coming rather further down the scale in importance. This is likewise a reflection of the different handling rates ports charge for import/export and for transhipment containers, with the former receiving priority.

In the pure transhipment terminal scenario the opposite is the case as mainline ships are totally dependent on feeder ships and vice versa, which implies that both receive a high priority as one is unable to function effectively without the other. In this scenario, land transport is almost an irrelevance. Importantly, land access constraints, so often a serious issue nowadays at major gateway port locations, do not really impinge on transhipment port efficiency.

Productivity is another important aspect where the transhipment terminal can generally offer superior benefits compared to a gateway cityport (Ocean Shipping Consultants 2005). Ship-to-shore crane productivity may be as much as one third better at a transhipment terminal due to:

- Yard equipment have a focus on supporting ship-to-shore quay cranes, rather than continually searching for boxes in the stack and moving them onto trucks and trains;
- Transhipment yard stacking areas tend to be closer to the quay, requiring shorter trips for yard equipment moving between the quay and the stack;
- More quay cranes used for longer periods on the same ship due to the greater container interchange typically associated with transhipment port calls;
- Fewer restows helps speed up turnaround; and
- Shorter container dwell times raises annual terminal handling capacity.

Research into the specific issue of container terminal capacity in Taiwan demonstrated that terminal capacity utilization is dependent on the following factors:

- The handling system adopted;
- Crane dimensions and in particular the stacking height of cranes;
- Container yard size;
- Average dwell time of containers and transhipment ratio;
- Characteristics of terminal operator in expediting the planning procedure of the terminal.
  (*Source*: Chu and Huang 2005)

As container dwell times for transhipment units tends to be less than for local import/export containers, this means that effective capacity is greater for a terminal with a higher transhipment ratio. In effect, container terminal capacity decreases as average dwell time increases. With a transhipment ratio of 50 per cent, maximum annual handling capacity of a terminal is estimated to be about 75 per cent. As the average transhipment ratio falls to around 30 per cent, this means average dwell time for the latter will be higher, which suggests a maximum annual handling capacity of around 70 per cent. However, at ports with a high transhipment ratio of 90 per cent or above, terminal capacity would be expected to be above 80 per cent.

Transhipment Port Traffic and Trade (Value) per Capita

Container volumes represent trade as well as empty container moves. In 2004, empty container units made up an estimated 22 per cent of global container port handling operations, equivalent to 78 million TEU, involving repositioning costs of US$ 23 billion, or 16.5 per cent of combined carrier income (see Hailey 2005).

Notwithstanding empty moves, the greater the container volume handled by a given port or country, the greater will be the value of trade moving through that port/ country. Thus, ports and nations handling very significant volumes of containers might be expected to also record substantial trade values across their borders, whereas ports and nations with less significant container volumes will see rather less trade.

Container traffic reflects the demand for production and consumption in traded goods, and of course this is directly related to GDP. Increases in GDP tend to be supported by increases in trade (The World Bank 2005), which helps explain why many nations, large and small, seek to facilitate greater trade flows, even through the interception of third country trade via transhipment. A useful, if rather obvious, hypothesis, may therefore be that a nation experiencing a rapid increase in container traffic (e.g. China) might also be expected to be witnessing rapid economic growth. Conversely, those countries recording far more moderate increases in container traffic would be expected to see rather less significant increases in economic growth.

Of course, how this works out in the case of transhipment-oriented ports will tend to be more complicated, as much of the trade is for third countries. Transhipment hubs seek to capture some of this trade value through developing added-value logistics competences and capabilities positioned close to the marine terminals. Indeed, virtually all transhipment-oriented ports, aided through the creation of Free Trade Zones, have become adept at intercepting some of this immense trade value, with knock-on benefits flowing through to the local economy.

Table 6.4 presents TEU-per-capita measures for countries split into three separate groups, *viz*: high (TEU-per-capita) ranked countries; low (TEU-per-capita) ranked countries; and G7 countries. Not surprisingly, all of the high TEU-per-capita ranked countries either have a significant container transhipment incidence (e.g. Bahamas, Malta etc.) and/or act as entrepot for third countries (e.g. Hong Kong SAR, Belgium, Netherlands). These are therefore countries in which the majority of the national ports' container traffic is neither produced nor consumed in that particular country, but is instead transported to/from other third countries throughout the region concerned.

What is also evident here is that high-ranking countries are all relatively small states in population terms, ranging from just 303,000 inhabitants in the Bahamas to 24.1 million in Malaysia: transhipment/entrepot ports are clearly handling an immense amount of trade relative to their rather modest populations. As almost all of the high ranking countries major container ports' are also Free Trade Zones, this implies that they are seeking to maximise opportunities, wherever possible, to add value to cargo intercepted for third countries through associated logistics and distribution functions.

Table 6.4 TEU-per-capita for selected countries

High Ranking Countries	TEU per Capita	G7 Countries (+ China/Spain)	TEU per Capita	Lowest Ranking Countries	TEU Per Capita
Singapore	4.160	Spain	0.183	Vietnam	0.026
Bahamas	3.491	Italy	0.146	Venezuela	0.023
Malta	3.377	Germany	0.128	Colombia	0.023
Hong Kong SAR	3.178	UK	0.118	Brazil	0.023
UAE	2.700	Japan	0.114	Peru	0.022
Oman	0.740	Canada	0.111	Indonesia	0.019
Belgium	0.633	US	0.110	Argentina	0.018
Taiwan	0.527	France	0.059	Iran	0.017
Panama	0.508	China (Incl HK)	0.047	Mexico	0.016
Netherlands	0.441	*Average G7*	*0.112*	Russia	0.007
Puerto Rico	0.426			India	0.004
Malaysia	0.418			Bangladesh	0.004
Jamaica	0.414				
Trin & Tobago	0.409				

The highest ranked countries (i.e. Singapore, Bahamas, Malta, Hong Kong SAR, and UAE) each have a TEU-per-capita ratio some 25 and 40 times higher than the G7 country average of just 0.112. Interestingly, all G7 countries have a rather similar TEU-per-capita ratio (i.e. about one tenth of a TEU per person/year), albeit with Italy and Germany somewhat higher than the average, reflecting those nations stronger role in the transhipment sector and in the handling of third country trade.

Contrasting the relatively small developed countries like Belgium and the Netherlands with G7 countries is also informative. The Benelux countries record TEU-per-capita ratios that are between 4 and 6 times greater than the G7 country average. This reflects the significant entrepot and added-value function of Benelux ports (primarily Rotterdam, Antwerp and Zeebrugge) in handling third country trade for various EU and neighbouring states, via both transhipment and inland transport. Italy likewise has a slightly higher ratio than the G7 average by virtue of its recent focus in developing new high transhipment incidence ports (e.g. Gioia Tauro, Taranto and Cagliari). Germany has a higher than average G7 ratio helped by a significant transhipment incidence at Hamburg (40.6 per cent) and Bremerhaven (30 per cent). Spain's slightly higher ratio reflects high transhipment incidences at Algeciras (85 per cent) and Las Palmas (56.8 per cent), and to a lesser extent Barcelona (30.5 per cent) and Valencia (27 per cent).

China's rapid economic growth resulted in a TEU-per-capita figure of 0.047 in 2004, which is about half the G7 average. Ongoing rapid economic growth should propel China forward and help the country to achieve a far higher TEU-per-capita ratio within the next few years. According to the China Ports & Harbours Association (Grinter 2005), by 2020 Chinese ports will have the capacity to collectively handle

6.5 billion tonnes of cargo and 240 million TEU. Should that transpire it would result in a four-fold rise to a TEU-per-capita figure of 0.183 (based on today's population), which is the same as Spain at current levels, and therefore higher than the G7 average.

Most of the ongoing port developments in China are being driven by state entities, though with significant opportunities for private sector investment and operation (Wang and Slack 2004). The view of the world's largest container terminal operator is informative in this respect. Speaking at a signing ceremony in 2005 at the Port of Yantian in Shenzhen, Hutchison Whampoa chairman Li Ka-shing stated that China will remain one of the fastest growing countries in the world, where economic development will continue to experience significant rates in growth, aided by continued expansion of the container port sector (Wallis 2005).

Lowest ranking countries include Russia, India and Bangladesh. Russia's rapid growth over recent years, with container traffic expanding 466 per cent during 1995–2003, suggests a highly positive trend. India's growth is lagging somewhat behind at 187.9 per cent over the same period.

Turkey is actively seeking to raise container traffic volumes, which are currently regarded as too low for a population of 70 million people (i.e. 0.040 TEU-per-capita). Container traffic in Turkey is expected to increase rapidly as the country's industrialisation process gathers pace, and rising levels of wealth encourage even more international trade (Fossey 2005). To meet this need, Turkey is planning major investments in its ports and transport system, with a focus on transhipment capacity to serve the East Mediterranean and Black Sea region.

Container transhipment ports clearly act as trade *interceptors*. Such ports function as gatherers of trade for third countries, as well as serving the trading needs of their own country. This has the effect of significantly increasing the volume and value of trade moving across a country's borders, inbound and outbound, and well beyond that which it might reasonably expect to handle based on the demands of domestic production and consumption alone. This additional trade not only creates employment locally, in port operations and related services, but importantly it leads to expansion of a nation's added-value infrastructure, services and capabilities. This in turn implies that the transhipment terminal hub-and-spoke function, and resulting connectivity, helps to enhance national competitiveness through allowing firms (indigenous and multinational) direct access to frequent, low cost, global and intra-regional transport services.

Such factors act as important levers in attracting inward investment into a country. Transnational firms now look to locate their regional logistics and distribution activities close to container transhipment hubs in order to take advantage of these benefits (Restall 2005). This helps to explain why national governments promote development of international container transhipment terminals and associated logistics infrastructure as a key element in what is a relatively low cost policy aimed at significantly enhancing the international competitiveness of the country concerned.

In this context it is useful to assess the value of containerised trade flows, by country, that may be 'intercepted' by a port/nation based on investments in transhipment capacity. According to the World Shipping Council (2005), international waterborne containerized cargo carried on liner vessels arriving at or departing from US ports in 2004 had a total value of $521.4 billion. Based on US international waterborne container volumes of 21.3 million TEU in 2004, this gives an average cargo value of $24,494 per TEU. Given that the US imports from and exports to virtually all parts of the globe, it is assumed that this average cargo value per TEU is fairly representative of the world container market. Indeed, while US ports account for about 10.7 per cent of world container port traffic, according to World Shipping Council data, at any one time there are more than 4.0 million containers in use in US trades out of a total of 13.0 million overall, implying that some 30 per cent of all containers circulating worldwide are based on US trade. This further suggests that the estimated figure for average value per TEU of $24,494 is reasonably representative.

Table 6.5 Value of container trade-per-capita for selected countries (US$)

High Ranking Countries	Trade per capita	G7 Countries+ China/Spain	Trade per capita	Lowest Ranking Countries	Trade per capita
Singapore	101,894	Spain	4,482	Vietnam	637
Bahamas	85,508	Italy	3,576	Venezuela	563
Malta	82,716	Germany	3,135	Colombia	563
Hong Kong SAR	77,841	UK	2,890	Brazil	563
UAE	66,133	Japan	2,792	Peru	539
Oman	18,125	Canada	2,719	Indonesia	465
Belgium	15,505	US	2,694	Argentina	441
Taiwan	12,908	France	1,445	Iran	416
Panama	12,443	China (incl HK)	1,151	Mexico	392
Netherlands	10,802	*Average G7*	*2,750*	Russia	171
Puerto Rico	10,434			India	98
Malaysia	10,238			Bangladesh	98
Jamaica	10,140				
Trin & Tob	10,018				

Based on this average cargo value, Table 6.5 presents the estimated value of (container) trade-per-capita for selected countries. The same three categories of countries analysed in regard to TEU-per-capita above are used, namely – high ranking TEU-per-capita countries, low ranking TEU-per-capita countries, and G7 countries.

As would be expected, high transhipment incidence ports and/or ports with a strong entrepot function also record very high trade-per-capita outcomes. The highest outcome in this regard is again Singapore, with a trade-per-capita figure of $101,894. Following closely behind Singapore are all the very high ranking transhipment incidence countries including Bahamas, Malta, Taiwan, Oman, and Malaysia, and the transhipment/entrepot hubs in Hong Kong, Belgium, and Netherlands. The relatively small populations and high TEU-per-capita for Malta and Bahamas provides for very high trade-per-capita figures of $82,716 and $85,508 respectively.

For the 14 highest-ranking countries the average transhipment incidence is estimated to be 64 per cent, which is well above the world average transhipment incidence rate of 28.2 per cent for 2004. An obvious conclusion from this analysis is that, for ports/nations exhibiting a high transhipment incidence (i.e. typically well above 50 per cent), this tends to translate into a very high trade-per-capita value.

The average container trade-per-capita figure for G7 countries is estimated at $2,750, with the highest of these being Italy with $3,576, followed by Germany with $3,135, and the lowest France with $1,445. Italy's relatively higher figure (compared with other G7 nations) again reflects its increased focus on developing transhipment hubs in recent years, and Germany's more positive outcome similarly reflects a significant transhipment incidence at Hamburg, slightly less at Bremerhaven. Spain likewise has a relatively higher trade-per-capita figure of $4,482, also reflecting its higher transhipment incidence ports.

China records a container trade-per-capita figure of $1,151, which is about 42 per cent of the G7 average. Further down the scale, Russia has a container trade-per-capita figure of just $171, and India $98. There is clearly a massive gulf between the highest ranked countries and the lowest ranked, and this tends to reflect the present economic reality. For countries like India, it has been argued that the desire to develop new transhipment ports must become a higher national priority (Paul 2005), and the evidence presented here would tend to reinforce that view.

Conclusion

World container port traffic virtually doubles each decade, placing pressure on ports and supply chains to expand capacity accordingly. Transhipment traffic is the fastest growing segment of the container port market, a consequence of increased ship size, a limit on the number of direct port calls per string, in addition to economic and operational efficiencies associated with relaying, interlining, and feedering of containers. The incidence of transhipment has risen steadily year-on-year since the early days of containerisation, and is expected to continue rising in the foreseeable future.

Reflecting this change, over the past decade or so a number of major new ports have been developed that have a primary focus on transhipment markets. Today, there are twenty ports amongst the world top-100 container ports at which the majority of traffic consists of transhipment, and many other ports also participate in transhipment traffic to varying degrees. Further new transhipment-oriented ports are currently at different stages of planning and development. Often these ports are located on islands or peninsula, remote from densely populated urban areas, positioned at strategic intersections between oceans and seas and/or major canals, the virtue of natural deep-water being highly advantageous, together with avoidance of congested and high cost urban centres (e.g. cityports) where access and environmental barriers are increasingly difficult to overcome. This ongoing trend itself results in a higher and rising transhipment incidence.

A state that develops a container transhipment hub, which then successfully intercepts third country trade, will thereafter inflate the value of its exports and imports out of all proportion to population size. Findings from this study demonstrate that high transhipment incidence nations handle far greater import/export trade value-per-capita than low or non-transhipment incidence nations. This interception of trade then generates opportunities (for transhipment port host nations) to become actively involved in that third country trade, particularly in the logistics and added-value activities flowing from its interception, enhanced by seemingly obligatory free trade zone capability.

As well as creating new employment opportunities locally, the superior competitiveness (both global and intra-regional) that a transhipment hub provides the host nation concerned (i.e. through access to lowest cost global and intra-regional transport connections, plus transnational logistics/distribution & free trade zone capabilities etc.) serves to enhance the attractiveness of the transhipment port location country itself. This will in turn be expected to make the host nation a more attractive location for inward investment, while simultaneously strengthening the competitiveness of indigenous export/import industries.

The financial cost of implementing such a policy for the host nation may be small, relative to the extensive trading and economic benefits, given the capital expense associated with developing a moderate-sized transhipment terminal, and taking into account the likely role of the private sector in helping to provide such capacity. Typically this involves the state supporting at least part of the costs associated with building a new transhipment terminal (infrastructure), with the private sector investing in superstructure (cranes and equipment). Transhipment terminals are predominantly operated by transnational terminal companies via long-term concession agreements arranged with respective local/national governments and/or port authorities (Baird 2002; Ocean Shipping Consultants 2005). The concessionaire will usually be asked to guarantee traffic volumes, and certain levels of investment, thereby further limiting risks for port authorities' and other state entities involved in the project (Notteboom 2006).

Successful container transhipment operations developed as a key part of a country's industrial development strategy can therefore permit host nations to develop an important regional and global strategic competitive advantage, and this is an advantage which is otherwise unlikely to exist.

Acknowledgements

The author is most grateful to the ports that responded to the survey on container port transhipment incidence, the latter forming an important part of this study. An earlier version of the paper was presented at the First International Workshop on New Generation Port Cities and their Role in Global Supply Chains, The University of Hong Kong, December 12–14, 2005.

Chapter 7

Mediterranean Ports in the Global Network: How to Make the Hub and Spoke Paradigm Sustainable?

Enrico Musso and Francesco Parola

Introduction

During the 1990s the transhipment revolution and the growth of Asian economies offered Mediterranean ports the opportunity of capturing a growing amount of cargo on the Europe-Far East trade.

European Mediterranean countries developed new transhipment hubs, close to the trunk routes and located outside the congested old port-cities. Their maritime tradition and expertise combined with strategic position increased the competitiveness of Mediterranean ports compared with Northern Europe port range. Nonetheless, their growth is now facing major structural bottlenecks: scarcity of space in the gateway or spoke ports, inadequate road and rail networks, no barge transport, geographical barriers. Growth is also hindered by the relative eccentricity from major EU final markets.

On the macroeconomic side, the risk of 'demaritimisation' of old port-cities cannot be avoided through quantitative growth, which combines a decreasing demand of labour and increasing land consumption and environmental effects. This raises the question of the sustainability of growing throughputs in the long term.

The chapter outlines some weaknesses and strengths of Med ports and some possible strategies for their sustainable development, based on value-added activities, cooperation between hubs and spoke ports of the 'Latin arc', opening to emerging markets in the Mediterranean. These strategies aim at decoupling the growth of value-added activities from the growth of throughput and outlining possible growth paths for old port-cities in anciently industrialised countries.

Med Ports and Deep-sea Trade: An Unbalanced Growth

The growth of Mediterranean...

Until the early 1990s the Mediterranean was almost excluded from major East-West routes. Shipping companies preferred to call North European ports both for Transatlantic and Europe-Far East services. Mediterranean ports were basically involved in short-sea shipping and secondary North-South routes. State owned ports, difficulties in labour management and land planning, poor intermodal links to the hinterlands had relegated for decades South European ports in a secondary role *vis-à-vis* the global maritime transport network.

Over the last 15 years this scenario changed significantly. Globalisation, relocation of manufacturing activities in countries with low labour costs, falling tariff barriers after the institution of Free Trade Agreements and Areas (EU, ASEAN, NAFTA, Mercosur, etc.) deeply affected the structure of deep-sea services. Transatlantic routes, although growing, reduced their market share compared to Transpacific and Europe-Far East routes. The share of Europe-Far East routes on East-West traffics rose from about 19 per cent in 1984 to more than 35 per cent in 2004. The Mediterranean Sea happened to be the heart of this revolution which gave services to/from Far East a key role in the main shipping networks (Zohil and Prijon 1999; Genco and Pitto 2000).

Mediterranean ports underwent profound institutional and management turn in order to face changes in international competition. Reforms aiming at overcoming the traditional 'state port' model started up in several countries, and some new important ports – such as Gioia Tauro – rose to match the growing demand for transhipment services, and to 'capture' substantial shares of Far East traffic previously addressed to the Hamburg-Le Havre range.

This survey, based on data from Containerisation International, includes the main ports of Mediterranean/Black Sea and of Northern Europe. Ports have here been grouped into ranges: Hamburg-Le Havre, UK, Baltic/Scandinavia and Atlantic range in Northern Europe; North-Med, West-Med, East-Med, Central-Med and Black Sea in the Mediterranean basin.[1]

A simple methodology is used to define port ranges: the first criterion is essentially geographical, based on geomorphological characteristics of the territory; while a further criterion is offered by the different gateway/transhipment ratio in ports which identifies different functions of ports and allows to analyse separately transhipment ranges (such as the Central-Med).

The usual comparison between Northern and Southern ports should actually avoid common misleading approaches. Traditional quantitative analysis between Northern and Southern range often neglects the nature of the different cargo flows (namely the distinction between gateway and transhipment functions) and can lead to unaffordable outcomes. In sum, is there really competition between North and South? How can we perceive and measure it?

Looking back at history, it appears that since 1980 the market share of Mediterranean considerably grew, from 24 per cent to about 40 per cent. Yet, a substantial share of this increase is due to the accelerated growth of transhipment

---

1   Atlantic range: ports from Gibraltar to Brittany; North Med: French Mediterranean ports and Northern Italian ports (from France to Civitavecchia and from Ancona to Trieste); West Med: Mediterranean Spanish ports; Central Med: Southern Italian ports (not included in the North-Med), Malta, Piraeus; East-Med: Middle East, other Greek ports and Mediterranean Turk ports; Black Sea: ports of Marmara Sea and Black Sea. Apart from Egypt, African ports have not been considered since they have no significant container throughput.

in the Mediterranean arena, and namely to its dramatic rise in hubs situated close to the 'ideal' Suez-Gibraltar trunk route. Transhipped containers, albeit giving place to additional moves of containers in hub ports (which are moreover counted twice), do not actually increase total import-export and land transport volumes. Therefore, they are likely to produce an overestimation of the actual competitiveness of Mediterranean ports (Trotta 2000). If we cut transhipment from these statistics, results are quite different: since 1980 the market share of Mediterranean ports in 'final' (import-export) traffic grew from about 23 per cent to the present 33 per cent approximately, and in recent years this was negligible.

... and inside the Mediterranean

If we refer to the 'final' import-export traffic, a far better indicator of port competitiveness than total throughput, the analysis of single Mediterranean ranges highlights very different trends (see Figure 7.1).

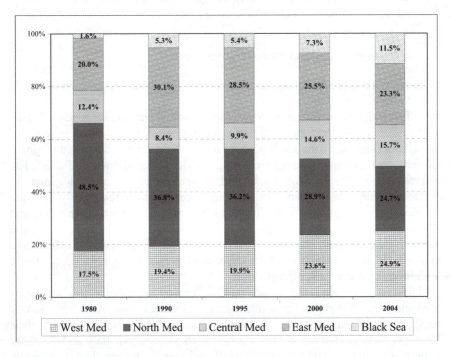

Figure 7.1 Market share of gateway traffic in different Med port ranges

Although referring to the sole 'final' traffic, these data show the ongoing growth of 'Central Med' – caused by a boost in transhipment and a contemporary growth of some Southern EU regions (Southern Italy, Greece) increasing also the final throughput – which reached in 2004 a market share of 16 per cent on the total of Mediterranean, transhipment not included (+87 per cent since 1990).

Also the West Med, thanks to the economic development of Spain and the effective port and land use planning of cities such as Barcelona and Valencia, has been increasing its market share to 25 per cent in 2004 (+28 per cent compared to 1990). Similar results are seen for the Black Sea, which took profit from the growing opening of Eastern Europe economies and increased its share to 11,5 per cent in 2004 (+117 per cent compared to 1990). East Med, on the contrary, although increased its overall throughput, reduced the market share down from 30 per cent in 1990 to 23 per cent in 2004 (-23 per cent).

Yet, the port range recording the worst fall in (final) throughput market share was the North-Med, i.e. French and Northern Italy ports. In spite of the relative proximity to the rapidly growing economies of Germany and Central Europe, these ports were not able to capture the increase in traffic from/to the Far East, and dramatically reduced their market share to 25 per cent, from 37 per cent in 1990 (-33 per cent) and almost 50 per cent in 1980 (-49 per cent).

It appears that Mediterranean ports, though they globally increased throughput and market share compared to Northern Europe, show a non-homogeneous path of different ranges, some of which seem to be in a phase of stagnation or even of fall.

The Strategic Positioning of Mediterranean Ports

In the current and the following section, a couple of possible explanations may help to find the rationale of these trends.

A first possible interpretation comes from strategic positioning of ports. Figure 7.2 summarises the strategic positioning of main Mediterranean ports in terms of throughput (surface of the circles), share of transhipment on the total throughput (X-axis), and diversion distance from the ideal Suez-Gibraltar route (Y-axis). The two main typologies for major ports – hub or gateway ports – are highlighted. As previously said, transhipment facilities have been growing remarkably over the last decade along the ideal route, thanks to the limited diversion distance: beyond Algeciras, Damietta and Marsaxlokk we now find Gioia Tauro, Cagliari and Taranto, in Southern Italy, while the Greek port of Piraeus plays a somehow 'hybrid' role thanks to the remarkable share (about 55 per cent) of import-export traffic, due to the leadership in the domestic market.

These remarks help to better understand differences in evolution between North-Med and West-Med ports. The former, quite far from the trunk route, hold low or negligible transhipment shares and mainly focus on import-export thanks to their closeness to fully developed final markets such as Northern Italy and Southern France; ports are mainly medium or small, and port authorities do not cooperate significantly. The West-Med based its rapid final throughput growth on the gateway ports of Barcelona and Valencia. Their geographical position, not far from the trunk route, allows them to attract also a significant share of transhipment.

The Black Sea is assuming an important role in deep-sea services. Ambarli (Istanbul), thanks to investment by foreign players (such as MSC) in its port facilities, is recording a rapid growth of its throughput (over 1 million TEU in 2004). On the contrary, the 'East Med' range fails to record a significant growth in final traffic, while, thanks to its position close to the Suez Canal, transhipment is constantly growing, drawing the interest of international stevedores (Littlejohn 2003).

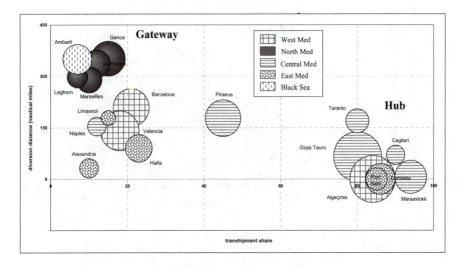

Figure 7.2 Diversion distance and transhipment share on total throughput of some selected Mediterranean container ports

While bringing some interesting insights, these remarks fail in depicting the overall trend. Transhipment ports emerge as a successful story of growth while gateway ports show contradictory results, with positive trends for some Spanish and Turkish ports and slow growth rates for main Italian container facilities. In the story of Gioia Tauro, the busiest transhipment port in the Med, the origin-destination cargo matrix surprisingly reveals that only 22 per cent of containers transhipped in 2004 (source: Contship Italia) had a 'hub-and-spoke relation' with Italian ports. In other words, this hub, although successful, seems to provide a 'poor leverage' for the growth of the gateway ports of its own country.

Traffic Dynamics and Port Lifecycle Theory

Differences in port trends may be addressed through an approach based on product lifecycle theory applied to ports. Pioneering studies for applying industrial lifecycle theory (Malthus 1798; Schumpeter 1939; Vernon 1966; Norton 1986) in shipping and ports were done by Sletmo (1989; 1999). We followed Sletmo's approach, supporting it with the Dicken's typology (1998).

The scarce involvement of international players in the North-Med and the stagnation of its import-export traffic suggest a reflection on the possible 'lifecycle' evolution for Mediterranean ports (see Figure 7.3). In which phase of port development do they take their place?

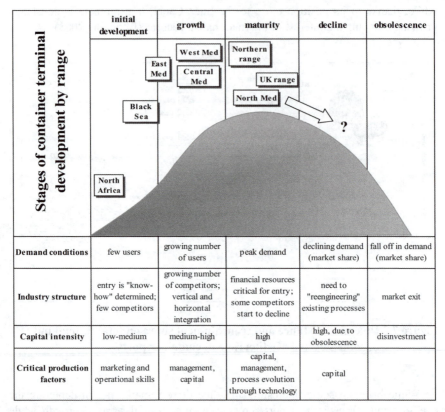

	initial development	growth	maturity	decline	obsolescence
Demand conditions	few users	growing number of users	peak demand	declining demand (market share)	fall off in demand (market share)
Industry structure	entry is "know-how" determined; few competitors	growing number of competitors; vertical and horizontal integration	financial resources critical for entry; some competitors start to decline	need to "reengineering" existing processes	market exit
Capital intensity	low-medium	medium-high	high	high, due to obsolescence	disinvestment
Critical production factors	marketing and operational skills	management, capital	capital, management, process evolution through technology	capital	

Figure 7.3 Lifecycle of port activities in selected port ranges

In Northern Europe, the Hamburg-Le Havre range, although well inside its maturity as for throughput and players' involvement, shows high throughput growth rates and a fair dynamism in investment and medium-long run planning.

The Mediterranean situation is quite differentiated. Insufficient national (top-down) policies slowed down port privatisation despite the (bottom-up) push from the stevedores to invest in a region considered as strategic, and the need of global carriers to acquire dedicated handling facilities in major South European ports. Unlike Northern Europe, where in historical port enclaves of local stevedores (such as ECT, Naties, BLG/Eurokai and HHLA) the entry (and takeovers) by big foreign players started recently (early 2000s) and grew very rapidly, due to the aggressiveness of newcomers, the entry of global players in South European ports, be they international stevedores (HPH, PSA, P&O Ports) or carriers (APM Terminals, MSC, CMA-CGM, Cosco, etc.) began in the 1990s but grew more slowly. Over the last few years, while the North-Med range appears scarcely dynamic, West-Med ports are more 'on the wavelength' of private players and have more aggressive marketing strategies. Black Sea ports opened only partly and recently to (some) privatisation, but the potential growth of the hinterland make them rapidly gain importance in deep-sea services. The hub-and-spoke system which developed mainly in Central Med caused remarkable growth in volumes but failed to support adequately North-Med ports, which are possibly running into a real decline.

Elements for a SWOT Analysis

This section analyses strengths, weaknesses, opportunities and threats of the main Mediterranean port ranges – with a special focus on North- and Central-Med, also in the perspective of a possible further readjustment of final (import-export) throughput compared to the Hamburg-Le Havre range, and in order to outline adequate policies to reinforce the growth or stimulate the recovery for critical cases.

Strengths and opportunities: a growing and reinforcing hub-and-spoke network

Thanks to its closeness to the trunk route, the Mediterranean with its peninsulas, namely Italy, and islands, can act as a geographical platform for Asian traffics addressed to the European heartland through land transport or short-sea shipping, as well as for future traffic for/to Africa.

This geographical advantage fostered the implementation of new hubs which were allowed to capture deep-sea services from/to the Far East. The hub-and-spoke network grew efficiently (Drewry 2000), as transhipped container in Central-Med range grew at a rate double the world average, rising from less than one million TEU in 1995 to over 6 millions in 2004. In this range activities initially concentrated in a few big ports (Marsaxlokk, Gioia Tauro) spread over other facilities where major global carriers invested to establish dedicated hub terminals in the Mediterranean. The dramatic rise in throughput provided the critical mass needed to create spin-off or satellite hubs such as Taranto and Cagliari (Slack 1999; Midoro *et al.* 2004). This trend is modelled in Figure 7.4.

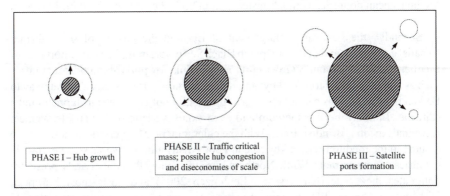

| PHASE I – Hub growth | PHASE II – Traffic critical mass; possible hub congestion and diseconomies of scale | PHASE III – Satellite ports formation |

Figure 7.4 Typical stages in fast-growing transhipment and gateway port systems
Source: our elaboration.

A similar evolution in transhipment port ranges occurred in Singapore, where the growing volumes caused the implementation, next to the historical hub, of new facilities such as Port Kelang, Laem Chabang and Tanjung Pelepas. Northern Europe showed a partly similar evolution, although transhipment is less common and most ports are gateway ports. Frémont and Soppé (2004) brought empirical evidence of this process, and showed that unlike previous evidence (Ashar 2000), in rapidly growing port systems carriers do not necessarily concentrate traffic in one or two facilities. In the Hamburg-Le Havre range big carriers such as Maersk, CMA-CGM and MSC, even when reinforcing their supply of hold in major ports, tend to maintain a good diversification of their calls in three to four ports. This strategy, pursued by major carriers, caused the fall of Rotterdam's market share over the last 10 years to the advantage of competing ports. New satellite of 'historical' load centres are now arising in Northern Europe, following the increase in throughputs: as a spin-off for Rotterdam, Antwerp, Hamburg, Bremen, Felixstowe, new terminals are arising in Amsterdam (Ceres), Zeebrugge, Wihelmshaven and London.

Beyond the geographical advantage and the efficient hub network, some Mediterranean countries (Italy, Greece) also boast a long tradition in the maritime industry, namely in some anciently established gateway ports. Notwithstanding their market share reduction (in Italy: Genoa, La Spezia, Leghorn, Trieste, all in the North-Med range), the richness of port clusters still provide a background able to attract traffic from/to a wide hinterland.

In perspective, Mediterranean ports can take profit of other competitive advantages.

First, the probable establishment of an Euro-Mediterranean Free Trade Area (Euromed FTA) (expected around 2010) should cut customs duties and tariffs and substantially increase trade inside and from/to the Mediterranean. The present efficient transhipment network would be able to tranship container coming from the Far East towards North Africa, being barycentric within the Euromed FTA. This is even more important since demographic and, in prospect, economic growth in South Mediterranean countries is much faster than in both Western and Eastern European ones.

Secondly, the Eastward enlargement of EU and the growth of some former socialist economies and of throughput in Black Sea ports strengthen the importance of Mediterranean hubs: namely Greek ports, as hubs linked to ports of candidate countries such as Rumania, Bulgaria, Turkey; and Italian Adriatic ports, as possible gateway to Balkan peninsula. This can represent an opportunity not only for transhipment hubs (Piraeus, Taranto), but for medium and even small Adriatic ports (Trieste, Venice, Ravenna, Ancona, Brindisi, Bari). With the enlargement, Mediterranean Europe may assume in the medium-term a key role in goods distribution towards some extra-EU countries or new entrants. While Northern Europe, namely the Netherlands, presently dominates the scene (Kuipers and Eenhuizen 2004) and hosts most European Distribution Centres (EDC) intended to serve the entire continental market, the EU enlargement might cause a general relocation of distribution processes, to serve more efficiently the emerging markets. Some manufacturing firms are restructuring their distribution and logistics organisation, from one to two continental EDCs or to several regional platforms supported by secondary distribution centres developing local distribution functions (Ferrari *et al.* 2006). The prospective establishment of a free trade area proposes South EU ports as candidates to host second and third level distribution centres capable to serve North African and South European countries (Italy and Greece for expansions towards East, Spain and France towards West Europe, all towards Northern Africa). This suggests a role for Mediterranean ports for both transhipment and import-export, as well as for a strategic location of sub-continental distribution centres. The creation of value-added distribution centres would certainly have a positive impact in terms of employment and for attracting further traffic.

Weaknesses and threats: from natural constraints to political slowness

Some serious weaknesses threaten the growth potential of Mediterranean ports, and/ or a fair balance between the growth in throughput and the local socioeconomic impact.

First, there are a number of geographic and demographic points:

- the South Mediterranean ports are distant from the European heartland; although the well-known 'blue banana' is no longer the only concentration of European wealth (Winkelmans 2005), the natural hinterland of North European (namely the Hamburg-Le Havre range) still concentrates the biggest part of EU manufacture and the demand for intermediate and final goods;
- apart from distance, barriers such as mountain ranges (Alps, Pyreneans), seas (for island) or political borders (Greece) increase the economic distance of Mediterranean ports from EU markets;
- unlike Northern Europe, there are very few ports on estuaries, and no significant inland waterways, and port development along rivers is not feasible (Musso and Benacchio 2002);
- space for port activities within little distance from terminals is often scarce, due to the intense coastal urban development and orographic conditions of most port regions; the consequent competition for alternative land uses (port related activities, urban development, tourism) makes coexistence of cities and ports difficult (Musso and Benacchio 2002; see also Baird 1996, for other European examples and Lee and Song 2005, for Hong Kong and Singapore);
- the scarcity of port spaces often induced a negative attitude towards dedicated port terminals (Haralambides *et al.* 2002) namely when governments and port bodies aim at maximising throughput and/or favouring local operators;
- for Italy (and to some extent for some Southern French and Spanish regions) geographical dispersion of relevant demographic poles (and markets) causes the breaking up of port activities.

This explains locally based pressures influencing transport and port policies (namely in Italy where some 25 ports are marked as 'majors' and host independent port authorities).

In most South European countries, moreover, the demand for transport infrastructure emerged mostly over the last 15 years as a consequence of booming traffic and clashed with increasing public financial straits resulting from constraints imposed by the Treaty of Maastricht. Therefore, land infrastructure (transport networks, inland terminals) often fails to match the growing demand. In Italy Maastricht financial restrictions turned to be particularly severe, due to the huge budget deficit. Main networks connecting Italian ports to their hinterland are now saturated, and even the significant improvements of Alpine passes (Loetschberg and Gothard) might turn, from an opportunity for contesting Central-European markets, into the threat of a more effective competition from North European ports in the Italian market.

The case of the 'North Med' range

Over the last decade, major global stevedores (Hutchison Port Holdings, PSA, APM Terminals, P&O Ports) have widened their networks worldwide and increased their market shares. Their growing demand for space has been seldom matched in the North Mediterranean, whose terminal supply is broken up into a number of independent port bodies, some of which are slow in modernizing their institutional framework (France), while port planning lacks coordination and governance. Also, the fierce competition within the range resulted in a weakness towards competing ranges.[2]

The traditional and somehow unrealistic attempt to compare the ports of the Hamburg-Le Havre range to some hypothetic European Southern Range mostly represented by North Italian and South French ports is mostly deceptive and misleading.

In Northern Europe spaces are concentrated in a few huge gateway ports. In spite of the fierce inter-port competition, the critical mass of each port can produce the economies of scale and synergies needed by the intermodal logistic chain, and provide a multimodal (road, rail and barge) gateway to/from the hinterland. The 'gravity force' of port size and logistic integration proved to be capable in attracting major global stevedores (namely from Far East).

On the contrary, the North-Med range has not been able to enhance its gateway to the European economic heartland. The breaking up of financial resources, and political criteria in their distribution, the lack of coordination between players involved in the intermodal chain (railways, motorways, inland terminals, etc.), and the lack of a common port and transport policy reduce the chances to attract major world 'pure stevedores' (HPH, PSA and Dubai Ports World) and integrated carriers-stevedores (APM Terminals, NYK-Ceres, APL-NOL, MSC, etc.).

North-Med ports may well fail to host logistics facilities, distribution centres and value-added service providers, with a gradual impoverishment of port-induced economy. The lowering local macroeconomic effects can cause the 'demaritimisation' of formerly port-oriented regions and the rejection of port activities by port-cities' land use strategies, what eventually results into an impoverishing production structure and maritime culture for historical Mediterranean port-cities.

---

2   The struggle among Ligurian ports to obtain the MSC terminal and throughput is an outstanding example.

What role for Mediterranean Ports?

Recent trends in containerised traffic, reflecting the organisation of supply but also the changes in demand, still offer positive prospects for Mediterranean. The remarks of the previous section help to identify some key factors on which Mediterranean ports might build their future development.

Reinforcing the growth compared to Northern Europe

On both main East-West routes of interest for Europe, representing the main commercial ways towards North America and Far East, Mediterranean ports still record a solidity or even a slight recovery compared to Northern Europe, in terms of full container traffic, as seen in Figure 7.5 (Cazzaniga Francesetti and Foschi 2002a). Drewry (2005) forecasts that Mediterranean Sea can increase its market share on the Europe-Far East route by another two per cent over the period 2003–2006.

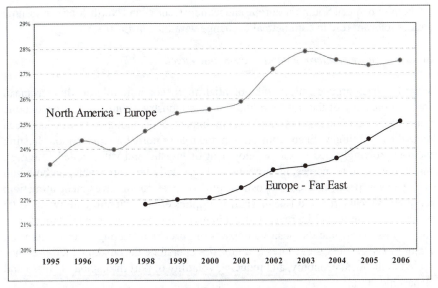

Figure 7.5 The growing traffic share of Mediterranean ports
Note: Figures for 2005 and 2006 are estimations.
Source: Our elaboration from Drewry (2005).

As for hold supply, some carriers are – although slowly and partly – repositioning their fleet from Northern to Southern Europe (Drewry 2001–2005). In 2001, 22 per cent of top carriers' slot capacity was deployed in the Mediterranean while 78 per cent called North European ports. In 2004 this share had risen to over 28 per cent and, at mid 2005, to over 30 per cent. This seems mainly due to the growing share of Eastern Europe, Black Sea and Adriatic Sea, increasingly direct-called by services from/to the Far East.

Traditionally, some European carriers such as CMA-CGM and MSC did give a substantial importance to Mediterranean ports in exchanges with Asia (40–50 per cent of slot capacity), while Maersk and members of top global alliances preferred to call North European ports. Today, this distinction is partly disappearing. If the CKYHS alliance has only began to (slightly) increase its operations in the Mediterranean, world top leader Maersk has increased its slot capacity in the Mediterranean from 11 per cent in 2001 to about 32 per cent in 2005. The involvement of APM Terminals in port projects in North Med and Eastern Europe confirms the interest of the AP Möller-Maersk group for the Mediterranean basin.

From the microeconomic point of view, as for the efficiency of transport and logistics industry, some South European ports could well develop logistics and value-added activities aimed at distribution in North African and East/South European markets. At the moment most distribution centres are located in Northern Europe but, after the EU enlargement and the perspective of a free trade Euro-Mediterranean area, even Med ports could host these distribution facilities, even if of second or third level.

In this prospect, Southern Europe and namely Centre- and North-Med can assume a more relevant role in commercial exchange with the Far East.

Synergies between micro and macroeconomic effects

What has been argued reflects the potential microeconomic role of Mediterranean for the efficiency of the transport and logistics industry. From the macroeconomic point of view, as the direct employment impact of handling activities has been dramatically falling with containerisation, the role of ports for cities/regions hosting them is growingly tied to the development of logistic and value-added activities, much more than to increasing throughput. These activities can develop in both hub and gateway ports, and cause positive effects in terms of investment attraction, job creation, catalytic and (Keynesian) multiplier effects, therefore allowing to (i) generate a quantitative increase and qualitative improvement of employment; and (ii) stabilise over time the positive impacts of ports by attracting investments from major global carriers, stevedores and logistics operators, thus making their presence rooted in the local economy, and reducing volatility of port throughput (Musso and Benacchio 2002).

Developing such activities and locating distribution centres is today the most effective strategy both at a microeconomic level, since they increase port competitiveness and make each port less easily replaced by competitors within the intermodal chain; and at a macroeconomic level, due to the increase and stabilisation of external benefits towards the local economy. The two levels interact, as the increasing competitiveness attracts investments from global port/logistics operators, and this in turn maximises local macroeconomic benefits over time. Port development is therefore contemporarily driven by micro- and macroeconomic forces, which must be coordinated and directed to give place to cumulative growth effects.

Macroeconomic policies should pursue a strategy (at least) at national level – and possibly international, at least in the EU – aiming at identifying and quantifying the demand for port space and infrastructure coming from the transport/logistics industry, and at finding locations capable to enhance the overall efficiency of the logistics system. Regional/local policies should also carefully consider the development of port facilities and other port related logistics infrastructure, in order to face increasing traffic, on one side, and to balance economic and environmental effects to ensure political and social consensus on port development projects on the other side. A strong coordination is therefore necessary between national and regional/local policies on transport infrastructure.

On the microeconomic side, concerning the industrial organisation and the efficiency of transport and logistics industry, the push for port development comes mainly from private firms entering the stevedoring industry (both pure stevedores and carriers) and investing huge capitals in more and more expensive assets and projects. These investments are allowed by the growing (horizontal and vertical) concentration both in stevedoring and in transport industry. The latter, after the integration of different transport modes thanks to containerisation and intermodality, has progressively extended its control to the port node, partly to search for profit but mainly to gain control on the whole transport cycle, and move competition upwards, at the level of integrated (and intermodal) logistic chains. The former (the stevedoring industry) either moves towards a network of dedicated terminals vertically integrated with a carrier (or an alliance of carriers, or a global logistic operator), or tends to horizontal integration, with international (and mainly private owned) 'pure' stevedoring groups.

These trends caused over the recent years profound institutional and management changes in ports, which brought about a rescaling of players and drivers, since stevedores – more than port authorities and governments – hold today a key role in a port community formed by many players aiming at the port's performance and competitiveness (Olivier and Slack, forthcoming).

Strategies and Policy Guidelines: Establishing Competing 'Transport Chain Solutions'

It is now worthwhile wondering which policy guidelines may help the competitiveness of Mediterranean ports, in order to match the opportunities coming from (i) recent and coming boom in Far East trades, and (ii) distribution opportunities in emerging Mediterranean markets (North Africa and East Europe). Possible strategies focus on three main areas:

- the reinforcement of hub-and-spoke structure in order to enhance network economies arising from (i) the geographical distribution of traffic and (ii) the characteristics of Mediterranean ports;
- the enhancement of North-South connectivity, in order to increase links with hub ports and between the two edges of the Mediterranean, and to overcome geographical and political barriers of Southern Europe (mountain ranges, seas, borders);
- the building of institutional and governance capacity in port communities, and in port-cities/regions of Southern Europe.

Hubs, spokes, and gateways

It is beyond doubt that one of the elements which allowed the growth of Mediterranean ports since the 1980s was the boosts of the hub-and-spoke system (Cazzaniga Francesetti and Foschi 2002b).

Even in perspective, the reinforcement of the hub-and-spoke network will allow to:

- pursue economies of scale and of network due to the multiplicity of destination markets (i.e. of the 'hinterlands', in some way) which can be reached through the big Central Med and trunk route hubs: European Union, Black Sea, North Africa, Middle East);
- establish dedicated terminals in hub ports, thus financing large infrastructure projects, attracting permanently major carriers in the Mediterranean region, reducing the volatility of traffic which normally affects hub ports due to competition;
- alleviate the volume growth in some 'traditional' Mediterranean ports, located in 'fragile' territories characterised by scarce space, intense coastal urban development, environmental and tourism assets, etc., and not able to sustain a growth rate proportional to the growth in seaborne trade on East-West routes;
- attract the location of distribution centres and logistic platforms (and logistics functions and value-added services) in 'spoke' and 'gateway' ports,[3] partly as a consequence of lower pressure on land use; this can reinforce local macroeconomic benefits (employment, value-added) per unit of throughput, and allow the 'decoupling' between throughput trend and local benefits; the reinforcement of the hub-and-spoke model emphasises the role of gateways ports by allowing the supply of value-added services for the shipper, while the presence of distribution centres makes more attractive (even for deep-sea direct-call services) the 'old' North-Med port-cities, with positive macroeconomic effects.

North-South connectivity within the Mediterranean and Southern Europe

The boost of Mediterranean hub-and-spoke system, while it significantly contributed to rebalancing port throughput between Northern and Southern Europe, indeed failed to bring benefits to the so-called North-Med Range, mainly characterised by gateway ports, which recorded a throughput growth rate far smaller than other areas, and a substantial market share fall. North Italian ports, namely, proved to suffer from geographical barriers and poor land transport infrastructure (namely railroad), which hindered them from gaining market shares beyond Alps.

Moreover, the connectivity of 'old' North Italian gateway ports grew far less than the average of spoke ports in the Mediterranean basin, in terms of links to Central

---

3   If space in ports is insufficient, as it happens in North Italian ports, this location can take place even at a certain distance from the terminal facilities, provided that it is within the same economic (and labour supply) region.

Med hub ports and to the Southern edge of Mediterranean. Therefore, increasing North-South connectivity towards hubs and Southern edge requires:

- the implementation of European North-South multimodal corridors (based on Trans-European Networks) mainly structured on railway links connecting North Mediterranean ports on the Northern edge (Spain, France, Italy, Greece, and in prospect the Balkans) to the European economic heartland; a key role should be played by the 'corridor of the two Seas' from Rotterdam to Genoa (via Simplon), the axis Berlin-Palermo (via Brenner), the railway link between Spain and Northern Europe and the European Corridor no.5 (from the Iberian Peninsula to Kiev), as well as the improvement of mountain passes through Appennine (new railway line from/to Thyrrenean ports) and Alps (Fréjus and Gothard);
- the establishment of an effective network of short-sea shipping services involving both South European coastal navigation (links between Spain, Italy, and France; between Greece and Adriatic ports; etc.), in the aim of decongesting land transport networks, and links with major islands and with the Southern edge of Mediterranean.

Institutional Capacity Building

In most Mediterranean countries a modernisation of the port institutional and governance is needed to match the deep changes occurring in port management patterns and the growing complexity, and variety of the port community and of the 'output' of port production.

Without going into details of specific national regulations, the definition of new institutional and governance models suitable for the new trends must match at least three major needs.

First, the geographic networking: the new models should be more flexible and capable to involve a mixed (public and private) partnership, including players not only belonging to the port community (cities, regional and central governments, land transport providers), for actions to be developed not only in port areas (e.g. inland terminals), possibly located in different countries. These networks must allow not the 'normal' synergy effects between terminals similar but located far away from one another (as it normally happens in a horizontally integrated global stevedore), but rather complementary links between nodes/ports geographically nearby but with different and complementary functions; these network must allow a more rationale land use, aiming at the development of the whole port range. In this perspective, it seems necessary to achieve a higher cooperation between neighbour ports in the same sub-range (i.e. North Tyrrhenian Sea and North Adriatic Sea) in order to attain the critical threshold needed to attract new clients, by providing a unique and integrated gateway to Southern Europe. Only a higher coordination between some functions (e.g. space allocation, marketing) and the implementation of an effective access to the potential hinterland beyond Alps (Switzerland, Austria, Bavaria), that the North Med range could recover an acceptable competitiveness and role within the Mediterranean basin.

Second, the financing of port and infrastructure investment: the involvement of private investors both in the implementation of terminal and handling facilities and in providing port nautical services must allow a substantial contribution to back the growing financial needs for port investment. Increasing financial constraints in most countries (namely in the Euro countries), as well as the efforts of the European Union to standardise public subsidies and pricing criteria for using infrastructure (Haralambides *et al.* 2001) require, in the medium-term, a higher capacity of the port industry of attracting private investors in the port venture, what in turn requires more courageous market rules in the production of port services (auctions, concessions and franchising for terminal management and public services).

Finally, dedicated terminals: in tight connection with the private financing of port infrastructure, the concession of dedicated facilities from port authorities to some top carriers, even in gateway ports, should allow to count on a solid cargo base not subject to the normal volatility. In a few years Northern Europe changed from negative to positive its attitude towards the traditional dilemma of dedicated terminals. Negative effects (non optimal land use, risks of unfair intra-port competition) have been emphasised in the past, positive effects (effective inter-port competition, stabilisation of cargo base over time, etc.) have been neglected.

Acknowledgements

The authors are grateful to Prof Claudio Ferrari of the Faculty of Economics of Genoa for his support in collecting data and information about European ports. The authors remain solely responsible for any errors remaining and for opinions expressed in the chapter.

Chapter 8

Northern European Range: Shipping Line Concentration and Port Hierarchy

Antoine Frémont and Martin Soppé

Introduction

Port concentration is a recurring topic in maritime transport studies. Can the organisation of maritime networks coupled with that of inland networks lead to the concentration of traffic at a small number of ports at the expense of the others? This question is of concern both to geographers and economists as the spatial configurations of transport networks and the terms of competition change completely from one scenario to another.

The problem of port concentration existed before containerisation, but the containerisation process has renewed interest in it. This is because in a context of strong competition between the various actors in the transport chain, which has become increasingly integrated and global in nature in order to meet the requirements of shippers, containerisation derives its strength from the economies of scale it generates through massification both on the sea and on the land. Throughout the last forty years, containerisation has inspired the wildest speculation with the recurring extreme hypothesis of a single mega-port on each seaboard. Each increase in the size of ships revives this scenario.

This chapter will re-examine the issue of port concentration from the detailed level of transport operators, in particular shipping lines running regular services, based on analyses of the authors' database on Weekly Containerized Transport Capacities. By focusing the investigation on the ports of the Northern European range which extends from Le Havre to Hamburg, this chapter will show that the apparent absence of an increase in port concentration along the seaboard in fact hides the fact that, on the scale of the network of each shipping line, real concentration processes exist which are also implemented by cargo handlers and freight forwarding agencies.

Towards a New Model of Port Concentration

Massification and port concentration

Many factors encourage the process of port concentration. Technically, the process is made possible by containerisation.[1] Containerised transport is standardised and has permitted a continuous reduction in unit transport costs as a result of major economies of scale. This massification process is most spectacular on the sea where there has been a continuous increase in the size of vessels. The massification process extends inland where companies seek to provide end-to-end transport solutions. Inland, massification is less marked than at sea due to the lower capacities of inland transport.

The technical possibilities of containerised transport have become genuine innovations because the actors involved in maritime transport have implemented them in the favourable context of globalisation. Globalisation has resulted in an increase in international trade volumes, in particular for products manufactured between the poles of the Triad. Shipping lines running regular services have followed, in a context of deregulation, this internationalisation of the processes of production and consumption. They have met the global demand of shippers with a global supply of transport. In order to control significant market share in relation to their competitors, considerable maritime resources have been brought into play. These imperatives explain the existence of mergers and alliances achieved by the pooling of nautical resources which have led to a high degree of concentration of the sector: in 2004, the twenty largest shipping lines accounted for 62 per cent of global containerised transport capacity as opposed to less than 33 per cent in 1989. These mergers and acquisitions were crowned at the end of the 1990s by the creation of three major alliances: the *Grand Alliance* with a capacity of almost 550,000 TEU (2002), The *New World Alliance* with almost 400,000 TEU (2002) and the *United Alliance* with slightly more than 300,000 TEU (2002).

So, logically, within each port range only those ports which are able to participate in the process of transport massification will be favoured by shipping lines. They must be able to face the concentration of maritime flows with access roads and infrastructure that can cope with large vessels and increasing traffic volumes.

The development, since the end of the 1980s, of the *hub and spoke* system is also contributing to port concentration. Like airline companies, the shipping lines concentrate the stops of their mother ships and feeders in pivot ports in order to be able to increase the number of possible destinations for containers, at both global and regional levels.

---

1   The term *port concentration* corresponds to statistical concentration of handled freight and shipping companies among the ports along a seaboard. It results in the reduction in the number of ports used and the highly dominant position of a small number of ports.

Integration of the transport chain and port concentration

The shipping lines have played a pioneering role in maritime massification and the reorganisation of maritime and inland networks. The other actors in the chain have followed the trend by obligation and opportunity, not only to withstand the growing power of the shipping lines but also to meet demand from shippers. The freight forwarders have responded almost instantaneously to the need for global coverage by forming large groups whose networks of agencies cover global markets. From the end of the 1980s, the cargo handling sector in its turn experienced a trend towards consolidation with the birth of large international cargo handling groups.

The largest cargo handling companies are creating networks of ports which also bring into question the concepts of port forelands and hinterlands. Comprehensive contracts are signed between the principal operators in the transport chain. These contracts help to modify the chains as a result of the economies of scale they generate. The benefits of network organisation then come into play. Competition between actors within the same terrestrial space and seaboard takes the place of competition between ports in which the geographical position and the performance of each port played a direct role. The *situation* of each port is now determined by the opportunities it provides for linking up with the networks of the various transport operators.

There is a reciprocal interaction between containerisation, container operators and globalisation which allows the setting up of globalised transport chains and these are expanding to operate on a global scale. Theoretically, these transport chains will encourage a new type of port concentration (see Figure 8.1). Indeed, several models for the development of maritime networks proposed by Taaffe, Morrill and Gould (1963) or Rimmer (1967) demonstrate that the process of concentration which can only be reinforced by containerisation. Hayuth (1981) has investigated the impacts of containerisation and concluded that the general trend towards port concentration will continue.

The advent of container ships with capacities over 10,000 TEU, or even the *malaccamax* type vessels (18,000 TEU) provides the opportunity for fresh speculation. The anticipated increase in the size of vessels would result in navigation being concentrated on an equatorial route, a reduction in the number of stops essentially for economic reasons and could, in Europe, result in the service of a single 'hub' port (Wijnolst 1999, 2000; Ashar 2002).

Port concentration or shipping line concentration?

Massification and the creation of networks of ports do not, however, on their own validate the hypothesis that maximum concentration will take place within a port range. Excessive port concentration, with in the extreme case a single port handling the majority of containerised traffic, goes against the stated and pursued interests of the operators. With annual growth rates of 7 to 8 per cent, it is inconceivable for a port to have sufficient capacity to meet demand both in terms of quay berths and storage capacity. In addition, capacities are subjected to a double pressure if the port functions as a hub. Excessive concentration would also pose the problem of inland feeder and distribution services with an obvious danger of inland networks becoming congested at different levels. Last, it would lead to a situation of increased competition between all the operators within a limited space. Inevitably the balance of power within the transport chain would shift in favour of ports by limiting alternative solutions and counteracting the advantages that accrue from the organisation of networks.

Massification also encourages the largest shipping lines to secure their port cargo handling operations. An increase in the number of hubs would require perfect coordination between the stops of the various mother or feeder ships. Any delay would constitute a threat to the entire system.

In a situation where benefits arise from massification and the creation of networks that encourages increased port concentration, and disbenefits necessarily result from excessive concentration, this chapter makes the hypothesis that transport operators, particularly shipping lines, are pursuing the trend towards concentration in another way, that of *shipping line concentration* at a port. The port ceases to be a mere pawn in the game (Slack 1993) and once again plays an important role. The objective of shipping lines is to possess dedicated terminals to secure their port operations, either by directly including this function in their activities or by making an alliance with a cargo handling company. In order to be viable, this solution requires the shipping companies' traffic to be concentrated at one or two specific ports on a maritime range. If this is not the case, the dedicated terminal will be under-used (Musso *et al.* 1999; Haralambides *et al.* 2002; Cariou 2003). If port concentration is not apparent on a given maritime range at the level of traffic as a whole, it will necessarily be apparent at the level of certain shipping companies, engaged initially in a process of massification and later in a process of securing their port services. A shipping line must logically attempt to have one or two 'dedicated hubs' on each maritime range. This search for security will lead the company to attempt to achieve a dominant position in the port in question in order to become a powerful and important interlocutor for the port administration and the cargo handling companies.

The consequences of shipping line concentration on hinterland services

A reorganisation of maritime networks obviously has an impact on inland services. The hypothesis of maximum concentration at a single port would have as a consequence that the whole hinterland would be dominated by this single mega-port. In the case where *hubs* are dedicated to a shipping line, close together, accessible and in competition, the scenario involves overlapping hinterlands or the merging of hinterlands into a single space with several maritime entrance points.

The shipping line concentration model situates the phenomena that have been observed since the start of the nineteen nineties in the process of change which is affecting the maritime transport network. The diagrams in Figure 8.1 illustrate in chronological order the changes suggested by the models. Diagrams 8.1.1 to 8.1.3 illustrate the process of concentration.

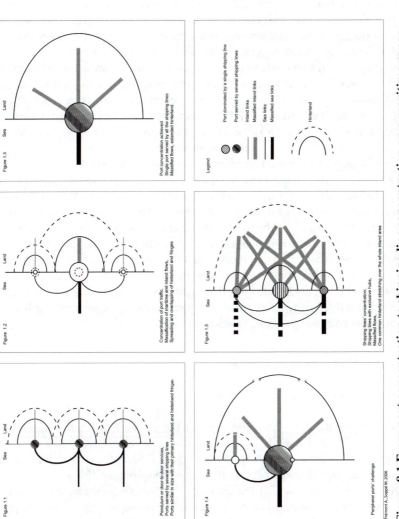

Figure 8.1 From port concentration to shipping line concentration on a maritime range

In the first phase, traffic is regularly distributed between the ports. The shipping companies serve all the ports on the seaboard. Each port relies on its fundamental hinterland and the margins where the hinterlands overlap are small. In the second phase, a trend towards concentration appears, with regard to maritime and terrestrial flows and port traffic. The peripheral ports lose traffic and their hinterlands become smaller to the benefit of the growing port. They are served by smaller shipping lines or *feeder* services operating from the *hub* port. Diagram 8.1.3 illustrates the extreme situation where the maximum concentration results in the complete disappearance of the secondary ports. All the routes converge on a single port on each seaboard which is served by all the shipping companies. The port is in a monopoly situation on the seaboard and its hinterland covers the entire zone. Figure 8.1.4 represents the peripheral port challenge described by Hayuth where the peripheral ports benefit from new dynamism as a result of the diseconomies generated by excessive concentration. The last diagram (see Figure 8.1.5) illustrates the shipping line concentration model described above. It represents one of the alternatives to the model of absolute concentration in the maritime transport system.

Does shipping line concentration at a port also extend to other operators? On the one hand, as the freight forwarding agencies and cargo handlers also operate in a globalised environment, they could consider concentrating their activities at a limited number of ports for the same reasons as the shipping companies. On the other hand, if the signing of comprehensive contracts between the major operators becomes common practice, the geographical repositioning of shipping lines would compel the other actors in the transport chain to follow them, *i.e.* to concentrate their activities at a selection of ports on the basis of their cooperation agreements. Thus, the ports would not only be hub ports dedicated to a dominant shipping line but also dedicated to a three-party cooperative structure consisting of the shipping line, the forwarding agency and the cargo handler.

The Example of the Northern Range

A movement towards shipping line concentration

An examination of containerised port traffic on the European Northern Range reveals a very high degree of stability. In the early stages of containerisation in the 1970s the port concentration index increased from 0.55 to 0.62, but since then it has varied only marginally and remained almost the same throughout the 1990s.

In order to test the shipping line concentration hypothesis we have analysed the port concentration indices not for traffic as a whole but separately for each shipping line. Table 8.2 shows the number of ports served and the concentration index for each shipping line for 1994 and 2002.[2]

---

2   Mergers between shipping companies are taken into account.

Table 8.1 Index of concentration (Gini coefficient) for the ports in the Northern Range*

	1970	1980	1985	1990	1994	1995	2002
TEU	0.55	0.62	0.56	0.62	-	0.60	0.61
WCTC	-	-	-	-	0.52	-	0.48

*Includes the ports in the northern range and the ports in the United Kingdom on the English Channel-North Sea seaboard.
Source: WCTC Database/INRETS.

For all shipping companies, with the exception of Hapag-Lloyd, the concentration index increased and the number of ports served remained almost the same. The highest concentrations were attained by European companies. Mergers between shipping companies have provided an opportunity for reorganising services to the Northern Range with the implementation of a port concentration policy which only existed to a limited degree in 1994 (Maersk group and P&O Nedlloyd group). MSC and CMA also illustrate this trend, but even more strongly, as a result of their extremely vigorous growth. In 1994, they served the ports in the Northern Range in a completely uniform manner. In 2002, growth has given rise to a reorganisation of maritime networks with greater port concentration.

In contrast, the Asian companies, except NYK, are characterised by concentration coefficients of zero in 1994 and which remained low in 2002. Again, in contrast with European shipping companies, the mergers carried out by Asian shipping companies, including the purchase of European companies do not result in a very marked increase in concentration. This confirms the hypothesis that European and Asian shipping companies have two different types of strategy (Frémont and Soppé 2004). The European companies, which are close to the market, innovate by implementing 'transport company' strategies. They rely on pivot ports and implement a *hub and spoke* strategy for the Northern Range, in spite of its small physical size. In contrast, the Asian companies concentrate on direct links, on the one hand because they lack sufficient transport capacity and on the other hand because of their specific approach which involves the exportation of national production towards centres of consumption.

Table 8.2 Change in the number of ports served and port concentration for different shipping companies in the Northern European Range, 1994–2002

Shipping line	1994		2002	
	Ports served	Gini coeff.	Ports served	Gini coeff.
Maersk-Sea Land and Safmarine	8	0.38	9	0.53
Maersk-Sea Land	7	0.36		
Maersk	7	0.28		
Sea Land	5	0.33		
Safmarine	6	0.12		
MSC	6	0.01	8	0.51
P&ONedlloyd	10	0.41	9	0.44
P&OCL	9	0.33		
Nedlloyd	9	0.40		
NYK	7	0.16	7	0.45
CMA-CGM	10	0.44	11	0.40
CMA	5	0.00		
CGM	9	0.43		
Hanjin+DSR	7	0.24	6	0.36
Hanjin	4	0.00		
DSR	7	0.21		
K-Line	4	0.04	6	0.25
Hapag-Lloyd	11	0.39	8	0.24
Cosco	5	0.00	6	0.23
Evergreen+Lloyd Triestino	5	0.00	7	0.23
APL	n.a.	n.a.	6	0.22
All shipping lines	7.05	0.52	7.54	0.48

The emergence of dedicated hubs

Our hypothesis is confirmed by an examination of the importance of the ports in the range in the port network of the shipping companies. The port concentration policy carried through by European shipping companies has resulted in a few ports on the seaboard being given preference to the others which only play a secondary role in the network.

Thus, Maersk (see Figure 8.2) has completely modified its port network in less than ten years by concentrating its traffic on Bremerhaven, to the detriment of Hamburg, and Felixstowe in addition to Rotterdam whose relative share has greatly decreased.

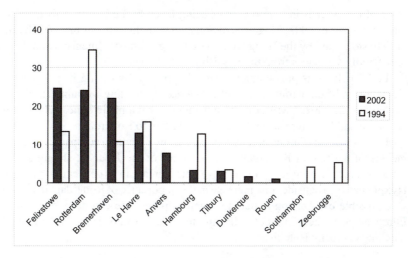

**Figure 8.2 The percentage of the WCTC of Maersk/SeaLand/Safmarine
handled by the different ports in the Northern Range**
Source: WCTC Database/INRETS.

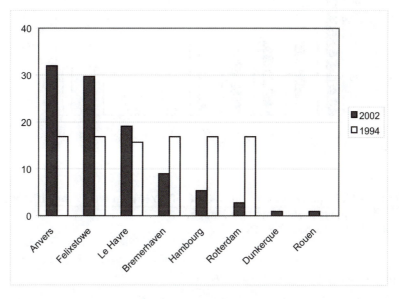

**Figure 8.3 The percentage of the WCTC of MSC handled by the different
ports in the Northern range**
Source: WCTC Database/INRETS.

MSC (see Figure 8.3) illustrates the transition from a non-differentiated port
network to one which focuses on two ports: Antwerp and Felixstowe. However, the

place of the latter is in the process of being taken by Le Havre. This is because in the second half of 2002, MSC was dissatisfied with the services provided by the port of Felixstowe and by the Hong Kong based cargo handler Hutchison and decided to transfer all its services from the English port to Le Havre.

P&ONedlloyd is pursuing an identical approach by basing its port network on Hamburg and Southampton and, like Maersk, by tending to minimise the role of Rotterdam. In 2002, CMA still did not seem to have made a clear choice, even if Hamburg and Le Havre seem essential in addition to Rotterdam.

In contrast to European companies, Asian shipping companies seem to be increasing the role of Rotterdam. The example of the Japanese shipping company NYK is particularly striking (Figure 8.4). The increase in its concentration coefficient is explained by a considerable increase in the importance of Rotterdam in its network. One possible explanation is that an Asian shipping line can not ignore the largest European port where in fact the leading terminal operator is the Hong Kong based handling company Hutchison.

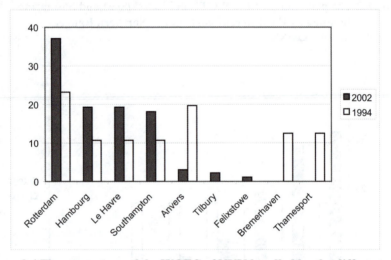

Figure 8.4 The percentage of the WCTC of NYK handled by the different ports in the Northern Range
Source: WCTC Database/INRETS.

A dominant position in dedicated hubs

The stability of port concentration in the Northern Range is therefore only superficial. The three largest shipping companies in the world are pursuing a strategy of concentration involving a very limited number of ports in addition to Rotterdam. There is a genuine *de facto* distribution of pivot ports as each shipping company relies on one or two different ports. This distribution explains why port concentration is stable at an overall level but increases when each shipping company is considered individually.

The shipping companies account for a very large share of the WCTC in their favoured ports (Table 8.3). Thus, Maersk alone accounts for 45 per cent of the transport supply in the port of Bremerhaven and MSC accounts for a quarter of Antwerp's port activities. In contrast, the shipping companies which have not concentrated on one port, such as CMA or the Asian companies, are not marked out from the others.

Table 8.3 Percentage of WCTC in 2002 handled by European companies and NYK and Hanjin DSR in the six largest ports of the Northern Range

Shipping line	Rotterdam	Hamburg	Antwerp	Felixstowe	Le Havre	Bremerhaven
Maersk/Sea Land*	**21.2**	4.2	11.3	**31.5**	16.4	**45.7**
P&ONedlloyd	11.5	**17.1**	8.9	3.8	7.7	5.5
MSC	1.5	3.9	**27.6**	**22.3**	14.2	11.7
CMA	6.7	10.8	3.4	2.1	11.0	0.0
NYK	4.2	3.2	0.8	0.3	3.1	0.0
Hanjin/DSR	11.5	10.8	0.7	12.7	8.8	3.3

* Including Safmarine.

These market shares in their dedicated hub confirm the hypothesis that the shipping companies in question are in a strong position to negotiate both with the port authorities and the cargo handler thereby securing their port operations in the long term.

The creation of port networks and the concentration of operators in Northern Europe

The hypothesis of shipping line concentration appears to be supported by our analysis, but what is the situation as regards cargo handlers and forwarding agencies? In this case, the analysis will be more qualitative. In 2004, five international companies handled 26 million TEU in the seven largest ports in the Range, which presented 84.6 per cent of the total traffic of these ports. Also, the way the presence of these groups is organised gives the impression that they are dividing up the market. Hutchison dominates in Rotterdam (ECT) and Felixstowe. PSA has added Antwerp to its network of 12 ports by acquiring local companies, Hessenatie and Noord Natie. This group has more than 90 per cent of the container market at Antwerp, the rest of the market being held by another major group, P&O ports. The cargo handler Eurogate which, although locally-based is nevertheless developing an international network, is present at Bremen and Hamburg where it shares the port with the local company HHLA, owned by the city. At Le Havre, the three major shipping lines, Maersk, MSC and CMA are allied with local terminal operators.

Table 8.4 Market share of the principal cargo handlers in the ports of the Northern Range in 2004

Terminal operator	Total		Rotterdam		Hamburg		Antwerp		Bremerhaven		Felixstowe		Le Havre		Southampton	
	TEU	%	TEU	%	TEU	%	TEU	%	TEU	%	TEU	%	TEU	%	TEU	%
Hutchison	7.6	29.2	5.0	60.9	–	–	–	–	–	–	2.6	100	–	–	–	–
Eurogate	5.7	21.9	–	–	2.3	32.8	–	–	3.4	100	–	–	–	–	–	–
PSA	5.6	21.5	–	–	–	–	5.6	93.3	–	–	–	–	–	–	–	–
HHLA	4.6	17.7	–	–	4.6	65.7	–	–	–	–	–	–	–	–	–	–
P&O Ports	2.5	9.6	–	–	–	–	0.4	6.7	–	–	–	–	0.7	33	1.4	100
Total throughput	26.0	100	8.2	100	7.0	100	6	100	3.4	0	2.6	100	2.1	100	1.4	100

Source: terminal handling companies' websites.

One can conclude that each major player decides to be present in one or two ports, if possible to the exclusion of other competitors of the same size, but perhaps sharing the space with companies of a more local nature.

The organisation of the forwarding agency sector is, geographically, more difficult to analyse due to a lack of data. The presence of forwarding agencies in European ports does not at first sight reveal geographical concentration at port level. In contrast, to shipping companies and cargo handlers, the activity of forwarders is not capital intensive, being principally based on the development of commercial networks. Forwarding agencies can increase the volume they handle by opening up offices in different geographical zones.

Table 8.5 Maritime activity of the five largest freight forwarding agencies in 2004

Firm	Millions of TEU in 2004	Market share in %
Kühne&Nagel	1.6	7.3
DHL Danzas Air & Ocean	1.1	5.5
Schenker	0.7	4.1
Panalpina	0.8	4.0
Exel	0.6	2.9
Subtotal	4.8	23.8
Total market	17.0	100.0

Source: Global Trade Databank, annual reports and company estimates.

Importance of Port Positions and Hinterlands with regard to Understanding the Stability of Port Hierarchy

The stability of port hierarchies

The emergence of shipping line concentration does not pose a fundamental threat to port hierarchies, even if the market shares of the large ports vary over time. In the case of the Northern Range, it is possible to identify four major types of change (Table 8.6). Rotterdam, which at the mouth of the Meuse is ideally located for serving the Rhenish heartland of Europe via the Rhine. It has exceptional nautical conditions for receiving the largest container ships and was, in the 1970s, in the process of asserting its position as the dominant port in the Northern range with a market share of more than 30 per cent in 1980. But between 1980 and 1995, its market share fell steadily, and then more suddenly between 1995 and 2000. This simple observation disproves the frequently repeated theory that all traffic will be concentrated on a single port in each range. On the contrary it probably indicates a refusal on the part of operators, both shipping lines and shippers to accept the possibility of dependence on a single port, however efficient it is.

Hamburg and Antwerp are continually gaining market share to the detriment of Rotterdam. They are nevertheless both located at some distance from the mouth of an estuary. They draw advantage from their inland location and their closeness to the market which seems more decisive than maritime accessibility. It is also undoubtedly the case that Hamburg is taking advantage of the fall of the Berlin wall in 1989 in order to extend its hinterland into Central and Eastern Europe.

Four ports come after this (Bremen/Bremerhaven, Felixstowe, Le Havre and Southampton). Although smaller than the previous ones, they are nevertheless important. They are affected by more uncertain trends with alternating phases of relative growth and decline. Their nautical conditions are excellent, but these ports are extremely dependent on a hinterland which is limited to their national capital for which other major ports are also competing. Lastly, small ports remain restricted to a secondary role; none of them has managed to move into the big league in the last 30 years.

Table 8.6 Change in the market share of ports in percentage of total traffic (TEU)

Port	1970	1980	1985	1990	1995	2002
Rotterdam	18.7	31.8	30.3	29.5	27.7	22.8
Hamburg	5.6	13.1	13.2	15.8	16.7	18.8
Antwerp	16.6	12.1	15.4	12.4	13.5	16.7
Bremen/Bremerhaven	15.0	11.7	11.3	9.6	8.8	10.5
Felixstowe	7.2	4.1	5.9	11.4	11.0	9.6
Le Havre	8.3	8.5	6.5	6.9	5.6	6.0
Southampton	1.8	6.0	2.4	2.8	3.9	4.5
Zeebrugge	5.4	2.6	2.2	2.8	3.1	3.4
Tilbury	12.0	4.5	4.4	2.9	2.0	2.0
Thamesport	0.0	0.0	0.0	0.1	1.6	1.8
Immingham	0.0	0.3	0.6	1.0	2.0	1.3
Hull	4.5	1.4	2.5	1.3	1.6	0.8
Dunkerque	0.9	1.1	0.8	0.6	0.4	0.6
Rouen	0.2	0.8	1.5	0.7	0.5	0.6
Goole	0.0	0.0	0.2	0.6	0.4	0.5
Amsterdam	2.2	0.9	0.9	0.6	0.5	0.2
Ipswich	1.8	1.1	1.7	1.1	0.8	0.1
Total	100.0	100.0	100.0	100.0	100.0	100.0

Source: Containerisation International Yearbook.

The role of the close hinterland

The stability of port hierarchies is also explained by the specific dynamics of the hinterlands. Concentration models are only concerned with the position of ports within networks, usually maritime, and ignore the centrality of ports in the operation of terrestrial space and its ties with maritime space (Debrie *et al.* 2005). The hinterland imposes a production and consumption market on the port and also inland transport infrastructure which remains constant for a long period of time. The hinterland imposes its specific demographic and economic potential on the ports of the seaboard and on maritime networks.

The ports in the Northern Range are developing some transhipment functions, but remain essentially hinterland ports. The potential of the hinterland is decisive in order to explain traffic flows and the stability of the port hierarchy in the face of the network approaches adopted by the operators. We are presenting the comparison of terrestrial accessibility based on statistical data from Eurostat at the NUTS3 level to illustrate the configuration of the European hinterland. Figure 8.4 shows the economic potential in GDP terms within perimeters ranging from 50 to 600 km around each of the four major ports in the range.

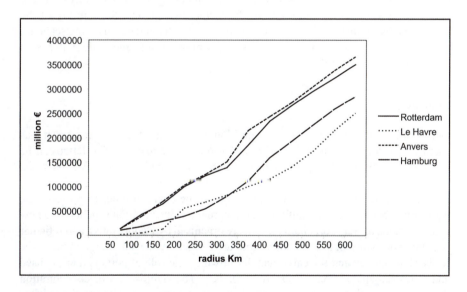

Figure 8.5 Cumulated GDP in concentric perimeters around the ports in 2002
© Frémont, Soppé.
Source: Eurostat 2005.

This figure clearly shows the difference between the centre of the seaboard which is supported by a very dynamic near hinterland (Antwerp and Rotterdam) and ports which are in more marginal geographical positions, Hamburg-Bremerhaven and Le Havre. The potential of the ports of Antwerp and Rotterdam is higher in absolute terms (by 25 per cent) than that of the geographically marginal ports. This superiority becomes more marked closer to the ports. This situation reflects the distribution of wealth and the potential for production and consumption of the Rhine axis and shows the advantage of the Dutch and Belgian ports with regard to the market. Hamburg has, however, staged a remarkable recovery since 1990 by managing to capture more distant inland traffic as a result of effective rail transport and by re-establishing historical links with the hinterland in Central and Eastern Europe. Thus, despite a relatively weak near hinterland, the port of Hamburg can rely on more distant potential.

The stability of the port hierarchy is also explained by the scale of the investments made by each Northern Range port in order to maintain or increase its potential traffic. All the large ports are currently engaged in programmes to develop their port spaces: Maasvlakte II in Rotterdam, Deurganck in Antwerp, Buchardkai and Altenwerder in Hamburg and Port 2000 in Le Havre. These investments on the part of the various ports and the fact that the capacities of ports are, in a context of increasing maritime traffic, perceived by operators as being limited, make any radical change in market shares impossible. Each port is thus trying to strengthen its connections with its hinterland. The principal aim of the improvements is to avoid excessive congestion which could lead to traffic being switched to a competing port. The rigidity of inland transport networks is therefore one of the factors that favours the stability of the port hierarchy by distributing the pressure exerted by the hinterland on the seaboard between the ports and by limiting the possibility of rapid and large-scale switches, in particular towards a single mega-port.

Conclusion

Our results confirm that port concentration process is still in progress. It has taken a new form which is that of *shipping line concentration*. The latter can be observed in the setting up of dedicated hubs. By extension, we have made the hypothesis that there is a process of *actor concentration*, due to the imitation or modification of strategies by the other actors in the chain in order to preserve the equilibrium between the strengths of each segment. Concentration is generating new configurations of transport chains which are organised by a cooperative and reticular structure consisting of a three-party structure formed by the shipping company, the forwarding agency and the cargo handler in which the role of ports is marginalised and terrestrial spatial constraints are secondary. The stabilisation of concentration from the comprehensive perspective nevertheless raises a fundamental question. The structure and limits of the terrestrial space and its seaboard must be included in the existing models. Ultimately, this amounts to a reinstatement of the port triptych which is often brought into question in the context of containerisation and theories of the complete dominance of networks. Terrestrial space exhibits inertia and moderates the more rapid changes that affect maritime networks. The proposed models of concentration are more able to explain aspects of a general trend than provide predictions. Thus, a 'revolution' of the European seaboard is not on agenda, at least in the medium term.

Chapter 9

Factors Influencing the Landward Movement of Containers: The Cases of Halifax and Vancouver

Robert J. McCalla

Introduction

It is now almost 50 years since Malcolm McLean began his New York to Houston box service on the *Ideal X*, thus launching the container revolution. Wholesale changes in how ships were built, how shipping companies operated, how trade routes were configured both on sea and land and how ports operated were to be made over the next 50 years. Those changes are ongoing today. No longer is international trade of general cargo thought of in discrete stages; rather, it takes place across many integrated modes linking inland origins on one continent to inland destinations on another. Thus we speak of *intermodal chains* of transportation. Of interest in this chapter is the landward portion of these intermodal cargo flows and just how accessible container terminals are to trucks and trains. The chapter focuses on Canadian intermodal operations at the ports of Halifax and Vancouver through the analysis of a questionnaire administered to key personnel in the two port-cities.

The efficient operation of intermodal chains follows Oram's (1968) First Law of Mechanisation: 'if you improve a stage in the process of cargo handling you will immediately have to improve the stage before and after that one.' It is not sufficient to have just the biggest and fastest ships, or the terminal with the most lifts per hour, or the most direct landward connections between terminal and inland origin or destination; all modes must run effectively and efficiently for the chain to be strong. Theoretically, all elements share the same importance, but in practice one element will assume greater importance when it is identified as the weakest link in the chain. If this one element fails to keep up with changes in the other elements then it takes on critical importance which must be addressed. It is not always the case that the same element is always the critical one. Over time as changes take place in the elements some will lead and some will fall behind. Each of the links in the intermodal chain – landward transport in the export foreland, offloading and loading at the export terminal, the sea link, offloading and loading at the import terminal and the land transport in the import hinterland – has undergone improvements over time. Ships are larger; terminals are bigger and more efficient; trains have the ability to double stack containers. Furthermore, managing the logistics of the connecting elements has developed into an industry itself.

Currently, the element driving improvements in intermodal chains is the container ship. As ships have got progressively larger, ports and terminals have been adjusting to accommodate them (Cullinane and Khanna 2000). It is also necessary that adjustments be made in land transportation infrastructure and operations. An 8000-TEU vessel requires three days of round the clock operation of six gantry cranes to offload all its containers (Mongelluzzo 2005). Assuming a 50/50 modal split between road transport and rail, each ship fills about six double stack trains and 2000 truck chassis which, with their tractors, would stretch almost 32 km. Of course, no ship unloads all of its containers in one port on the range of ports it is calling. Consequently, the numbers suggested are theoretical rather than actual, but they do indicate the demands large ships put on land facilities. A port, to be successful, serving these ships must have terminal space, cranes, water depth, labour *and* intermodal transportation connections. Land access by road and rail transportation has taken on critical importance in moving containers to and through container terminals. It could be seen as the weakest link in the chain. Evidence from the 2004 delays in moving containers through the North American West Coast ports points to this conclusion (Mongelluzzo 2004). Reasons to account for the weakness are related to the shipping industry itself including the location of container terminals as well as the development of the urban region in which the port sits and through which the linking land transportation modes must pass.

In terms of the shipping industry, several reasons can be cited that indirectly affect the importance of land access. The first has to do with container ships themselves. They have become larger and larger, but the land modes which serve the ships have had difficulty keeping up. This is especially true for the trucking industry. Rail responded initially with the double-stack rail wagon and train, but since their introduction in the 1980s increases in train capacity have been met with longer and more frequent trains and not an increase in the actual carrying capacity of a train wagon. So also, the response of the trucking industry to cope with the increasing capacity of container ships is to add more trucks to the system. For the most part this increased number of trucks and trains use the same road and rail infrastructure that existed when container terminals were built in the 1970s. This is especially the case with access to 'downtown' terminals, as opposed to 'greenfield' sites where new transport infrastructure had to be built to connect the new terminals to existing road and rail systems.

The very fact that downtown sites were chosen for the first container terminals is now compounding the land accessibility issue. These terminals were not sited with land access in mind; rather they were located on port lands that had deep water and good sea access. In the beginning of containerisation land accessibility was not such a critical issue. With low volumes the existing road and rail infrastructure could cope. This is not the case today. Another development which has put pressure on land transportation is the necessity to move containers away from the terminals as quickly as possible. Terminals themselves have had difficulty keeping up with the increased ship size. Although they have expanded in size over time and have added more cranes, the expansion has not been as fast as the increasing ship size. This is particularly the case in the last five years. The terminals need to process containers as quickly as possible and send them on their way; also terminals have less room to store empty containers. When empties show up at a terminal they must be trucked away from the terminal, stored, and then returned to the terminal to be loaded onto a ship, an action which puts further pressure on the limited road infrastructure serving the terminals.

Changes in the cities in which container terminals are located have also contributed to the land accessibility issue. Cities have increased in size, not only in population but also in size. Car ownership is at an all time high; traffic congestion is the norm. In the larger cities public transit in the form of buses on roads and commuter trains on rails is encouraged. As a result container trucks are competing with space on roads with cars and buses and intermodal container trains must share the rails with other goods trains as well as passenger and commuter trains. Citizens are also much more aware of environmental issues and they are concerned with their own safety as they coexist with commercial vehicles. Noise and exhausts associated with trucks and trains are undesirable. So also are dangerous goods in containers on city streets and railroads. Finally, as cities increase in population, some people want to live 'downtown' for a variety of reasons – to lessen their commuting time or to be close to the entertainment and cultural amenities the downtown offers. The downtown waterfront has become an attractive place to live. The response by developers is to build condominiums and support shopping and entertainment facilities. Land has become very expensive and harder to justify for port and transportation use.

But just how true are the statements above? How do port users see the importance of land transportation in the intermodal chain? This question, along with others, was asked of transportation industry and city officials in the port-cities of Vancouver and Halifax. This chapter reports on those findings. The chapter first outlines the growth of containerisation at Canadian ports with emphasis on Vancouver and Halifax over the past twenty years including a summary of terminal developments during that time. Also a description of road and rail infrastructure serving Vancouver and Halifax is provided. The chapter then goes on to show the results of the interviews *vis à vis* the importance of land access and its impediments in the two port-cities.

Containerisation at Canadian Ports

Canada's most important container ports are Vancouver, Montreal and Halifax. Since 1980 these three ports have handled approximately 90 per cent of all Canadian containers. Their relative importance, though, has changed over that time period. Whereas in 1980 Montreal was Canada's busiest container port followed by Halifax and Vancouver, by 2003 Vancouver had replaced Montreal as Canada's busiest container port with Halifax trailing (see Figure 9.1).

All three ports, but especially Vancouver, have experienced significant absolute increases in container throughput. During the period Vancouver increased its throughput from 0.127 million TEU in 1980 to 1.539 million TEU in 2003 (Table 9.1). The rise of Vancouver can be largely explained by the shift in world manufacturing to Asian Pacific countries, especially China, and Vancouver's relatively advantageous location on the North American West Coast to handle import containers for both Canada and central United States markets.

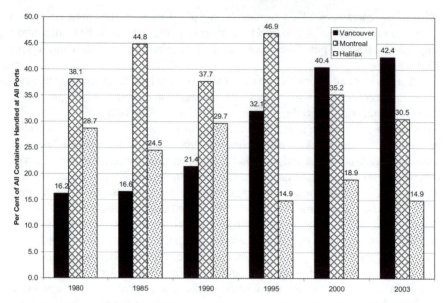

**Figure 9.1 Container throughput at Canada's most important container
          port in percentage terms**
Source: Data from *Containerisation International Yearbook*, various years.

Each of the three ports has added significantly to terminal infrastructure. Table
9.1 summarises these developments. As throughput has increased so also have the
land dedicated to container handling and the number of cranes. Increases in container
throughput, terminal size and lifting capacity have been reasonably well matched
in Halifax (Table 9.2). In Vancouver, though, there is strong mismatch between
increases in throughput, terminal size and number of cranes. TEU increased by a
factor of 12.1, terminal space increased by a factor of 4.4 times and crane numbers
increased by a factor of 5. Although the growth rates are different in each of the
ports in all the measures, in all three cases the ports have increased terminal size and
lifting capabilities to be able to handle more containers. The fact that terminal land
and cranes has not kept pace with throughput in Vancouver especially has meant that
on a per-ha or per-crane basis greater efficiencies in container handling have been
achieved. In all three ports more TEU are being handled per ha. The difference in
Vancouver is quite startling: 12,300 TEU per ha in 2003 vs. 4,500 in 1980 (Table
9.1). The increased throughput has put pressure on inland transportation to get the
containers to and from the terminals as quickly as possible.

Table 9.1 Container terminal characteristics at Halifax, Montreal and Vancouver

Year	Halifax					Montreal					Vancouver[0]				
	mTEU	ha*	Cranes†	TEU/ha	TEU/cr	mTEU	ha*	cranes†	TEU/ha	TEU/cr	mTEU	ha*	cranes†	TEU/ha	TEU/cr
1980	0.226	24.3	3	9,325	75,470	0.300	27.5	7	10,932	42,948	0.127	28.4	3	4,513	42,649
1985	0.263	45.7	5	5,756	52,611	0.481	45.6	10	10,559	48,152	0.178	50.3	5	3,542	35,635
1990	0.447	45.7	7	9,789	63,855	0.568	69.5	13	8,174	43,700	0.322	50.8	7	6,345	46,052
1995	0.229	50.5	7	4,553	32,829	0.726	74.1	Nd	9,803	Nd	0.496	50.8	Nd	9,770	Nd
2000	0.545	56.9	8	9,578	68,126	1.014	75.5	14	13,432	72,439	1.163	100.1	13	11,620	89,475
2003	0.541	56.9	10	9,519	54,154	1.108	79.6	14	13,930	79,202	1.539	125.1	15	12,302	102,603

* ha refers to size of all terminals in each port

† Cranes refer to number of ship-to-shore cranes in all terminals in each port

[0] Includes only the terminals (Centerm, Vanterm and Deltaport) within the Vancouver Port Authority. Does not include Fraser Port terminal.

Nd = no data

Source: Containerisation International Yearbook, various issues.

Table 9.2 Growth factors in throughput, terminal land and cranes at Halifax, Montreal and Vancouver, 2003 vs. 1980

	Halifax			Montreal			Vancouver		
	TEU	Ha	cranes	TEU	Ha	cranes	TEU	ha	cranes
2003/1980	2.39	2.34	3.33	3.69	2.89	2.0	12.1	4.4	5.0

Source: Derived from Table 9.1.

The Container Terminals of the Ports of Halifax and Vancouver and their Road and Rail Access

The focus of this chapter now turns to land access issues in Halifax and Vancouver. Figures 9.2 and 9.3 (note different scales) show the location of container terminals in the two ports and the road and rail infrastructure serving these facilities. A brief description of the terminals and road and rail links follows for each of Halifax and Vancouver.

Halifax (Figure 9.2)

Halifax has two container terminals: Halterm in the south end of the city and Fairview Cove in the north. Halterm was opened in 1970; Fairview Cove in 1982 (McCalla 2004). The former was sited on reclaimed land next to the existing break-bulk facilities at Ocean Terminals. Its location, adjacent to the commercial port waterfront, was excellent for sea access with deep water alongside. Fairview Cove was also sited on reclaimed land in the only vacant space on the Halifax peninsula waterfront. Unlike Halterm, Fairview Cove did not have good sea access, but it did have deep water in Bedford Basin.

Both terminals have direct rail access to the CN transcontinental line and on-dock intermodal transfer facilities. This rail access has served both terminals well especially in their early years when over 90 per cent of containers reached or left the port by rail. The modal split today between rail/road is still heavily weighted to rail with 80 per cent of Halterm containers and 60 per cent of Fairview Cove containers handled by that mode. Good accessibility by road cannot be equally claimed. All trucks entering or leaving Halterm must proceed through the narrow two-lane city streets of downtown Halifax. Trucks accessing Fairview Cove also must compete with space on city streets but these streets are wider (usually four-lane) and the distance from Fairview Cove to limited access highways is less than the distance from Halterm to these highways (3 kilometres vs. 8 kilometres).

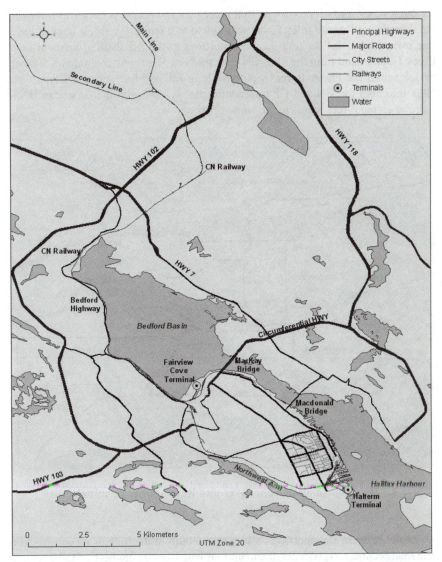

Figure 9.2 Overview map of Halifax and its container terminals

Vancouver (Figure 9.3)

Within the Vancouver Port Authority there are three container terminals: Centerm and Vanterm in Burrard Inlet and Deltaport in the Straight of Georgia. The first purpose-built terminal was Vanterm which opened in the fall of 1975. Previously, containers had been handled at Centennial Pier which eventually in the 1980s grew into Centerm. Deltaport opened for operation in 1998. Both Vanterm and Centerm were established in the commercial south shore of Burrard Inlet – the traditional cargo handling waterfront of Vancouver. In this area CP rail access is excellent following the shoreline of Burrard Inlet; CN is not as good as it relies on a single track at-grade line owned by BNSF to connect the waterfront to the marshalling yards at False Creek Flats. Inland from the Flats CN uses the New Westminster single track swing bridge across the Fraser River. A purpose built railroad line serves Deltaport and links into both the CN and CP transcontinental systems and the American BNSF railroad giving direct access to the United States.

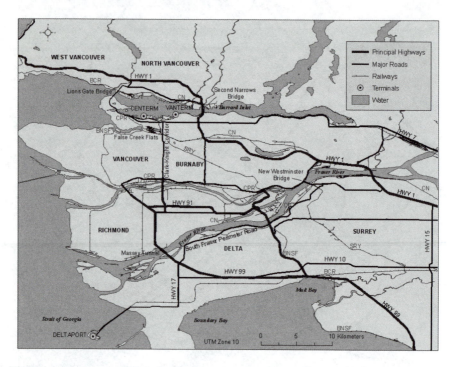

Figure 9.3 Overview map of Vancouver and its container terminals

Road access to Deltaport was also purpose built at the time of its construction. The roads connect to HWY 99, the main four lane freeway connection to Vancouver and the United States, and to HWY 10 connecting to the Trans Canada Highway (TCH) and the rest of British Columbia and Canada. These roads bypass much of the commercial and residential land use in Delta (the municipality in which Deltaport is located) but do cut across valuable agricultural land. Road access to Centerm and Vanterm is through existing Vancouver city streets. Connections to the TCH near Second Narrows Bridge which allow for limited access road travel to North and West Vancouver as well as Langley and beyond to the East is along a port controlled access road, but connections to Vancouver City and municipalities to the south (Richmond, Delta, Surrey) and onward to the United States is primarily through the Clark-Knight Corridor, a designated truck route arterial with numerous traffic lights and parking along the street.

In sum, each port has varied rail and road access, with strengths and weaknesses associated with each mode and each terminal.

Transportation Access to Container Terminals: A Questionnaire

In order to discover how both Halifax and Vancouver perceived the land access problem (if indeed it is a problem at all) and what was being done to alleviate any problems, an approach was made to port operators and users in the two port-cities. In addition a representative from municipal transportation or engineering departments was also asked an opinion on the accessibility issue in their respective ports.

Three questions

Three general questions were asked to gauge the feelings of each of the respondents about accessibility to the container terminals in the two ports.

   i. How would you describe the importance of land accessibility to the container terminals in the future of the port?
  ii. In general terms how would you describe road accessibility to the container terminals?
 iii. In general terms how would you describe rail accessibility to the container terminals?

In Halifax these questions were asked of the port, the two terminal operators, the city and the trucking industry. Unfortunately, a response was not received from the rail industry. In total, five individuals were interviewed. In Vancouver, the questions were asked of the port, the three terminal operators, the City of Vancouver (in reference to Centerm and Vanterm), the Municipality of Delta (in reference to Deltaport) and a representative of the trucking industry. Again, no response was gathered from the rail industry. Seven people were interviewed. Although the number of respondents is small, and the survey can in no way be described as a scientific sampling methodology, the people interviewed are key players in each of the ports and their opinions carry heavy weight in any analysis of perceptions of port issues.

The responses to question *i.* indicate all respondents identify land accessibility as a major issue in their ports. Table 9.3 summarises the responses. In Vancouver, particularly, land accessibility is seen to be critically important to the future of the port. Although it is a major issue in Halifax, it would seem it does not have as high a profile as in Vancouver. The 'score' for Vancouver is +0.928; for Halifax it is +0.650 (out of a maximum of +1.0. See note at the bottom of Table 9.3).

How the port communities see accessibility of the container terminals by road and rail is shown in Table 9.4 and 9.5 respectively. There are major variations in how modal accessibility is viewed – by respondent, by terminal and in summary terms overall. As a way to deal with the different views, attention is drawn to Table 9.6 where the 'scores' for each mode, city and terminal are recorded.

Table 9.3 Summary of responses to the question 'How would you describe the importance of land accessibility to the container terminals in the future of the port?'

HALIFAX
Score* 6.5/10 = 0.650

	Critically Important	Very Important	Important, but on a par with other factors	Somewhat Unimportant	Unimportant
Port	X				
Terminal Op 1		X			
Terminal Op 2	X				
City (Halifax)			X		
Trucking Industry	X				

Terminal Operator 2 responded between critically important and very important.

VANCOUVER
Score* 13.0/14 = 0.928

	Critically Important	Very Important	Important, but on a par with other factors	Somewhat Unimportant	Unimportant
Port	X				
Terminal Op 1	X				
Terminal Op 2	X				
Terminal Op 3		X			
City (Vancouver)	X				
Municipality (Delta)	X				
Trucking Industry	X				

* In an attempt to quantify the responses, points were awarded for each response. As can be seen there were five possible categories for response. Assigned values varied from +2 through 0 to -2 depending on the category of response chosen. For the middle category 0 points were assigned. For categories to the left of middle, positive points were awarded. Critically Important = +2, Very Important = +1. For categories to the right of middle, negative points were assigned. Somewhat Important = -1, Unimportant = -2. The maximum raw value of responses that the question could have depends on the number of people responding. For questions with seven people responding the maximum value would be +14 (all respondents giving a "critically important" response). The raw values were divided by the number of respondents to give a "Score" for the question. Scores range from +1 to -1.

Table 9.4 Summary of responses to the question 'In general terms how would you describe road accessibility to the container terminals?'

HALIFAX
Score: 0/16 = 0.000

HALTERM
Score -2/8 = -0.250

	Excellent	V. Good	So/So	Poor	V. Poor
Port			X		
Terminal Op 1			X		
City (Halifax)					X
Trucking Industry			X		

FAIRVIEW COVE
Score +2/8 = +0.250

	Excellent	V. Good	So/So	Poor	V. Poor
Port		X			
Terminal Op 2		X			
City (Halifax)			X		
Trucking Industry			X		

VANCOUVER
Score -2.5/24 = - 0.108

Deltaport
Score: -0.5/8 = -0.0625

	Excellent	V. Good	So/So	Poor	V. Poor
Port			X		
Terminal Op 1		X			
Municipality (Delta)				X	
Trucking Industry				X	

VANTERM
Score: -1.5/8 = -0.1875

	Excellent	V. Good	So/So	Poor	V. Poor
Port			X		
Terminal Op 2				X	
City (Vancouver)			X		
Trucking Industry				X	

CENTERM
Score: -0.5/8 = -0.0625

	Excellent	V. Good	So/So	Poor	V. Poor
Port			X		
Terminal Op 3			X		
City (Vancouver)			X		
Trucking Industry				X	

Table 9.5 Summary of responses to the question 'In general terms how would you describe rail accessibility to the container terminals?'

HALIFAX
Score: 9/16 = 0.563

HALTERM
Score: 5/8 = 0.625

	Excellent	V. Good	So/So	Poor	V. Poor
Port	X				
Terminal Op 1	X				
City (Halifax)		X			
Trucking Industry			X		

FAIRVIEW COVE
Score: 4.0/8 = 0.500

	Excellent	V. Good	So/So	Poor	V. Poor
Port	X				
Terminal Op 2		X			
City (Halifax)		X			
Trucking Industry			X		

VANCOUVER
Score: 6.5/18 = 0.361

DELTAPORT
Score: 2.5/6 = 0.417

	Excellent	V. Good	So/So	Poor	V. Poor
Port					
Terminal Op 1	X		X		
Municipality (Delta)			X		

VANTERM
Score: 2.5/6 = 0.417

	Excellent	V. Good	So/So	Poor	V. Poor
Port					
Terminal Op 2	X		X		
City (Vancouver)			X		

CENTERM
Score: 1.5/6 = 0.25

	Excellent	V. Good	So/So	Poor	V. Poor
Port					
Terminal Op 3		X	X		
City (Vancouver)			X		

Note: The trucking industry representative did not offer an opinion on rail accessibility to the terminals in Vancouver.

Table 9.6 'Scores' associated with perceptions of road and rail accessibilities in Halifax and Vancouver, overall and for each terminal

	HALIFAX			VANCOUVER			
	Overall	Halterm	Fairview Cove	Overall	Deltaport	Vanterm	Centerm
Road	0.000	-0.250	0.250	-0.108	-0.063	-0.188	-0.063
Rail	0.563	0.625	0.500	0.361	0.417	0.417	0.250

The following observations about modal accessibility can be made:

- Rail 'scores' higher than road in both ports overall and for each terminal.
- No respondents gave a negative response for rail for any of the terminals in either of the ports.
- Overall, road accessibility is seen as neutral to negative in the two ports, in contrast to the positive rail accessibility measures.
- Particularly, road access is seen to be particularly negative for Halterm in Halifax and Vanterm in Vancouver.

For Halifax, the city response for Halterm road access is more negative than any of the industry responses including the trucking industry. For Vancouver, poor road access is expressed by various respondents depending on the terminal. Consistently, the trucking industry thought that road access was poor to all three terminals.

There would seem to be general agreement from all parties that rail accessibility in the ports is not of great concern. How that mode actually performs in serving the needs of the terminals and ports is not in question – this was not the question asked. Rather, the reality of the accessibility is seen to be acceptable. The conclusion for road access is not positive.

Halterm, Vanterm and Centerm have similar problems of road access. All three terminals were built in the heart of commercial port waterfronts in the 1970s with little consideration of how trucks were going to gain access to the terminals. The terminals were built in the infancy of containerisation in Canada when the future of containerisation and intermodality was uncertain. They represent the lack of integrated thinking in intermodality. The ports and *cities* of Halifax and Vancouver are now paying the price of that piecemeal thinking. The other two terminals (Fairview Cove in Halifax and Deltaport in Vancouver) were second generation terminals located in sites away from the original port waterfronts. There was better integrated thinking in their location to take account of not only land availability and sea access but also land accessibility. However, issues of road accessibility still exist.

What is Being Done to Address Access Concerns?

In the course of collecting answers to the three major questions posed, it became obvious that, although opinions may differ on the exact dimensions of land accessibility issues in the two ports, in both places there was general awareness that accessibility by road and rail to the container terminals was an issue deserving attention. In both ports, studies have recently been commissioned to shed light on the problem and ways to address it.

In Halifax there have been studies undertaken to assess the feasibility of building a rail-transit-truckway in the CN rail cutting along the Northwest Arm to/from the south end of the Halifax peninsula. A study in 2004 commissioned by the Halifax Regional Municipality, recognises 'the need in Halifax to improve the trucking connections to and from the [southend] port facilities' (Marshall *et al.* 2004, 1). Two options were recognised as a feasible way, operationally, to divert container truck traffic from downtown Halifax streets to the rail cutting: 1) a one-way roadway parallel to the existing one-track railway and 2) a two-way roadway with the rail embedded in the roadway. An earlier study (Atlantic Road and Traffic Management 2003) recognises that 'virtually all truck traffic to the South End Ocean Terminals travels from north Barrington Street to the Cogswell Interchange and then on Hollis Street to the Ocean terminals'. The number of trucks inbound and outbound from Ocean Terminals averaged 40 trucks per hour at that time. The disadvantages of a combined transport corridor are construction costs ($40–50 million) and who will pay, loss of railroad container storage areas, scheduling concerns of rail, trucks and buses so as to not interfere with existing trains, and incompatibility of such a vehicular transport corridor with a walking trail that had designs on using the corridor.

The combined rail-transit-truckway is still being considered. A recent study commissioned by Halifax Regional Municipality and Halifax Port Authority with the participation of CN, gives further consideration to the corridor option, and also studies the possibility of an inland container transfer facility where all road containers would be transferred to rail (Marinova Consulting 2005). Such a facility would not only remove most of the container truck traffic from downtown Halifax streets to/ from Halterm, but also truck traffic to/from Fairview Cove would be affected. Of significance is the fact that the study is a cooperative effort of city and port indicating that there is general agreement that a real problem exists that requires the combined resources and vision of more than one party.

Vancouver has also been involved in developing better land access to its container terminals. In July 2003 a report commissioned by the Greater Vancouver Gateway Council (GVGC), an industry led organisation of transportation related service providers, identified the need for a defined multimodal major commercial transportation system (MCTS) that would 'maximize the use of existing infrastructure and provide a blue print for investments in new infrastructure for the movement of goods, services, and people'. (GVGC 2003, E-1).

In the report, major and minor road and rail infrastructure improvements are suggested and analysed for their effectiveness in contributing to the development of the MCTS. Of these the following major road improvements are particularly relevant to improving access to and from Vancouver container handling terminals:

- Widening of the South Fraser Perimeter Road linking the TCH to Highways 91 and 99 including a new highway interchange at HWY 99 and HWY 17.
- Construction of two new lanes of the Massey Tunnel under the Fraser River.
- Upgrading of Highways 10 and 15.

For the most part these suggestions would favour road accessibility to Deltaport.

Suggestions for minor road improvements were focused on the existing arterial road network under municipal control. Many would directly impact on access issues to Vanterm and Centerm on Burrard Inlet. As an indication of how traffic has increased in this corridor, the 24 hour average annual daily traffic southbound (away from Burrard Inlet) has increased on Clark-Knight Street from 14,347 vehicles in 1984 to over 24,000 in 2003. Similar numbers are found for northbound traffic. Not all of these vehicles are trucks, of course, but it is estimated that 'truck volumes comprise 9 per cent to 13 per cent of traffic volumes which is the highest number of trucks of any City street in a day. This represents 2,200 to 3,000 trucks per day, with heavy trucks comprising 47 per cent to 60 per cent of truck traffic' (City of Vancouver 2005).

The rail improvements suggested vary from the major initiative of replacing the 100 year old New Westminster single-lane swing-bridge railroad bridge across the Fraser River to minor improvements involving grade separation of rail and road at key points in the greater Vancouver area, two of which would directly affect access to Centerm and Vanterm on Burrard Inlet.

Of significance in studies on modal accessibility being undertaken in both ports is the fact that they are being done cooperatively between port and city and involving the modal carriers themselves. This cooperation indicates the importance attached to intermodal transportation in the port-cities and the recognition that no single player has control over improving the modal accessibility to container terminals.

To assist in coordinating the needs and concerns of ports users, each port has established various working stakeholders committees. In Halifax, the port authority has recently created *Smart Port*, a port-industry-government association interested in not only promoting the port but making it work better. There are over 70 members contributing to three working groups: Marketing & Strategy, Competitiveness & Productivity, and Security & Technology. In Vancouver, as an example, there is a Stakeholders Working Group on Container Traffic consisting of representatives from ocean carriers, terminal operators, off-dock terminal operators, trucking companies, rail carriers, general merchandise shippers, freight forwarders, forest product shippers and the Vancouver Port Authority.[1] Both ports also are key members to the so-called Gateway Councils of their respective cities. The Halifax Gateway Council was created in the fall of 2003 to provide a forum for regional transportation

---

1 See   (http://www.portvancouver.com/trade_shipping/services/stakeholder.html), accessed on 6 September, 2005.

stakeholders to work together to improve the competitiveness and efficiency of the movement of goods and passengers through the Halifax region. It took as its model the Greater Vancouver Gateway Council created in 1994 to build and act on a vision for Greater Vancouver as a world transportation gateway.

Conclusion

Canadian containerisation trade is concentrated at three ports: Vancouver, Montreal and Halifax. Over the years of involvement in container traffic each port has had to respond to changes in the dimension of global containerisation development. They have done so by building new terminals, expanding existing ones and adding new lifting capacity. They have attempted to accommodate the needs of intermodality to make more efficient the transfer of containers from ship to shore and *vice versa*. The seamless operation of intermodal chains not only depends on the efficiency of the terminals, it also depends on efficient sea and land transport. It has been suggested that Oram's First Law of Mechanisation applies in the successful operation of intermodal chains. The development of larger and larger container ships has put a strain on the land operations to keep up with the demand for seamless intermodal flows. Of particular concern in this chapter has been the perception of land transport accessibility to container terminals in the ports of Vancouver and Halifax.

Although the respondent base is small – five from Halifax and seven from Vancouver – all respondents to the major questions posed are key people in the intermodel industry in the two port-cities. There is almost complete unanimity in Vancouver that land transportation accessibility is critical, over and above other factors, to the future of container operations. The Vancouver agreement on criticality *may* be because at the time of the interviews a strike by Vancouver independent container truck drivers had brought the movement of road containers to and from the terminals to a stop (Tower 2005). However, the evidence of cooperation between port, city and transportation modes in the past points to recognition that land accessibility has been an ongoing focus of the industry in the port-city. In Halifax accessibility is seen as important, but it does not rate as highly as in Vancouver. The lower 'score' in Halifax is mainly accounted for by the view from the city that land accessibility, although important, is on a par with other factors affecting container operations. This viewpoint is not consistent with the port's strongly held belief that land accessibility is critical. The Halifax city inconsistency is surprising given that recently the port and the city have been cooperating in studying how improvements can be made to road accessibility to the port's container terminals.

As for the condition of road access and rail access in the two port-cities, each saw rail being superior to road. There were real concerns with road accessibility in both ports.

Can other ports learn from the Canadian experience represented in this small study? One lesson that can be learnt is that many interests in a port-city have opinions and vested interests in land accessibility issues associated with the movement of containers to/from ports. This is not a new observation. What may be new is the degree of unanimity that such an issue may have among the different stakeholders, and that the shared viewpoint may be seen as more critical than other issues in the port's future. Since there is no single player that has sole responsibility for land accessibility issues, solutions require cooperation. It is heartening to see that ports, terminals, transportation companies and city governments are cooperating to find ways to not only highlight the importance of container movements through their cities and ports but also to seek solutions that will be acceptable to all users. It is this cooperation that other ports and their cities can learn from. A successful outcome of cooperation is what is required to ensure that land transportation keeps up with the dictates of Oram's First Law of Mechanisation as applied to the intermodal transportation industry.

PART 3
Inserting Port-Cities into Global Supply Chains

Chapter 10

Globalisation and the Port-Urban Interface: Conflicts and Opportunities

Yehuda Hayuth

Introduction

Seaports and the port-city interrelationships have always been a multidimensional phenomenon. Maritime technologies, port-operation systems, site and location, economic considerations, as well as environmental concerns are some of the agents of change in the process of the evolution of the port-city interface. A port is a dependent element of the transportation system within which it operates. Port functions have always aligned in direct relationship to the services they performed for vessels, commodities, and land-transportation modes. Developments in the transport industry and international trade forced modifications in the modus operandi and the physical and economic structure of the port, with a consequent great impact on port-cities.

Since the early 1970s, the port-city relationship has witnessed substantial changes (Hoyle and Hilling 1984). The scale and the dimensions of these changes can be characterised more as revolution than gradual evolution. This phenomenon is derived from several key factors: the development of shipping technology, such as containerisation; the vast back-up land required for modern terminals, and the dependence on the accessibility of inland transport networks. The changes in the traditional functions of the port caused a decline in port-related employment and a revolution in the public's attitude toward environmental issues in general and waterfront developments in particular.

One of the most distinct changes in the port-urban interface was the spatial and functional segregation of the historical ties between cities and ports. The development of 'out ports' in north-west Europe and the downstream development of ports in Britain (Bird 1963) were two early examples that illustrated the trend to ports abandoning the traditional waterfront areas of cities. In the 1970s and the 1980s, the development of maritime trade and the modernisation of port operations, accompanied by increasing public concern over coastal areas greatly accelerated the phenomenon (Hayuth 1982). Obsolete terminals in the historical waterfront areas were replaced by modern facilities located away from the traditional port-cities. This trend became globally common.

The dynamics of the interrelationship of ports and cities at the turn of the twenty-first century created yet another wave of new developments at both ends. Liner shipping began facing a continued growth in vessel size. The 11,000-TEU vessel is already under constructions in shipyards. Recently, a classification society and a large Korean shipyard published a design study for a container vessel with a carrying capacity of 13,000 TEU which might enter service in the year 2009. Both vessels present a major challenge to existing container terminals. Meanwhile global container terminal operators continue to increase their share of the port industry. The four leading global operators manage more than one third of all container-terminal throughput. This trend, combined with growing concentration in the liner shipping industry, presents a new challenge to the port-city interface, especially though not solely in the infrastructure dimension.

Since the mid-1980s, intermodal transportation has altered the basic function of a container port (Hayuth 1987). The transition from a 'port-to-port' to a 'door-to-door' concept has eliminated many traditional port activities, such as warehousing, packaging and repairing. Ports became another link in the transport chain from the origin of the cargo to its final destination. This development, in turn, negatively impacted on the economic relationship of the port to its city and region. In the last few years, shipping lines, ports, transport and logistics companies, employing new developments in logistics, which have made it possible to integrate the port and its region into the supply-chain operation. This trend introduces a new phase in the evolution of port-urban relationships.

The objective of this chapter is to analyse the potential implications of key recent developments in global trade and transportation for the evolution of ports, specifically the conflicts and opportunities offered to the port-city interface. The drawbacks and opportunities for seaports and port-cities are evaluated. The analysis also attempts to highlight a new relevant research agenda and provides directions for new policy decisions. Particular emphasis is given to the shipping lines' point of view. One should remember that liner shipping companies were the catalyst behind the revolution of the port-urban interface at the beginning of the containerisation era, and they still occupy the same position as key agents for further changes.

The Growing Port-urban Interface Conflict

Since the late 1960s, in particular with the introduction of containerisation in maritime transportation, both the spatial and the economic ties between cities and ports have been loosening. Moreover, the common interest that traditionally characterised the relationship between most ports and their cities often turned into a conflictual relationship. These conflicts stemmed from the existence in the same confined space of two spatial entities, whose basic interests and goals, in many cases, were radically different (Amato 1999). Ports, as a dependent element of the maritime transportation system, were and are committed to competition, productivity, technological advance, business development, and profitability. The port-city, for its part, strives to fulfil such other objectives as promoting the well-being and quality of life of its residents in an accommodating environment and responding to the priorities of its citizens in regard to the urban waterfront, among other things. Such different goals easily result in conflicts of interest, which can cause many difficulties in the compatibility of the two entities, whether on a daily basis and in regard to the development of future plans.

Without a doubt, the port and the city share some common goals, most of them relate to economic issues. Port operations and the economic impact multiplier provide direct and indirect employment and business development opportunities that certainly benefit the city and the region. The cities, in turn, provide the port with multiple urban services, port-related activities, transportation infrastructure, and in many cases port-promotion support. However, there are many issues that cause friction and disagreements between the two entities, ranging from the demand for expansion of port space, noise and air pollution, aesthetics, urban traffic congestion, waterfront redevelopment, control over the waterfront, and transport access corridors. The reconciliation of the divergence of the vision and the need to balance technological development, the port's requirements that reflect the shipping lines' demands, urban planning principles, and environmental constraints can restrain necessary decision-making in the dynamic shipping and transport industry.

Several key developments, most of them related to technological and organisational changes in the maritime transport industry and some being the result of computerisation and communication advances in general, are responsible for weakening ties between ports and port-cities. The new cargo-handling methods introduced by the containerisation revolution and greatly improved productivity resulted in a major reduction in port labor. Moreover, many of the traditional port-related activities, and jobs, were relocated to inland locations.

With containerisation, many general cargo ports became obsolete. The physical layout, the land-use configuration of the conventional terminals, and the access to inland transport systems were totally inadequate for container handling. During the 1960s and 1970s, the process of the separation of ports and cities or, as was phrased by Hoyle (1989), 'the retreat from the waterfront', became a worldwide phenomenon. The relocation of terminals from the finger-piers of Manhattan to Port Elisabeth, New Jersey, from San Francisco to Oakland, and from Marseille to Fos provides just a few examples.

For many cities, vacating valuable waterfront land was a bonus for the urban mosaic, particularly if an adjacent location could be found for the new marine terminals. Many cities, though, lost numerous jobs and employment opportunities with the relocation of terminals. With the advance of communication technology, shipping lines also began relocating their headquarters and main offices away from the waterfronts and their ports of call. MSC, the second largest container line, based its headquarters in Geneva as CGM and Zim shifted their main offices in the US to Norfolk, Virginia. This development constituted yet another blow to the traditional economic ties between cities and their ports.

For the last several decades, ports and shipping lines have faced environmental legislation that has presented many constraints to their development (Hershman 1978). The current rapid growth of containerised trade and the parallel development in the dimensions of cellular vessels have intensified the environmental conflicts between ports and port-cities, with severe implications for the potential development of many ports. As a direct response to the growth in container port throughput, environmental agencies, supported by the growing public concern over the increase in air pollution, road congestion and the pressures on additional waterfront land, have introduced new constraints. One such example is the 'Green Terminal' in Long

Beach, which requires vessels to shut down their engines completely during the handling of the containers and to hook themselves up to an external source of power during loading/unloading. These conflicts may fuel a new wave of segregation between existing urban waterfronts and new container terminals.

The Growth in Containerised Trade and its Impact on Shipping and Ports

World container trade and port throughput have grown at double-digit rates over the last three years, surpassing the average growth rate of over the last two decades. Globalisation, which is responsible for the shift of manufacturing mostly to the Far East, the sudden emergence of China as a massive exporter of containerised cargo, and the accession of China to the World Trade Organization (WTO) in early 2002 are the main factors responsible for the growth in trade. This growth, which to a great extent had taken the world by surprise, has put the shipping lines, and existing terminal facilities, under considerable strain. In 2004, the volume of world container throughput reached more than 350 million TEU (including empties and transhipment), more than twice the throughput of ten years ago. Table 10.1 provides an overview of container activity by region since 1996, along with estimates for 2004. The dominance of port activities in Asia is striking, and reflects the concentration of industrial production in the region. Far East and South East Asia ports handled more than 170 million TEU in 2004, compared with a throughput of 69 million TEU in Western Europe and 40 million TEU in North America (Table 10.1). Perhaps more significant to our discussion is the fact that between 2002 and 2004, the annual rate of growth in container handling in the three regions amounted to 11.5 per cent, 13.0 per cent, and 14.1 per cent respectively. The annual rate of growth of the Far East ports was even higher than the world's average, reaching 18.0 per cent in 2003 and 17.4 per cent in 2004.

Shipping lines have responded to the boom in containerised trade with an unprecedented order of new vessels. Most of the large shipping yards are fully booked for the next three years. On 1 October 2005, the cellular fleet could count 3,554 ships, with a capacity of 7.97 million TEU. On the same date, the order book numbered 1,243 ships, with a capacity of 4.55 million TEU, representing 57.1 per cent of the existing fleet (Alphaliner 2005). Furthermore, container terminals can be expected to handle about 50 per cent more vessel capacity between 2005 and early 2009. Not only has the cellular vessel fleet grown, but the dimensions of the vessels serving in the main trade routes have already reached record size. At the beginning of October 2005, the percentage of vessels over 7,500 TEU amounted to 7.3 per cent of the total fleet capacity. Based on the new orders contracted with the shipyards, this figure will rise to 16.6 per cent of the fleet by the beginning of 2009.

Currently, the largest container vessel in service is the Emma Maersk with a capacity of over 11,000 TEU. In early 2007 a series of 10,000-TEU vessels, for China Ocean Shipping Co. for example, will join the world fleet. Container vessels with 9,200-TEU capacity have currently joined the trade on a monthly basis. In early October 2005, Germanischer Lloyd, the German class society, and Hyundai Heavy Industries (HHI) of South Korea unveiled a design for the largest containership ever, capable of carrying 13,000 TEU. HHI is now accepting orders for 2009. The twin-propeller vessel will be 382 m long and 52.2 m wide and have a draught of 13.5 m and a speed of 25.5 knot. (ITJ Daily 2005).

Table 10.1 Container activity by region (million TEU)

	1996	1998	2000	2002	2004(e)
North America	22,813	26,401	30,824	34,212	40,357
Western Europe	35,304	44,381	51,707	57,350	69,467
North Europe	23,172	27,331	31,661	34,403	41,301
South Europe	12,131	17,049	20,047	22,947	28,166
Far East	44,899	52,192	71,096	87,541	121,254
South East Asia	23,353	28,020	34,320	41,105	52,112
Mid East	7,243	8,849	11,092	13,642	19,378
Latinamerica	10,893	15,112	17,802	19,212	24,569
Carib/C.Am	5,852	8,206	9,925	10,464	12,472
South America	5,041	6,907	7,877	8,749	12,097
Oceania	3,583	4,155	5,019	6,023	7,037
South Asia	3,824	4,661	5,481	6,586	7,646
Africa	5,049	5,707	7,150	8,454	11,271
Eastern Europe	908	978	1,080	1,796	2,523
World	157,868	190,456	235,571	275,850	355,612

Source: Drewry Shipping consultants Ltd (2005).

The stress on container terminals and inland infrastructure will only grow with the new mammoth vessels. Ship-to-shore operations and handling comprise one issue that must be dealt with. Another is the back-up land and inland transport infrastructure needed to accommodate such vessels; these elements constitute a greater problem. Consider the 8,000–9,200 TEU ship. Approximately 150 of them are expected to be deployed in East-West trades by 2008. A single vessel discharging 4,000 containers in a hub port might on average require 2,000 truck-moves and 10 stack-trains of 200 containers each (Koch 2005).

The rapid expansion of containerised trade has put the squeeze on the shipping lines, which, as illustrated above, responded with a huge wave of new ship orders. However, with the influx of the new, large vessels, the pressure has shifted to the marine terminals and also to the inland distribution systems. The stress on ports, inland infrastructure, shippers, and supply-chain management will only become greater in the coming years. With the deployment of mega vessels, the continued expansion of export containers from China and other Asian countries to Europe and North America, and the rapid growth of the intra-Asia trade, ports are facing perhaps their biggest challenge since the introduction of containerisation. Seaports have to find solutions to the multiple problems that they are facing. Lack of capacity, a physical inability to handle the new generation of vessels while maintaining an acceptable level of service, inadequate inland transport infrastructure and, on top of all this, the commitment to safety and security – all these issues and more the port industry must address. In light of such challenges, 'out-of-the-box solutions' will be required.

Generally, the strength of a chain is measured by its weakest link. In the present evolving situation, ports are becoming a weak link, adversely affecting the entire supply chain from supplier to consignee. One of the most visible indications of the emerging crisis was the recent spate of port congestion, causing 2004 to be probably one of the worst on record for container ports since the introduction of containerisation. The congestion hot spots were mostly, but not only, in developed countries. Among the ports most affected were, perhaps ironically, some of the most modern and well equipped, like Los Angeles and Long Beach, Vancouver B.C., Rotterdam, Southampton, and Antwerp. Most of these ports were not prepared to handle the unexpected volumes of Chinese exports.

In Southern California, during the holiday shipping season of September-November 2004, there were more than 80 container vessels waiting at anchor to be unloaded at any given time. On the average, it took six to eight days to handle each of those ships, which was twice as long as when the port was operating under normal capacity. On top of the longshoreman's strike which caused ship-to-shore delays, trucks were not available to shift containers inland, and the double-stack trains were operating at near capacity. Labour shortages in the terminal and a shortage of drivers were prime factors that brought about long delays at the ports of Los Angeles and Long Beach. The credibility and reliability of the 'just in time concept' for maritime transportation came into question after years of trust building among producers and shippers.

The special measures that were taken in the Fall of 2005, such as more longshore-men, longer gate-hours, and the diversion of vessels to other ports along the coast or to all-water services provided temporary relief in the peak season, but in no way resolved the basic problems. Port and rail operators are scrambling for ways to increase physical capacity or to improve productivity in existing terminals. However, there is little space left for new terminals in Los Angeles and Long Beach, the largest port complex in the United States, and none is currently under construction. (Damas and Gillis 2005). Only one terminal (Pier S in Long Beach) is even in the design stage. For most West Coast ports, any further development of new terminals involves environmental and land-use conflicts and is subject to lengthy government review, not to speak of expected public opposition.

Port capacity shortage

SSA Marine, one of the largest stevedoring companies in the United States, has painted a rather grim picture of the capacity problem facing the port industry in the United States. In 2005, container-handling demand in the United States (including Vancouver, B.C.) was already exceeding the capacity of the country's container terminals by about 1.5 per cent. In 2010, the situation is forecast to become much more difficult. The total capacity of US ports, which includes the additional capacity of new development projects in Tacoma, in the US Gulf, in Savanna, in Virginia, and in New York/New Jersey, is estimated to fall short of demand by almost 6.0

million TEU (Table 10.2). This shortage represents 13 per cent of the total projected containerised trade in 2010. The forecast is based on a moderate growth projection of 5 per cent per year during the 2006–2010 period.

Table 10.2 US port throughput and capacity (2010)

	2010 Capacity	2010[1] Volume	2010 Used capacity
West Coast Ports			
Vancouver	1,395,000	2,358,020	(963,020)
Seattle	2,016,000	2,358,047	(342,047)
Tacoma	4,437,000	2,484,455	1,952,545
Oakland	3,415,000	2,807,067	607,933
Los Angeles	6,493,500	10,514,244	(4,020,744)
Long Beach	5,562,000	7,791,820	(2,229,820)
Total	*23,318,500*	*28,313,658*	*(4,995,158)*
Gulf Ports			
Houston	1,327,000	1,795,748	(468,748)
Miami	1,143,000	1,434,946	(291,946)
Total	*2,470,000*	*3,230,694*	*(760,694)*
South Atlantic Ports			
Savannah	1,912,500	2,198,770	(286,270)
Charleston	1,800,000	2,446,192	(646,192)
Virginia	2,991,572	2,441,909	549,663
Total	*6,704,072*	*7,086,871*	*(382,799)*
East Coast Ports			
Baltimore	1,237,500	724,496	513,004
New York/New Jersey	5,827,500	6,161,997	(334,497)
Total	*7,065,000*	*6,886,493*	*178,507*
Grand Total	39,557,572	45,417,716	(5,960,144)

(1)   Projected +5% per year growth 2006-2010.
Source: SSA Marine.

Even if the definition of capacity can be contested or internal productivity and longer gate hours improved, congestion will remain a major challenge for the liner industry. Moreover, the capacity problem in United States puts the whole freight system at risk (Borrone 2005). A US Chamber of Commerce study indicates that the

US intermodal freight system is currently operating at many areas near the limits of economically sustainable capacity (National Chamber Foundation 2003). Several interesting options are currently being exercised in the congested US West Coast. Canadian National (CN), Maher terminals, and the British Columbia Government are currently converting a bulk terminal into a container terminal at the Port of Prince Rupert, some 800 km north of Vancouver and close to the border with Alaska. The first phase of the 160-acre terminal, which has a water depth of 16.7m, will start operating in early 2007. This new terminal, located away from a congested urban area, will transfer Far East imports to North America's Midwest. In the South, Hutchison Port Holdings and Union Pacific are involved in building a large Mexican West Coast terminal gateway south of Ensenada, just 80 km south of the US border. Another container terminal feasibility study is being conducted in Punta Colonet, in Mexico, about 240 km south of San Diego.

Congestion has become a major problem in European ports, as well, and threatens more serious problems in the next few years, should the shortage of capacity not be addressed. Congestion at ports not only delays container vessels, but it also damages the entire supply chain. Moreover, it has a negative impact on the European Union's efforts to shift containers from the highways to intra-Europe short-sea services. In the UK, the pressure on the government to build a 'London Gateway' new container port is expected to yield positive results in the near future. The port will be built and operated by P&O Ports in Thurrock, Essex, and is planned to be operational, with a capacity of 3.5 million TEU, in 2008. The plan includes the development of a logistics and business park. Additionally, a proposal to build a new deep-sea port away from the congested ports and urban areas of South East England was advanced by the private sector. Teesport in North England, Hunterston in Scotland, and Orkney Islands were considered. Critical congestion levels at the port of Rotterdam has triggered several new projects for adding capacity to container-handling facilities in order to keep pace with the surge in traffic that is threatening to gridlock the largest port in Europe. In 2004, the Port of Rotterdam won government approval for a $3.5 billion project to build a container terminal with a yearly capacity of 8.5 million TEU. The project, which will be built on land reclaimed from the North Sea, will include a distribution hub.

In Asia, despite the massive development of container terminals in the last few years, congestion is still a problem in some areas. India is one of the countries that has suffered from a shortage of port capacity in light of fast-growing throughput demand. The Port of Mumbai, for example, restricted shipping lines throughout 2004 to volumes they handled the previous year. In order to relieve some of the pressure resulting from demand, Mumbai Port Trust has issued a tender to build an offshore container terminal for the port. The terminal, to be located some 800 m from shore, is to have two container berths (Containerisation International 2005).

By far, the largest off-shore container terminal is currently being built by the Port of Shanghai. The Yangshan terminal, located 30 km from shore and 100 km from the Port of Shanghai, will be connected to the mainland by a bridge. Yangshan, will offer a maximum draft of more than 15 m thereby, providing relief from the draft limitation restricting the Port of Shanghai. The new island terminal is being built to accommodate the largest container vessels currently under construction, and with 50 berths when completed it will have an annual capacity of 15 million TEU, thereby doubling the capacity of the port, the first phase is scheduled to open in 2006 (Damas 2005).

The Dominance of Global Terminal Operators

During the past 10–15 years, a new trend has emerged in the control of container terminal throughput (Heaver and Van De Voorde 2001). Both public and private sectors controlled container terminal handling since the 1960s. Since the 1990s, however, there has been a sharp decline in public sector involvement in the operation of container terminals. As Figure 10.1 illustrates, the proportion of throughput handled at public terminals has declined from an estimated 42 per cent in 1991 to only 22 per cent by 2003. At the same time, with a few earlier exceptions, a relatively small number of companies have started to operate container terminals in more than one geographical region. These companies are known as global terminal operators. Most of these operators are private-sector companies although several important state-owned operators, such as Singapore's PSA Corporation, Dubai Port Authority, and Hamburg-based HHLA, are exceptions.

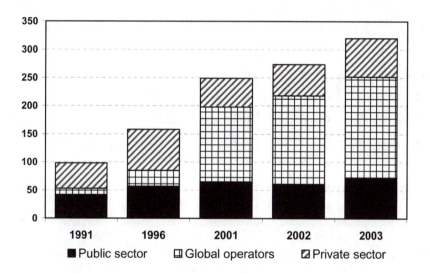

Figure 10.1 Public/private control of container terminal throughput, 1991-2003 (Million TEU)

Source: Drewry Shipping Consultants Ltd (2004).

Table 10.3 The 25 largest global terminal operators (2004)

	Operator	Total Throughput 2003 (m TEU)	Total Capacity 2003 (m TEU)	Geographical region of operation						
				North America	Europe	Far East	South East Asia	Middle East	South & Central America	Others
1	HPH	41.5	48.9	–	16.3	64.3	11.6	1.5	5.8	0.5
2	PSA	28.7	37.2	–	20.8	12.4	66.7	–	–	–
3	APM Terminal	21.4	24.4	28.7	24.5	12.6	19.1	9.4	5.4	0.3
4	P&O Ports	16.0	21.5	11.7	23.2	19.0	32.5	–	2.7	10.7
5	Eurogate	10.8	12.9	–	100.0	–	–	–	–	–
6	Cosco	7.4	9.4	13.4	5.2	80.1	1.3	–	–	–
7	Evergreen	6.7	9.2	30.4	9.9	47.9	6.2	–	5.7	–
8	DPA	6.5	8.3	–	–	–	0.4	95.4	–	4.1
9	SSA Marine	5.4	7.7	59.2	–	–	–	0.6	40.1	–
10	APL	4.9	7.5	50.3	–	26.0	23.7	–	–	–
11	HHLA	4.6	5.9	–	90.3	–	–	–	9.6	–
12	Hanjin	4.1	5.9	41.1	–	58.9	–	–	–	–
13	MSC	4.1	5.5	12.8	–	87.2	–	–	–	–
14	NYK Line	4.0	4.7	46.8	1.0	–	35.5	16.7	–	–
15	OOCL	3.4	4.0	74.0	–	26.0	–	–	–	–
16	CSXWT	3.1	3.9	–	–	84.6	–	–	10.7	4.6
17	MOL	2.9	3.8	35.4	–	41.2	23.4	–	–	–
18	Dragados	2.5	3.7	–	97.4	–	–	–	2.6	–
19	K Line	2.1	3.6	46.2	–	53.8	–	–	–	–
20	TCB	2.0	3.4	–	74.9	–	–	–	25.1	–
21	ICTSI	1.6	2.8	–	18.6	–	77.9	–	3.5	–
22	P&O Nedlloyd	1.4	2.7	35.5	20.6	–	43.9	–	–	–
23	Yang Ming	1.4	2.2	48.4	–	51.6	–	–	–	–
24	Hyundai	1.2	1.5	69.1	–	30.9	–	–	–	–
25	CMA CGM	0.6	1.1	–	100.0	–	–	–	–	–

Source: Drewry Shipping Consultants Ltd, 2004.

The global terminal operators have been increasing their share in the world container throughput. In 2004, global container operators handled over 234 million TEU, which was more than a 24-per-cent increase over 2003 levels (ITJ 30 September 2005). This figure represents almost 60 per cent of the world container throughput. Moreover, the four largest global companies, known in the industry as 'the big four' – Hutchison Port Holdings (HPH), PSA Corporation, APM Terminals, and P&O Ports – handled in 2004 about 135 million TEU, which represents one-third of the global container terminal throughput. Table 10.3 presents the ranking of the largest 25 global terminal operators, based on their throughput, capacity and main geographical region of operation (Drewry Shipping Consultants 2004).

The global terminal operators do not form a homogenous group, and they can be divided into three sub-groups. The first and largest group, accounting for 65 per cent of global operators' throughput in 2003, consists of 'global stevedoring companies' whose primary business is port operations. Among the largest companies in this sub-section are Hutchison Port Holdings, a Hong Kong-based company the majority of whose operations are in the Far East and Europe; PSA, a Singapore-based operator that concentrates its activities mostly in SE Asia and Europe; Dubai Ports Authority, a fast-growing operator that has recently taken control of P&O ports to become the third largest global port operator, with terminals Asia, Europe, and North America, the Middle East and the Caribbean; Eurogate, which operates only in Europe; and, the veteran SSA Marine, which is based in Seattle with operations in North and South America.

The second sub-group contains the 'global carriers', companies whose primary business is container shipping. This group represents a growing trend in liner shipping to secure terminal facilities, first of all for their own cargo. This is particularly true in light of the shortage in capacity of container-handling facilities and a growing interruption in scheduling because of port congestion. The sub-group also represents another trend among container lines, which is to extend their business involvement along the total transport chain. Carriers can gain greater efficiency by integrating the terminal into the seaborne trade services. The terminal operation is mainly run by the shipping lines as 'cost centres'.

The third sub-group of terminal operators is the 'global hybrids'. These companies' main business is container shipping, but they also operate terminals throughout the world for other shipping lines as an independent business. APM Terminal, a Copenhagen-based company is the leading operator in this group, followed by the Chinese Cosco Pacific, NYK, and OOCL.

The phenomenon of the global terminal operator, the dominant position that they have gained over the traditional public and private operators, and the magnitude of the container throughput that they handle represent a structural change in the global port industry. This relatively new trend doubtlessly has considerable implications for port development and operations. However, its impact is also felt on the evolution of the city-port relationship. With the emergence and strengthening position of global container operators, the control and influence of the relationship between the city and the port has been shifting away from the local and even the regional level to the global level. The selection criteria guiding shipping lines have been changing, as well, and go beyond such conventional factors such as productivity and port tariffs. These criteria extend to new factors, such as flexibility and reliability of global scheduling, the importance of maintaining the 'just-in-time' commitment, the availability of 'added-value' services, and IT capabilities. Securing terminal facilities in a capacity-short industry, particularly in the main trade areas, is yet another criterion.

The global terminal operator trend parallels, and to a great extent, highly correlates with two other known trends – the globalisation of international trade and the globalisation of supply chain management. However, despite the growing research on the role of ports in supply chain management (Carbone and Martino 2003), there are difficulties in understanding the logistical chains that ports find themselves embedded. Even port managements are struggling to define the new core business of the port in the new logistics environment (Robinson 2002).

The Shipping Lines' Point of View

Shipping lines, like any other participant in the transport chain, must decide on their strategic choices in light of the dynamic changes taking place in the market environment, particularly the globalisation of trade and logistic operations. The organisational structure of liner shipping is currently being reshaped. Whereas the 1970s and 1980s were marked by the emergence of strong outsiders, which weakened the standing of the conference system, most of the 1990s was characterised by the formation of strong global industry alliances. Since the late-1990s, the trend has been changing once again, this time involving takeovers, acquisitions, and mergers (Notteboom 2004); this trend has greatly intensified in the past two years. At the turn of the twentieth century, the liner shipping industry was still highly fragmented. No single carrier controlled more than 8 per cent of the global container slots, and the top 20 operators controlled just about 50 per cent of the global fleet capacity (Ahlander and Rehling 1999).

In September 2005, just five years later, liner shipping is a much more concentrated industry. Following the recent takeovers of P&O Nedlloyd by A.P. Moller-Maersk and, Delmas by CMA CGM and CP ships by Hapag-Lloyd, the five largest carriers alone control 45.4 per cent of the world fleet capacity. The two largest carriers, Maersk and MSC, individually control, after the takeover, 18.2 per cent and 12.8 per cent, respectively, of the capacity. The twenty largest carriers control 80.7 per cent of the global slot capacity (Alphaliner 5 October 2005). Considering that on top of these recent acquisitions the global alliances are still operating (Slack *et al.* 2002b), the bargaining position and the competitive arena for seaports and city-ports are very difficult indeed.

Regarding other liner shipping strategic decisions, carriers have to position themselves in the total transport chain in terms of both their involvement in assets and their value-added services (Baird 2003). Shipping lines are highly motivated to extend their activities in the vertical integration system of global transport and trade. They have several good reasons to do so. In light of the persistent congestion in ports, the prospects of an increasing shortage in capacity and the prolonged delays in their scheduling, carriers want to have greater control over their ports-of-call, beyond the traditional practice of leasing terminals. Moreover, as a result of soaring port costs, shipping lines want to exert more control over one of the largest expenditure items in their budgets.

Shipping lines, in addition to their greater investments in terminal operations, are buying shares in strategic hub terminals. Maersk, for example, has substantial shares in the Malaysian Port Tanjung Pelepas (PTP), in Salalah, and in Felixstowe. Recently, MOL, because of its concern at the state of terminal infrastructure in the US West Coast, the growing demand for all-water services between the US East Coast and Asia, and the expanding trade between North America and South America, has reached an agreement with the Jacksonville Port Authority to build and operate a 160-acre container terminal at the port's Dames Marine Terminal.

Carriers have also been expanding their involvement to other fronts along the transport and supply chain. Many of the largest shipping lines are deeply involved in logistical activities. Some of the largest carriers have established inland container terminals away from the port areas in order to help streamline the flow of their containers and the distribution of both full and empty containers. Other shipping lines are involved in land transportation. Recently, for example, Hyundai launched an express rail service from Slovakia to Rotterdam to complement its Far East-NW Europe service. Moreover, it is a common policy and a recent trend among carriers to take full control of their agencies around the world, replacing the general agents whom they appointed and worked with for years.

All these land-based activities of shipping companies have several common denominators. Carriers need, more than ever, to penetrate logistical and supply chain management activities for several reasons. First, the potential rate of return for logistics activities is higher than compared with their maritime transport services. Second, having a greater mix in their business portfolios helps spread the risks of operating in a volatile industry. Thirdly, greater vertical integration in the flow chain of the commodities gives them an advantage *vis-à-vis* their customers, in addition to better control over the coordination and synchronisation of the various links of the chain. Furthermore, carriers that invest heavily in new vessels cannot afford to depend on freight forwarders or NVOCCs (Non-Vessel Operating Common Carriers) for the mix and the freight rates of their cargo. They must be functionally closer to the shippers in order to ensure the optimum booking for their vessels and improved customer services.

Again, how does all this affect the port-urban interrelationships? Ports and port-cities were always dependent on the decisions of shipping lines regarding their development. There has been no change in this dependency today. However, as already noted, there are certain changes in the criteria according to which the carriers now make their port-selection decision. From the carriers' point of view, port location is more often being viewed in relation to the distant hinterland than to the local port-city. Global considerations often surpass local factors. The dependence on the availability of an intermodal infrastructure plays a critical role in the selection process. Shipping lines, which themselves are looking for a niche in the supply-chain journey, are now searching for logistics-related services, existing or potential, to add to their portfolios.

This perspective of the shipping lines in regard to port-selection criteria may not be promising for port-urban interface development for some ports. Indeed, this new perspective might further weaken the city-port interrelationship. Nevertheless, policy makers in ports and port-cities should concentrate on the potential opportunities being presented to them with the changes in transportation and logistics services. Ports and port-cities are strategically located on the transportation route from producer to consignee. The gateway position of many hub ports offers opportunities for the development of value-added logistics (Notteboom and Winkelmans 2001). The port region has the potential to serve as a platform and centre for information systems, which provide the common denominator and prerequisite for many logistical functions. Cities may greatly benefit from cooperating with ports in the establishment of information system centres, since port operators control valuable information about the cargo and its destination.

Cooperation between the city and the port is essential and beneficial to both parties. Most often, the logistical parks will not be located in or near the waterfront. The vast amount of land required and the access needed to interior markets will prohibit such development. In addition, the high demand for waterfront areas from alternative uses and environmental interests will make a waterfront logistical parks a tough objective to achieve. In order to promote logistical parks and distribution centres within their jurisdiction, cities must provide adequate infrastructure for such activities, perhaps at the outskirts of the urban area. Carriers and global port operators, for their part, are eager to enter into such activities, and financially they are capable of doing so.

At the same time, port and urban authorities must be realistic with their assessments of the potential of integrating themselves into the transport and logistic chains. There might be cases in which the market place location away from the ports has relative or absolute advantages over a coastal location. Even then, there might be alternative opportunities for port-city interactions not always based on seaborne trade. The waterfront is an attractive, prime location much in demand for tourist activities, entertainment, business, real estate, and housing. This land might add to a city's economic base, on one hand, and provide resources for port-related activities with clear advantages, on the other. The Pentaport concept, which was developed in Inchon, Korea, provides an example of multiple, non-conventional, urban land uses (Chang 2003). The Pentaport combines five ports in one port project – airport, business port, technoport, and leisure port.

Seaports and port-cities have always been affected by the dynamic changes that the world economy and international trade have brought about. Some have managed to remain as operational ports and successful hubs, despite the turbulence. Others have had the opportunity to modify and revitalise the port-urban interface areas, sometimes with great success to the city and its community.

Conclusions

The evolution of the port-urban interface since the 1970s can be divided into three different phases: the first phase, containerisation, dominated the changes in the interrelationship of seaports and port-cities throughout the 1970s and most of the 1980s; the second phase, intermodality, is responsible for another set of changes that occurred from the second half of the 1980s and throughout the 1990s; and the most recent phase, which started at the beginning of the twenty-first century, and particularly in the past three years, is being shaped by the impact of globalisation.

The containerisation phase was characterised primarily by technological innovations that completely revolutionised the structure of vessels, cargo-handling methods, and the physical layout of ports. During that phase, the long-standing spatial ties between the city and the port were interrupted, and geographical segregation between the two entities emerged, subverting the traditional land-use characteristics of the urban waterfront. The phase of intermodality was more of an organisational revolution in which a segregated transportation system was converted into a total transport system. Coordination and synchronisation of transport systems supplied the focus here, rather than technology. In that phase, the main function of the port as terminus – a final stop in the port-to-port operation – was converted: the port became another link in the transport chain. Deregulation of transportation in the United States, inland penetration of seaborne trade, and the shifting of traditional functions, such as storage and warehousing from the waterfront to inland locations, form some of the key components of this phase.

In the past few years, particularly since the emerging of China as a major producer of containerised cargo, seaports and port-cities have been confronted with a more mature globalisation process. This, third and present phase of the port-city interface is characterised by an unprecedented volume of trade and container throughput, record-size container vessels, the dominant position of a relatively new component of the globalisation process – the global port operator – and finally, the intensification of the globalisation process of logistics, distribution, and supply chain management. The control and influence of the relationship between cities and ports are shifting away from the local to the global level.

At least four continuous trends, related to the interrelationship of seaports and port-cities, have followed each of the three phases: a weakening of economic ties, a loosening of the spatial relationship, increasing environmental pressure, and in general, growing conflicts of interest.

Reconciliation of the friction, the disagreements, and the divergence of visions between ports and cities are both necessary and possible. However, this requires different and sometimes non-conventional solutions, some of which have already emerged. It seems that in many cases, terminal and inland transport infrastructure are currently operating close to their capacity. Adding new terminals within existing ports is quite difficult to achieve, at least on the congested US West Coast and in NW Europe. However, building container terminals in new locations is a feasible option. The Port of Salalah in Aden, the new terminal in Prince Rupert in northern British Columbia, and to some extent the new terminals in Mexico, south of the US border, may be signalling the new direction: most of these new facilities are located away from congested urban areas. Offshore container terminals, such as Yangshan near Shanghai and off the coast of Mumbai, might provide another solution to resolve conflicting and common port-urban demands for waterfront land and in regard to related environmental issues.

However, the most important challenge for seaports and port-cities is to respond to the great opportunities that are currently presented to them. Both entities should cooperate and coordinate their actions in order to benefit from their strategic location along the supply chain and to be able to carve out their niche in the emerging global logistics systems. Port-city managements should recognise the business and employment opportunities that are presented, and actively assist in providing the necessary infrastructure – land, accessibility and communication – mostly at the outskirts of the city. These will trigger a chain of actions. Financially, global operators and ocean carriers, which are already engaged in logistics themselves, have the ability and the interest, to invest in 'logistics parks' and 'value-added' activities. Ports that could offer or facilitate such added services in their vicinity would have a competitive edge *vis-à-vis* the carriers and the global operators. The integration in the global logistic systems will enhance port-city interrelations, reduce the conflicts around the sensitive urban waterfront and should turn around the prevailing trend of declining port economic impacts.

Chapter 11

A Metageography of Port-City Relationships

César Ducruet

1. Introduction

It is now generally recognised that maritime networks have had an increasing influence on ports and port-city relationships over the last three decades, following the container revolution and the new spatial distribution of industrial activities. Although containerisation has spread globally and homogenously, it has also encountered a regional diversity of heritages and practices. The responses of port-cities to global economic change reveal important differences between world regions, notably in terms of waterfront redevelopment in Europe and America (Hoyle 2000) and port-city planning in the Northern and Southern hemispheres (Carmona 2003a; 2003b). Thus, transport players that are willing to insert the port-city within the global transport chain must cope with normalised logistics systems which are managed by an ever-reducing number of powerful global companies (e.g. shippers, shipping lines, freight forwarders, logistics agents) and local and regional specificities in terms of economic development and spatial planning. Between global insertion and local impediments, a wide variety of situations can be found.

This chapter seeks to determine whether or not homogenous port regions exist, and, if so, what factors define such regions from arbitrary spatial divisions (Braudel 1979; Lewis and Wigen 1997). Studies on the world system and regionalisation have not paid much attention to ports (Lloyd 1992; Durand *et al.* 1993; Dollfus *et al.* 1999); while most studies focus on the world's largest cities when examining transport globalisation (Dogan 1988; Keeling 1995). Port geographers have addressed a number of models usually separating developed and developing countries at different periods from colonial cities to global logistics (see Lee *et al.* 2006 for a synthesis), but their application has remained limited to collections of case studies rather than macro-regional or global analysis (Slack *et al.* 2000).

In this respect, port-cities seem to be an original ground on which to study the local and regional factors affecting globalisation. Important contemporary changes have been widely described by scholars, such as the decline of mutual economic benefits (Benacchio *et al.* 2001) and the increased spatial separation (Hoyle 1989) between ports and cities resulting from technological and managerial change in global transportation. In order to verify the linkages between global and local factors affecting port-cities, a large-scale analysis is needed.

This research analyses the relationships between functional attributes (demographic size, logistics activities, port infrastructures, traffics and land-sea connections) and locational attributes (latitude, longitude), so as to test the hypothesis of a regional coherence underlying the insertion of port-cities in the global transport chain. Previous works have been limited in undertaking such verification without the inclusion of geographical attributes (Ducruet 2004a; Ducruet and Jeong 2005). Geographical coordinates appear to be the only objective parameter available to express a regional belonging. It has the advantage of being neutral and unique to every place, and also it avoids the subjective definition of regional entities.

2. Models of Port-City Relationships

The port-city does not refer to a specific scientific category or methodology because of the diversity of port-city issues and the usual separation of port and urban studies (Broeze 1989; Reeves 1989; Chaline 1994; Morvan 1999). Thus, it is still an 'unidentified real object' (Brunet 1997) which, without a universally recognised definition, remains only broadly addressed by scholars as a circulation node between land and sea where specific functions develop (Bastié and Dezert 1980; Brunn 1983; White and Senior 1983; Brocard 1994).

2.1 Urban and port models

In port and maritime geography, the city has been given particular importance dating back to the works of Vigarié (1979). However, urban-related issues are often disregarded in the general literature on ports and transport (Banister 1995), which is more focused on technical (network and node performance) and/or institutional (transport players and their strategies) issues. Reasons for this focus include the traditional separation between urban geography and transport geography and the contemporary phenomenon of port-city separation which has become a very fertile ground for waterfront-related issues among planners, geographers, and economists.

The city appears to be a constraint to port expansion because of the technological transformations in the maritime world (e.g. the growing size of ships). The outports depicted by Perpillou (1959) and systematised in the anyport (Bird 1963) and European estuary (Brocard *et al.* 1995b) models show the shift of port facilities from the upstream city to deep-sea downstream locations. Hoyle (1989) also illustrates the successive stages of port-city spatial separation.

Urban functions are considered secondary factors to explain the strategies of shipping lines, port operators and freight forwarders which focus on cost and time efficiency of transport systems regardless of the location of port infrastructures. Additional issues regarding dry ports and inland multimodal platforms tend to reinforce the idea of the urban constraint within coastal cities. Port models have doubted the local benefits of new port facilities, like in the case of remotely located ports (Stern and Hayuth 1984).

The port is also poorly represented in urban models. Port function is often considered as disturbing the regularity of the central place theory, due to its effect on the urban system (Bird 1977). Thus, it has been neglected for a long time, for instance at the local level in urban models (Gleave 1997). At least port activities confer to the economic structure some specialisation in transport functions, with a higher share of employment in the transport sector than in non-port-cities.

For such reasons, port-cities have often lower ranking in urban classifications (Hautreux and Rochefort 1963; Noin 1974; Pumain and Saint-Julien 1976). Bird (1973) reacts to this by considering gateway and central place functions as equally important for cities and regions. Such argument was further developed through the idea of multiplier effects, described by Vigarié (1979) as a 'reciprocal breed' between ports and cities. Vallega (1983) also developed a theory on the interaction between port growth and local economic diversification, even though port and urban dynamics remain of a different nature. More recent researchers still consider ports as advantageous locations for trade and urban development (Fujita and Mori 1996; Fujita *et al.* 1999). The everlasting debate about the direction of the influence between ports and urban systems (Boyer and Vigarié 1982) raises the problem of causality: 'does the port develop the city and its economic activities, or is the city the engine of port expansion?' (Verlaque 1979). Goss (1990) condemns this question, arguing that 'it serves no useful purpose to ask which functions came first or are the more important: they go together'.

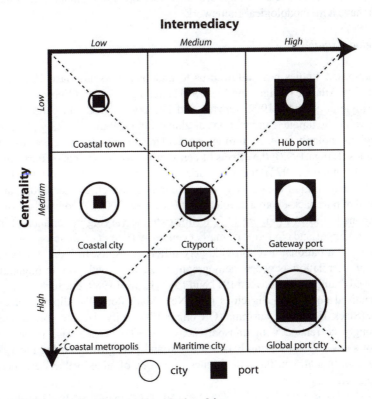

Figure 11.1 A matrix of port-city relationships
Source: Adapted from Ducruet (2004b).

2.2 The port-city matrix

The absence of a universal definition or model of port-city relationships is balanced by several typologies, of which the port-city matrix is a synthesis. In Figure 11.1, an upper left-lower right diagonal illustrates the hierarchical combination of centrality and intermediacy[1] (Fleming and Hayuth 1994) while the lower left-upper right one marks their opposition. The *cityport*, as defined by Hoyle and Pinder (1981; 1992) is a state of equilibrium between the coastal town and the global port-city in terms of size and between the hub and the general city in terms of function. This underlines the fact that, in reality, few port-cities might be considered cityports because of the recurrent disequilibria between these two main orientations.

3. A Global Approach

Most port studies on a world scale are limited to port traffics (Marcadon 1995; Brocard *et al.* 1995a), while others use original methodologies such as the application of graph theory to maritime systems (Joly 1999), and the calculation of a weekly containerised transport capacity from the main shipping lines' services (Frémont and Soppé 2003). Port-city relationships are more developed in regional studies but few of them have a methodological framework.

3.1 Regional studies

Regional-based studies have allowed us to understand Asian (Basu 1985; Broeze 1989; 1997), Atlantic (Knight and Liss 1991; Konvitz 1994) and European (Konvitz 1978; Hoyle and Pinder 1992; Lawton and Lee 2002) trends. In particular, some authors value the unique combinations of global and local trends taking place within port regions, notably in Asia, through particular land patterns (McGee 1967) and hinterlands (Banga 1992); the effects of dense urban environments on port activities (Ness and Tanigawa, 1992); the urban-oriented policies of Asian port-cities (Okuno 2000); the evolution of the port-city interface in hub port-cities (Lee 2005); and the new trend of port back-up area development (Lee *et al.* 2005). A comparison of main port regions is shown in Figure 11.2, to illustrate the varying importance of inland and coastal hinterlands in terms of market centrality (Lee *et al.* 2006).

Studies at a national level provide very different results. In India, for example, the linear correlation between demographic size and total port throughput has diminished dramatically between 1911 and 1981 (Kidwai 1989) due to the emergence of specialised ports from big cities (e.g. New Mangalore, Paradip). Inversely, in Canada (Slack 1989) and Australia (O'Connor 1989), city size and port throughput are strongly correlated with transport activities. The French case (Steck 1995) does not show any correlation between urban and port growth during the 1975 to 1990 period. In addition, the growth rates in Europe of added value were identical

---

1   Centrality is defined as a local/regional trade generation power (endogenous) while intermediacy is defined by external player's election of a place for serving their networks (exogenous).

between port-cities and non-port-cities between 1975 and 1985, but became stronger for non-port-cities between 1985 and 1996 (Lever 1994), illustrating the economic advantage of inland location in the European central place system (IRSIT 2004). In China, although new ports are distant from inner cities, they become industrial growth poles while port activity is still important for inner ports (Wang and Olivier 2003).

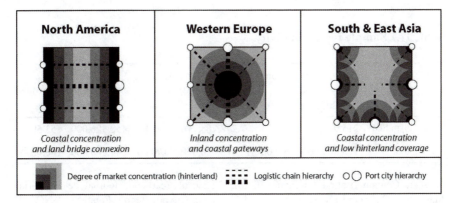

Figure 11.2 Regional models of port-urban organisation
Source: Lee, Song and Ducruet (2006).

3.2 Measuring port-city relationships

The lack of relevant sources for measuring these relationships through international comparisons (Ducruet 2003) has restrained the quantitative approach to 'approximate measures of economic benefits deriving from port activities' (Wang and Olivier 2003). In fact, port-city relationships are more of a qualitative issue but a number of authors have proposed some indicators to allow a comparative approach.

The relative concentration index is proposed by Vallega (1976) to compare Mediterranean regions, by simply dividing the regional share of throughput by the regional share of population. Similar index are used by Vigarié (1968) to measure maritime dependence (number of merchant marine tons per inhabitant) and Kenyon (1974) to measure the relative importance of transit function and urban magnitude amongst US port-cities (number of general cargo tons per inhabitant).

The works of Witherick (1981) and Gripaios (1995) remain based on specific data collected from national censuses. Recent works on port-related employment in British travel-to-work areas (Gripaios and Gripaios 1999), air-sea employment in European port-cities (Ducruet *et al.* 2005), the port-city interface in Europe and Asia (Ducruet and Jeong 2005), and global-local forces affecting global hub port-cities in Asia (Lee 2005) have provided useful outcomes motivating the pursuit of a global approach.

4. Application to a World Sample

4.1 Global analysis

As a result of data collection on a world scale, the sample covers approximately 96 per cent of container throughput, 60 per cent of port tonnage, and 53 per cent of coastal urban population (Table 11.1).

Table 11.1 Sample representativity

	Container throughput (2000)		Total tonnage (2000)		Coastal urban population (1990)	
	TEU	%	Metric tons	%	No inhab.	%
Sample studied	215,915,760	95.83	7,248,765,716	59.84	452,306,000	53.59
World total	225,300,000	100.00	12,113,000,000	100.00	844,000,000	100.00

Sources: Containerisation International, ISL Statistical Yearbook, Journal de la Marine Marchande, Moriconi-Ebrard 1994, World Gazetteer, Citypopulation, Populstat, UNCTAD 2002, Noin 2000.

The criterion used to select ports is their participation to regular container services of the world's major shipping lines, regardless of a demographic or traffic size (Frémont and Soppé 2003). This criterion has the advantage of assessing the participation of the port-city to the global logistics chain. Moreover, containerisation implies a higher value of the goods transported, a potential intermodality, and a set of logistics functions which are not common with ports specialised in bulk or oil products. The resulting sample consists of 348 ports located throughout the world.

Available data have been selected through their relevancy: geographical coordinates (Lloyd's Maritime Atlas 2005), urban population (Helders 2006; Lahmeyer 2006; Brinkhoff 2006), container-related businesses (*Containerisation International Online* 2006), freight forwarders and logistics agents (*International Transport Journal* 2006), highway and railway connections (Microsoft 2006), container throughput, maritime connections, nautical accessibility, and total length of the container terminals (*Containerisation International* 2006). Although other indicators exist at a global scale, they have not been included to avoid redundant values (e.g. ton traffic, total quayage, administrative and suburban population, surface of the metropolitan urbanised area, and ship-owners' headquarters).

The original values are transformed into logarithms to lower extreme values, except for geographical coordinates, which contain negative numbers. In Table 11.2, eigen values and cumulated variance show the results of the factor analysis with four main factors, accounting for 76 per cent of the original information.

The first factor (F1) is the concentration of the transport chain, based on logistics activities, port throughputs and infrastructures. In this hierarchy, geographical coordinates do not play an important role. Then F1 can be defined as a gradient of insertion in the global transport chain.

Table 11.2 Main characteristics of the principal components

	F1	F2	F3	F4
Eigen values	5.2	1.3	1.0	0.8
Cumulated variance (%)	47.2	59.1	68.3	76.0
	Contribution of the indicators to the factors (%)			
	Transport chain concentration	*North-south landside gradient*	*East-west urban gradient*	*North-south logistics gradient*
Coordinates > 0	Logistics Activities (14%) Container Throughput (13%) Container Terminals (12%) Freight Forwarders (12%)	Rail Connections (19%) Road Connections (18%) Latitude (15%) Urban Population (3%)	Longitude (51%) Urban Population (14%) Logistics Activities (3%) Rail Connections (1%)	Logistics Activities (10%) Urban Population (7%) Latitude (3%) Freight Forwarders (3%)
Coordinates < 0	–	Container Throughput (6%) Maximum Depth (11%) Maritime Connections (11%) Longitude (13%)	Container Throughput (2%) Container Terminals (5%) Latitude (7%) Maximum Depth (13%)	Longitude (10%) Rail Connections (15%) Road Connections (17%) Maximum Depth (30%)
	East-west maritime gradient	*North-south port gradient*	*East-west intermodal gradient*	

The second factor (F2) is an opposition between two trends. On one side, maritime connections and maximum depth of the container terminals are related to longitude (east-west maritime gradient), while on the other side, inland connections are related to latitude (north-south landside gradient). This opposition is recurrent in port geography, as it refers to the 'port triptych' model (Vigarié 1968) where foreland and hinterland are two major components of the transport chain, along with the port itself; few ports embrace a dominant position on both sides of the triptych. Aside these two major factors which account together for almost 60 per cent of the analysis, two other ones worth attention.

The third factor (F3) brings a complementary opposition: on one side is the interplay of demographic size and longitude (east-west urban gradient), and on the other side is the one between container infrastructures and latitude (north-south port gradient). The opposition between city size and port performance is a recurrent issue as stated previously. It means that the efficiency of port operation contradicts the importance of the urban centre, because of growing congestion at the port-city interface. Although coastal location has been an advantage in attracting population and industries close to ports for economic reasons, the spatial effects of such concentration have increasingly led to diseconomies of scale and of agglomeration. It also confirms in some way the opposition between the hub port, dominated by maritime shipments, and the coastal city or metropolis, dominated by central place functions (Figure 11.1). The north-south port gradient also recalls the works of Zohil and Prijon (1999) and Boske (2003) on the interdependence of transhipment volumes and distance to major sea lanes. Port planning on a world scale is highly influenced by the shortest path used by bigger ships, linking the three main economic poles of the world: ports located away from the circumterrestrial artery cause a deviation and are used as feeder ports instead of as direct ports of calls for mother vessels.

The fourth factor (F4) opposes two different trends: the interplay of logistics activities, population and latitude (north-south logistics gradient); and the combination of nautical, inland accessibility with longitude (east-west intermodal gradient). Urban economies are important for logistics activities because urban systems remain the *raison d'être* of production and consumption activities. If the local relationship between ports and port-cities undergoes growing pains (McCalla 1999), ports and transport players cannot ignore the markets they serve and nor their location patterns. The opposition to an intermodal potential means that the efficiency of transport systems has its own logic but, in the end, transport players are more likely to follow the urban hierarchy.

The absence of a gradient of port-city interdependence shows that on a world-scale, there is more of an opposition than a combination of urban and port functions.

4.2 Regional analysis

The spatial distribution of the gradient of transport chain concentration (F1) reveals the three dominant economic regions: North America, Europe and East Asia (Figure 11.3, upper). The cores of the world economy are also in the south: Callao-Lima, Buenos Aires, Rio de Janeiro, Abidjan, Capetown, Durban, Australian cities, Auckland, and the important metropolises of the Middle East (Jeddah, Dubai) and South Asia (Karachi, Mumbai, Colombo, Visakhapatnam). These port-cities are the most connected to the global transport chain although the principles of their insertion differ in terms of market centrality and urban systems (as shown in Figure 11.2). Thus, unsurprisingly, the organisation of global logistics corresponds to the world pattern of economic wealth and port concentration, dividing the world into two distinct hemispheres.

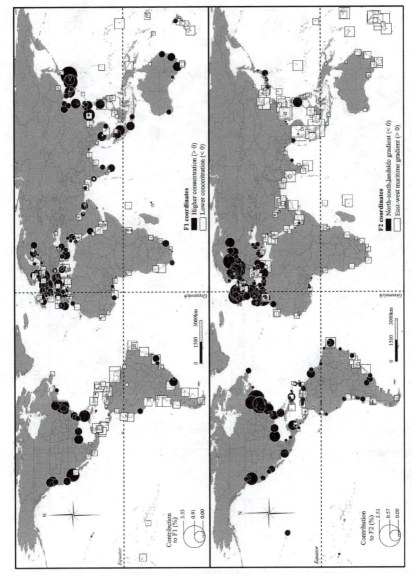

Figure 11.3 Spatial distribution of the results (1)

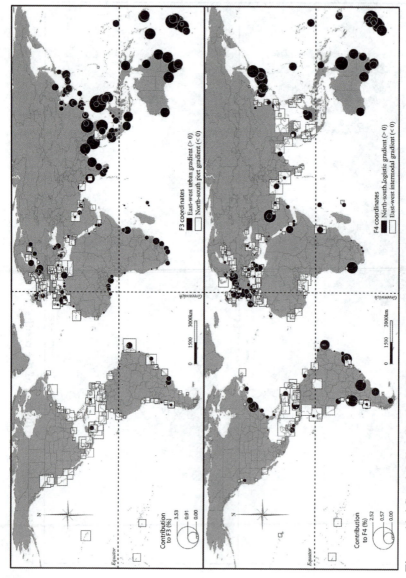

Figure 11.4 Spatial distribution of the results (2)

The first opposition (F2) reveals the contemporary shift of maritime and port activities to the East, the new gravity centre of the world economy (Figure 11.3, lower). Thus, the concentration of shipping lines and modern port infrastructures follows an east-west gradient, with most important scores located in East Asia. It also indicates the lack of inland connections, a main characteristic of Asian ports resulting from the extraversion of port activities and the coastal concentration of markets (Figure 11.2). Inversely, for the Western (Atlantic) world, the concentration of shipping lines is lower and the importance of inland connections is higher. This is particularly true for North America as well as for Europe, where ongoing regional integration is mostly based on the interaction between EU member countries within the continent. It also confirms that North America and Europe are more continental while Asia is more maritime.

The second opposition (F3) shows a complementary reality (Figure 11.4, upper). The east-west gradient shows the importance of city size in South and Southeast Asia (from Karachi to Manila), Oceania, Western and Southern Africa, and to a lesser extent in Northeast Asia and South America. In other regions, city size is relatively less important than port functions; this indirectly indicates the fact that Western urban economies have also developed inland, especially in Europe where the heartland of the continent is the core of the regional economy. Thus, European port-cities compete to sustain their accessibility and welcome the highest cargo volumes for serving overlapping hinterlands.

The third opposition (F4) has a more complex spatial distribution (Figure 11.4, lower). Broadly speaking, the east-west intermodal gradient concentrates on port-cities along the circumterrestrial trunk line: Caribbean, West and North Africa, East Mediterranean, and South and East Asia. The north-south logistics gradient lies north or south of this trunk line with South America, Northeast America, Western Europe, Japan and Oceania. Although the two gradients exclude each other, the importance of logistics activities in Europe does not mean a lack of intermodal potential. This trend can be explained by the historical importance of logistics activities in Europe, alike Japan and Northeast America. In other regions sharing this trend, the lack of intermodal potential is probably the main explanation. Thus, the remoteness to major shipping lines lowers the need for intermodal operations but accentuates the importance of local economies and logistics.

4.3 Exceptions

According to the east-west maritime gradient (F2), any port-city located westbound of the Greenwich meridian should indicate a relatively lesser concentration of shipping lines compared to the level of its landside connections. This is not true for some port-cities of the Caribbean (Kingston, Puerto Cabello, Cartagena and Colon) and South America (Rio Grande, Paranagua, Sao Francisco do Sul, Santos, Sepetiba and Suape). In Europe, port-cities located close to the heartland also contradict the trend, like those of the Northern range (Le Havre, Zeebrugge, Rotterdam, Tilbury and Felixstowe), northern Italy (Genoa, La Spezia, Venice, and also Koper in Slovenia) and the Mediterranean hubs (Algeciras, Gioia Tauro, Marsaxlokk, Piraeus and Limassol). Their direct connection to the global economy through the world's major shipping lines overwhelms the importance – or accentuates the lack – of inland connections. In contrast, some port-cities located eastbound of the Greenwich meridian have a lower concentration of shipping lines compared to the importance of their inland connections, such as Japanese and South Asian port-cities (e.g. Bangkok, Chittagong, Yangon, Visakhapatnam and Batangas). For Japan, this can be explained by the absence of one unique load centre and to its Western character due to earlier industrialisation than other Asian countries.

Similarly, the north-south landside gradient is not matched by several south American port-cities (Paita, Ilo, Chanaral, Caldera, Coquimbo, Buenos Aires, San Lorenzo, Montevideo, Rio de Janeiro, Ilheus, Recife, Fortaleza, Belem, Georgetown, Degrad-des-Cannes and Guanta, Maracaibo). Such exceptions are not found in Oceania, despite the distance to major shipping lines, because of the insular character of the port-cities.

According to the east-west urban gradient (F3), port-cities located westbound of the Greenwich meridian should see their city size less important than their port functions. Again, South America has several exceptions (most Brazilian cities, Talcahuano, and Coquimbo). Some Eastern cities show a lesser importance of city size as compared to their port functions (Laem Chabang, Jawaharlal Nehru and Port Mohammad Bin Qasim). These ports were recently created to reduce the congestion problems in their older neighbours (Bangkok, Mumbai and Karachi).

The distribution of the north-south port gradient (F3) is contradicted by several UK port-cities (Cardiff, Belfast, Glasgow, Edinburgh, Tyne, Hull, London) and Baltic (Copenhagen, Malmo, Rostock, Szczecin, Stockholm, Gdansk, Riga, Klaipeda and Saint-Petersburg), as well as in the south (Bordeaux, Sevilla, Malaga, Alicante, Algiers, Tunis, Messina, Bari, Volos, Thessaloniki, Izmir, Istanbul and Varna). Economic diversification, remoteness to major shipping lines, and congestion at the port-urban interface are main factors which explain the precedence taken by urban functions over port functions.

The last factor (F4) shows the spatial division of Europe, with logistics importance in the west and intermodal potential in the east. The logistics importance may correspond to the strategies of operators, to concentrate on few dominant ports to serve the continent.

5. Policy Implications: Strengths and Weaknesses of Port Cities

Although the factor analysis shows the different oppositions of variables and regions, an important question remains: how do port-cities integrate land and sea networks; port and urban functions; logistics activities and intermodal potentials? Because the particularity and efficiency of a port-city are more to combine different elements of the transport chain in a single place, a complementary approach is needed. The lower the contribution of a port-city to an opposition between two trends, the higher its participation to both opposing trends will be. Port-cities having less than 0.1 per cent contribution to a factor are considered more equilibrate within different functions and networks. A selection is proposed in Table 11.3, with (+) for contributions under 0.1 percent (equilibrium) and (-) for contributions above 0.1 percent (disequilibria).

Results are interpreted as strengths or weaknesses regarding the insertion of port-cities in the transport chain, with Figure 11.5 as a framework.

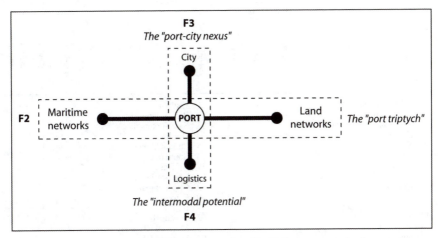

Figure 11.5 A system of port-city integration in the transport chain

Port-city integration in Europe is observed only for places located away from the heartland (Amsterdam, Liverpool, Dublin, Glasgow, Gothenburg, Oslo, Lisbon, Leixoes, Naples, Piraeus and Thessaloniki). European gateways are more efficient for triptych and intermodal integration (Rotterdam, Hamburg, Aarhus, Dunkirk, Southampton, Trieste, Genoa, Valencia and Leghorn). This confirms that the closer that ports are close to the heartland, the less their port-city equilibrium will be realised, given the concentration of flows and the indirect dependence on inland markets, which accentuates port specialisation.

Elsewhere, port-city integration reveals the specificity of Asian hub port-cities (Hong Kong, Singapore and Port Klang) combined with intermodal logistics (Busan, Incheon, Qingdao, Kaohsiung and Colombo). Such cities manage to keep a profitable equilibrium between urban and port functions by overcoming the risk of congestion at the port-city interface but suffer from the lack of hinterland. Except for hub port-cities, Asian places are mostly concerned with port triptych integration (Osaka, Nagoya and Hakata), which combines with intermodal logistics in the case of south-eastern metropolises (Bangkok, Jakarta and Chennai) but cannot maintain a sustainable port-city equilibrium.

In North America, 13 port-cities among 17 integrate logistics and intermodality, except for Halifax, New York, Boston and Philadelphia. Similar to European gateways, North American port-cities have grown into powerful integrators of transport networks, allowing the formation of land bridge strategies across the continent. However, the absence of port-city integration stems from the diversity and size of local economies.

Table 11.3 Types of transport chain integration at the world's main 100 port-cities

Rank on F1	Port-city	Sea-land	Port-city	Logistics-intermodal	Rank on F1	Port-city	Sea-land	Port-city	Logistics-intermodal
		Integration type					Integration type		
1	Tokyo-Yokohama	-	-	-	51	Durban	-	-	+
2	Osaka-Kobe	+	-	-	52	Rio de Janeiro	-	+	-
3	Rotterdam-Europoort	+	-	+	53	Saint-Petersburg	-	-	+
4	Hamburg	+	-	+	54	Dublin	-	+	-
5	New York-New Jersey	-	-	-	55	Philadelphia	-	+	-
6	London	-	-	-	56	Southampton	+	-	-
7	Antwerp	+	-	-	57	Brisbane	-	+	-
8	Los Angeles-Long Beach	-	-	+	58	Leixoes-Porto	-	+	+
9	Hong Kong	-	+	-	59	Copenhagen	-	-	+
10	Barcelona	+	+	+	60	Felixstowe	-	-	-
11	Miami-Port Everglades	-	-	+	61	Beirut	+	+	+
12	Busan	-	+	+	62	Savannah	+	-	+
13	Singapore	-	+	-	63	Mumbai (Bombay)	+	-	-
14	Shanghai	-	-	-	64	Portland OR	-	-	+
15	Bremen-Bremerhaven	-	-	-	65	Callao-Lima	+	+	-
16	Valencia	+	-	+	66	Chennai (Madras)	+	-	+
17	Genoa	+	-	+	67	Jacksonville	-	-	+
18	Nagoya	+	-	-	68	Fremantle-Perth	+	-	-
19	Seattle-Tacoma	+	-	+	69	Incheon-Seoul	-	+	+
20	Houston	-	+	+	70	Qingdao	-	+	+
21	Manila	-	-	+	71	Cape Town	-	-	+
22	Montreal	-	+	-	72	Abidjan	+	+	+
23	Bangkok	+	-	+	73	Trieste	+	-	-
24	Melbourne	-	-	-	74	Leghorn (Livorno)	+	-	+
25	Buenos Aires	-	-	+	75	Tanjung Perak-Surabaya	+	-	-
26	Vancouver BC	-	-	+	76	Ho Chi Minh City	+	-	-
27	Piraeus-Athens	-	+	+	77	Dalian	-	-	+
28	Marseilles	+	+	+	78	Haifa	+	+	+
29	Kaohsiung	-	+	+	79	Casablanca	+	+	-
30	Tanjung Priok-Jakarta	+	-	+	80	Boston MA	-	+	-
31	Baltimore	-	-	+	81	Izmir	+	+	+
32	Le Havre	-	-	-	82	Taichung	-	-	+
33	Lisbon	+	+	+	83	Zeebrugge	-	-	-
34	Port Klang-Kuala Lumpur	-	+	-	84	Auckland	-	-	+
35	Sydney-Port Botany	-	-	-	85	Algeciras	-	-	+
36	Gothenburg	-	+	+	86	Keelung-Taipei	-	-	-
37	Oslo	-	+	-	87	Hakata-Fukuoka	+	-	-
38	Helsinki	-	+	-	88	Thessaloniki	-	+	+
39	Dubai	-	+	-	89	Dammam	+	+	+
40	Bilbao	+	+	+	90	Aarhus	+	-	+
41	Oakland-San Francisco	-	-	+	91	Halifax	+	-	-
42	Charleston	+	-	+	92	Kitakyushu	-	-	-
43	Tianjin	+	-	+	93	Karachi	-	-	-
44	Colombo	-	+	+	94	Santos	-	-	-
45	New Orleans	-	-	+	95	Port Said	-	-	+
46	Jeddah	-	+	+	96	Lagos-Apapa	+	-	-
47	Amsterdam	-	+	-	97	Dunkirk	+	-	+
48	Haydarpasa-Istanbul	-	-	-	98	Limassol	-	-	-
49	Naples	-	+	+	99	Glasgow	-	+	-
50	Liverpool	-	+	-	100	Xiamen	-	-	-

Finally, the integration of all three factors is quite rare and spatially restrained. In fact, this profile is seen only in the south European-Middle Eastern area, except for

Abidjan. Lisbon, Bilbao, Barcelona, Marseilles, Izmir, Beirut, Haifa and Dammam are the only port-cities to maintain a total equilibrium. Thus, they can be attributed the identity of cityports. Inversely, the total absence of integration does not have a specific geographical logic. It is more of a functional matter, like the absence of consistent local economy, inland connections and intermodal logistics (Le Havre, Zeebrugge, Felixstowe, Limassol, Keelung, Xiamen and Santos), or the dominance of urban functions combined with the lack of space (London, Tokyo, New York, Shanghai, Bremen, Brisbane, Melbourne, Sydney, Istanbul, Kitakyushu and Karachi). These cities cannot be cityports because their situation in the transport chain gives advantage to only one of the elements of the system at a time.

6. Concluding Remarks: The Transport Chain is not Ubiquitous

Starting from the hypothesis that a world regionalisation underlies port-city relationships, this research has overcome the difficulty of gathering relevant data from a vast sample of port-cities throughout the world. Another difficulty of such an approach is the systematic measurement of a complex phenomenon which is not well defined in the literature; port-city relationships are often hampered by the institutional and physical separation between urban and port authorities, transport modes, and operators. Far from ignoring this reality, the focus was placed on a geographical rather than on an economical perspective. Arguing that the combination of different variables in every place is not unique, this chapter searches for wider levels of organisation, where port-cities face a number of common challenges inherited from similar stages of development (e.g. colonial period and the first Industrial Revolution), physical constraints (e.g. islands vs. continents and distance to trunk lines) and settlement patterns (e.g. types of urban systems), defined as long-term factors.

The first part of the results verifies the respective weight of long-term and short-term factors, with the latter being the strategies for inserting port-cities in the global transport chain (Robinson 2002). Unsurprisingly, long-term factors have a strong influence on the distribution of port and urban variables, which are in line with east-west and north-south patterns. This confirms the recurrent separation between port and urban functions, but this separation does not have the same meaning according to macro-regions. There are important distortions of regional patterns, caused by recent strategies of port concentration, new port construction and hub-feeder networks.

Following the horizontal analysis, based on the search for a bi-dimensional coherence of port-city relationships, the second part of the results is more a vertical one. Although port and urban variables are systematically opposed (land/maritime, port/city or logistics/intermodality), there are several cases for which these functions are articulated. This is a useful qualitative complement to usual port rankings based on sole traffics. The synthetic expression of strengths and weaknesses of port-cities addresses several policy implications. In the end, it provides some evidence about the relativity of universal issues, such as the transport chain, which are far from being ubiquitous. Results can also be a tool for port and urban players to position themselves in the world system.

Annex 11.1 Most representative port-cities

(+)	North–south landside gradient	East–west urban gradient	North–south logistics gradient
↑	Boston	Auckland	Nagoya
	Philadelphia	Ho Chi Minh City	Yokkaichi
	Glasgow	Wellington	Tokyo-Yokohama
	Stockholm	Melbourne	Osaka-Kobe
	Montreal	Sydney-Port Botany	Philadelphia
	Portland OR	Adelaide	Hakata-Fukuoka
	New York-New Jersey	Chittagong	Adelaide
	Bristol	Brisbane	Brisbane
	Bordeaux	Cebu	Buenos Aires
	London	Bangkok	Bremen-Bremerhaven
	Copenhagen	Tanjung Perak-Surabaya	Kitakyushu
	Houston	Fremantle-Perth	Gwangyang
	Liverpool	Mumbai (Bombay)	Fremantle-Perth
	Nantes	Tanjung Priok-Jakarta	Nantes
	St. Petersburg	Tokyo-Yokohama	Melbourne
	Belfast	Belawan-Medan	Glasgow
	Teesport	Karachi	Sydney-Port Botany
	Tunis	Shanghai	Wellington
	Baltimore	Dar-es-Salaam	London
	Riga	Hakata-Fukuoka	Shimizu
	Jacksonville	Kitakyushu	Amsterdam
	Amsterdam	Chennai (Madras)	Vigo
	Miami-Port Everglades	Tunis	Boston
	New Orleans	Stockholm	Trieste
	Rouen	Penang	New York-New Jersey
	Gothenburg	Osaka-Kobe	Liverpool
	Leixoes-Porto	Ningbo	Southampton
	Alicante	Buenos Aires	Shuwaikh
	Dublin	Haydarpasa-Istanbul	Gioia Tauro
	Oslo	Nagoya	Bordeaux
	Zeebrugge	Southampton	Mersin
	Belawan-Medan	Aarhus	Mina Zayed
	Incheon-Seoul	Jacksonville	Limassol
	Puerto Cabello	Port Said	Tunis
	Dalian	Veracruz	Haydarpasa-Istanbul
	Algeciras	Rio Grande	Penang
	Taichung	Portland OR	Santos
	La Spezia	Rotterdam-Europoort	Puerto Cabello
	Limassol	Vigo	Ravenna
	Santos	Trieste	Cadiz
	Gioia Tauro	Antwerp	Felixstowe
	Dubai	La Spezia	Cebu
	Manila	Bremen-Bremerhaven	Dubai
	Busan	Le Havre	Ho Chi Minh City
	Keelung-Taipei	Kingston	Dar-es-Salaam
	Penang	Savannah	Belawan-Medan
	Auckland	Charleston	Dakar
	Rio Grande	Santa Cruz de Tenerife	Mombasa
	Wellington	Tilbury	Kingston
	Colombo	Puerto Cabello	Venice
	Port Said	Oakland-San Francisco	Casablanca
	Chiwan (Shenzhen)	Algeciras	Callao-Lima
	Xiamen	Halifax	Chittagong
	Port Louis	Los Angeles-Long Beach	Hong Kong
	Felixstowe	Honolulu	Singapore
	Kaohsiung	Felixstowe	San Juan
	Qingdao	Gioia Tauro	Lagos-Apapa
	Port Klang-Kuala Lumpur	Vancouver BC	Mumbai (Bombay)
	Hong Kong	Seattle-Tacoma	Guayaquil
↓	Singapore	Zeebrugge	Karachi
(-)	East–west maritime gradient	North–south port gradient	East–west intermodal gradient

Chapter 12

Chinese Port-cities in Global Supply Chains

James Wang and Daniel Olivier

Introduction: China's New Generation Port-cities

Current global outsourcing trends in favour of China could not exist without supporting transport infrastructure. China has made spectacular leaps in upgrading its container port facilities in the past decade. Coastal container ports have averaged annual throughput growth rates in the order of 30% during the period 1991–2004 (Research and Markets 2005), and the overall volume of container throughput of mainland Chinese seaports reached 56 million TEU in 2005. However, while a growing literature has been documenting the rise of containerisation along China's coast (Cullinane *et al.* 2004) and the growing role of international terminal operators and shipping lines in Chinese port business (Wang *et al.* 2004), a piece of the puzzle remains missing: how do port-cities (beyond individual ports themselves) interact with global supply chains in the context of China's manufacturing boom?

There is now a pressing need to consider ports as core constituents of modern supply chains. Seaports – or more importantly the firms and cities that run them – are among a number of players interacting together to make global supply chains competitive. This chapter aims at empirically substantiating possible ways modern port facilities insert themselves in global supply chains in the context of China's evolving port-cities. Our argument is that regimes of supply chain governance are key to understanding the role seaports play in such global chains and which paths they can opt to insert themselves and their cities in global supply chains (GSCs) most productively.

The chapter begins by introducing a model of GSC governance from which we derive implications in terms of port-city strategy. Second, we discuss three types of buyer-driven GSCs that are found in hub port cities, and the role of Free Economic Zones (FEZ) in China in facilitating these GSCs. Third, we analyse an empirical case to illustrate how a supplier-driven GSC finds its way for government support and leads to a new seaport city being built. Finally, we address the role of governments at various levels in changing the port-city infrastructure and influencing the choice of various GSCs in China.

2. Port Development and the Global Supply Chain Approach: Some Conceptual Issues

2.1 The governance of GSCs

Ports are important components of GSCs: they are integrated within the overall production and distribution process. There is a pressing imperative to study ports within the context of GSCs (Robinson 2002; Carbone and De Martino 2003; Hesse and Rodrigue 2004). GSCs may be understood as an integrative concept seeking to account for the complex spatial segmentation of production across national and sub-national borders. Similar notions have emerged under different banners: global logistics chains, global supply chains, global value chains (Gereffi *et al.* 1994; 2005), global production networks (Hendersen *et al.* 2001), etc. The literature on global production governance being still in its infancy, several of the models on offer are found to be either empirically difficult to substantiate or methodologically weak.

Among such models, Gereffi *et al.* (2005) have developed the most comprehensive and methodologically workable. The model is premised on the firm and its strategy as a primary unit of analysis, whether chains are supplier-driven or buyer-driven. Gereffi et al. have proposed four sub-variants in the governance of value chains (Figure 12.1). Developed by economic sociologists, the model takes into account social-relational questions behind economic action and corporate networks. It is especially suited to the Chinese context where relational business contacts are largely present (Davies *et al.* 1995; Yeung 2004). The authors have substantiated the model against a number of industries worldwide.

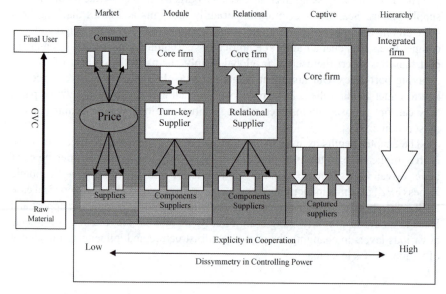

Figure 12.1 The Global Value Chain (GVC) governance model by Gereffi *et al*

However, such early models are yet to find general applications in transport and logistics sectors. This is rather surprising given the theoretical parallels between GSCs and the nature of logistics *per se* as 'network integrators'. Two early attempts to test the validity of the GVC model in the maritime industry have been made recently. Hall & Olivier (2005) have tested the model against evidence from the automobile transport industry and found it to have a high interpretative power. Implications for port logistics were singled out as one of the most promising axes for further research. Elsewhere, we have taken the idea a step further by empirically exploring the role of marine terminals in GSCs through the case of Tianjin, China's largest Free Economic Zone (FEZ) (Wang and Olivier 2006). We derive a conceptual model inspired from GSC literature by integrating current trends in China's coastal development which consists of integrating gateway ports with FEZ. In this chapter, we extend the explanation to more types of GSCs and their interplay with more port-cities in China.

2.2 The nature of GSCs: implications for port-city strategies

At this stage, some notional precisions are important in the context of GSCs' application to the port sector. Gereffi *et al.*'s (1994) earlier models of GSC governance included distinctions between supplier-driven and buyer-driven chains. Buyer-driven chains were found to be characteristic of some industries, namely consumer goods such as toys or televisions, while supplier-driven chains refer more to those industries that produce semi-final products such as machinery, electronic parts/components, and petrochemical products. From a port development standpoint, the retailer (buyer)-driven GSC differs from supplier-driven GSC in that the former is mainly associated with container shipping, while the latter more with bulk cargo shipping. More importantly, the two kinds of GSCs have different demands for a port. Retailer-driven GSCs are rarely vertically integrated in full (as in the 'hierarchy' sub-variant in Figure 12.1) and tend to be more flexible and more sensitive to accessibility of container terminal facilities. They are also more sensitive to such elements as:

- the trade agreements between the countries of buyers and that of suppliers;
- availability of comprehensive logistics and trading services; and
- service quality of a port such as the frequencies of calls and multiple destinations provided by shipping lines.

By contrast, supplier-driven chains tend to be less sensitive to such components since processing of bulk or raw commodities is at their core. Table 12.1 summarises the two kinds of GSCs, by considering six key dimensions. Naturally, container ports' capacity to respond to time sensitivity of GSCs is critical and questions of flexibility are important to smooth flows of circulation.

Table 12.1 Different GSCs and their relationship with port development

Requirements for ports and shipping	Retailer-driven final-product GSCs	Supplier-driven semi-final product GSCs
Type of cargo	Mainly by containers, some bulk and break-bulk	Mainly bulk (dry or liquid) cargo, such as ores, oil, steel
Volume	Uncertain, unstable, varied	Relatively consistent in time
Timing needs	Sensitive to delivery time of each individual batch, therefore sensitive to any possible time constraints such as customs check or call frequency to specific destinations	Sensitive to consistency and regularity of supply
Flexibility in using alternative port or terminals	Variable, may be highly dependant on the GVC governance models	Low, as large amount of capital are fixed assets or facilities for fairly long term usage
Environment considerations	Limited concerns	Sensitive, not only the cargo itself, but also directly related productions
Vertical integration including port facilities	Often low, normally not including port, terminal, or ships, therefore more flexible in choosing alterative transporters	High, firms tend to be large and to have their own terminal or berth, own or contracted ships, own or contracted fields of resource
Horizontal clustering in space	Yes, and particularly likely to places near a container port	Less likely, due to the scale of core firms

To countries like China that have a clear role as a world factory of final products and at the same time rely more and more on importing raw materials and fuel to support such export-oriented manufacturing, there are parallel and very fast developments of these two major types of GSCs. Two paths of port development are possible: (1) more multi-functional ports to deal with both kinds of GSCs, and (2) more port specialisation, i.e. each having specific functions, focusing on either containers, or other types of cargo. As required by today's vessel size, both possible development paths need deep-water conditions, but the landside requirements could be quite different. In the case of retailer-driven goods producers and container terminal operators, hub container ports in major cities that generate high traffic volumes are preferable. On the other hand, cities with some deepwater sites but with limited containerised cargo availability (or limited resources for container-cargo-generating industries) might be attractive more to vertically-integrated business seeking their own bulk-cargo terminals as part of their global supply chain. This is the difference between 'interactive development' and 'synchronised development' in industry-port-city dynamics. Here, interactive development is meant as a mutual reinforcing process between container terminal development and the concentration of industries that generate containerised cargo. Synchronised development refers to a development approach considered by those industries that see a specialised terminal – often purposely built and owned – as an integrated component when establishing themselves near a port. We now turn to empirical cases found in China to illustrate these concepts and distinctions.

3. Linking Port-cities and Buyer-driven GSCs: the Interactive Development

3.1 GSCs with captive local shippers in major port cities

We suggest there are three types of interactive development in the major Chinese cities with container hub ports. The first type is characterised by power imbalances typically in favour of powerful TNCs whose influence is such that they achieve substantial control over the entire chain, typically a captive shipper with capacity to generate massive freight volumes. Following trends in global outsourcing, many such manufacturing TNCs have naturally found their way into China. A large firm of this kind is likely to enter into stable arrangements with a specific shipping line and, in turn, to use a specific group of ports.

A case in point is Wal-Mart in South China, which has its own or long-term contracted factories in Shenzhen and Huizhou, two cities near Yantian port in the Pearl River Delta (PRD). Wal-Mart imported to the USA more than 576,000 TEU a year (Stalk and Waddell 2006, 23), three times more than the second largest retailers in the USA (Brenner *et al.* 2006). Among the goods it imported, roughly 10 per cent is made in China, procured directly or indirectly (Brenner *et al.* 2006). For this reason, it has a 'special relationship' partnership with Maersk, for shipping and overseas logistics services (Bonacich 2004). Interestingly, the latter purchased a minority stake in Yantian International Container Terminals Ltd. (YICT) from Hutchison Whampoa, the major shareholder of Yantian port. In this case, the three largest firms in their respective fields – retailing, shipping, and container terminal operation, are inter-locked to form a strong GSC without much involvement of independent freight forwarders and 3PLs. Similar 'big league' TNC-led GSCs involving Wal-Mart, Maersk and Hutchison Whampoa is found also in Shanghai and Ningbo. Since the three giant firms lock-in each other in a GSC alliance, their behavior matches Gereffi's 'GVC captive module'. This type of GSC seeing inter-corporate arrangements among some of the world's largest TNCs involves massive shipment volumes.

Spatial consolidation tends to follow corporate consolidation of GSCs, and logistics processing facilities are increasing in scale to meet large scale distribution requirements resulting from such shipments. For example, Wal-Mart and Maersk have become the largest customers of Yantian Port as shipper and carrier, respectively. Both companies have global networks of distribution facilities on both import and export sides of the GSC. Large shipments concentrate in a limited number of port-cities possessing advanced logistics processing facilities on the export side in emerging economies such as China. Leading mega-carriers like Maersk also tend to use large hub ports on the import side of shipments such as Los Angeles in the United States to meet distribution requirements of its giant retailing partners. Spatial configuration of such GSCs is a matter of increasingly consolidated corporate decision-making.

3.2 The role of Free Economic Zones in China

The second type of industrial-port interactive development applies to those GSCs that have relatively diversified markets (many EU countries, or both international and the domestic market in China) and have some significant amount of imported components from other countries into China for further processing. Examples in point are Samsung Electronics and Motorola, who have their R&D and core components produced in their home country but prefer setting up their production lines in China for both export and China markets. The ideal places to house such firms are Free Economic Zones (FEZ). FEZ is a valid theoretical and empirical intersect between ports, port-cities and GSCs. Ever since China's economic opening in the 1980s, a majority of the transnational corporations involved in GSCs have established themselves in China's coastal Economic and Technological Development Zones (ETDZs). As of 2003, China's top-15 ETDZs accounted for almost 90 per cent of China's foreign trade volumes (Wang and Olivier 2007b). It is the case in China that new greenfield container terminals seek greater spatial integration with ETDZs while disconnecting themselves from the old urban core. Furthermore, China has pursued a deliberate policy of port-FEZ bundling, whereby ports and FEZs geographically and functionally integrate. The port-FEZ complex is thus highly appropriate as first unit of enquiry into the understanding of ports relationship with GSCs. In fact, virtually all coastal port-city ETDZs have grown in tandem with their respective container port.

In a recent paper, we have examined more closely this integration process between ports and spaces of global production using the case of Tianjin Economic Development Area (TEDA) (Wang and Olivier 2007a). TEDA is China's largest and most successful ETDZ. Over 80 TNCs of global recognition have made TEDA their China base, of which 40 have Fortune 500 standing; such foreign presence accounts for over 40 per cent of Tianjin's total GDP. Some of China's largest TNCs are present with such high-profile global names as Toyota Motor, Matsushita, Motorola, Samsung Electronics, and IBM. TEDA's growing manufacturing strength is illustrated by the fact that in 2005 over 50 per cent Tianjin Port container throughput was generated in TEDA and surrounding districts, which confirms Song and Ducruet's (2006) findings on hinterland characteristics of Asian port cities (see also Chapter 11 of this book).

We have found that transport functions, especially the entry of private foreign terminal operators, are a major factor facilitating TEDA's integration in GSCs. While Hong Kong, the US and Japan rank first, second and third respectively as sources of inbound FDI for TEDA as a whole, port inbound FDI has followed this broader pattern with Hong Kong and US operators leading private entry and appointed to carry out commercial operation of new container facilities. Hong Kong operators include New World Ports Management, COSCO Pacific and China Merchants International Holdings, the latter two being in fact Hong Kong branches of mainland-based conglomerates. US operator CSX World Terminals (now under Dubai Ports World) had been present at the port of Tianjin since 1999 (CSX Orient Terminals) and renewed investments in new terminals in 2004 (Tianjin Five Continents International Container Terminal). Japan's leading stevedore, Kamigumi, maintains a presence in Tianjin through subsidiary Tianjin Toyota Logistics Co. Ltd. and has showed a continuous logistical commitment to TEDA-based Japanese firms (www.kamigumi.co.jp).

Functional links between the ETDZ and the port have thus an intrinsically spatial character and play an exceptional role in coastal urban economies. Yet, such spaces are at the same time disconnected from mainstream local economies to create a 'splintering effect' (Graham and Marvin 2000). Indeed, these FEZs in China function as self-contained enclaves that are closely knitted to their foreland, while their ties to the hinterland are more selective. ETDZs are custom-designed production enclaves with levels of internal coherence sharply contrasting their integration with mainstream urban economies. Functional and spatial links between the various components of FEZs determine to a large extent the efficiency and attractiveness of such zones. There is indeed a spatial logic of juxtaposition of sub-areas following production and customs requirement logics, as illustrated in Figure 12.2 for the case of TEDA and Tianjin Port. GSCs associated with firms operating inside TEDA find strategic niches between TEDA and the port according to their own global or local logistics needs. Policy frameworks governing such zones are such that there exists a layering of spaces associated to specific logistics and/or customs procedures following real cargo flows.

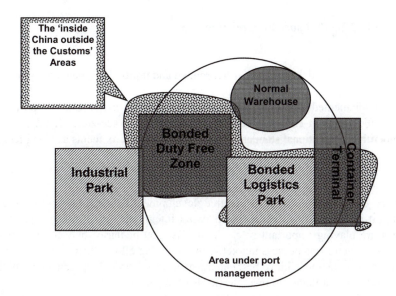

Figure 12.2 Tianjin port-FEZ relationship

Similar processes of developing port-FEZ complex can be found in many other Chinese coastal cities, notably among the 14 'open coastal cities'. However, it is important to note that there are variations in the success of the FEZs, and not all ETDZs have followed TEDA's success. Zhuhai in Guangdong Province is a case in point, where the bonded duty-free zone is spatially dislocated from the actual port site (Figure 12.3). The city is much less attractive for buyer-driven GSCs that require smooth processes in performing the sophisticated task of converting finished or intermediate goods from 'international' to 'domestic' status (or vice versa) within a GSC logic of production.

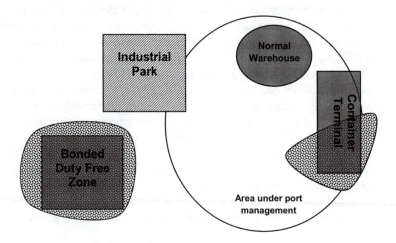

Figure 12.3 Zhuhai port-FEZ relationship

The Tianjin model has been further refined and uplifted to a new policy from the Chinese government called 'zone-port integration (*qu-gang-liandong*)' that began to be implemented at the beginning of 2005 in eight major Chinese port-cities. This policy aims at enhancing current FEZ true free-trade-zones (FTZs) to meet competitive international standards (emulating such environments as Hong Kong).

3.3 Network integrators and GSC management centres

We see the third type of the interactive development between buyer-driven GSCs and port in Hong Kong, where the 'network integrators' or 'turn-key suppliers' in GSCs are playing important role. Acting as intermediaries between buyers and suppliers, such firms possess market knowledge that allows them to tap into a free trade environment to achieve best chain performance through optimal combinations of outsourcing strategies to meet the needs of buyers.

Hong Kong-based Li & Fung Group is a typical case in point. At a macro-level, the firm plays a role of 'virtual manufacturer' and total supply chain manager, linking more than 7000 real manufacturers – mainly in China (over 80 per cent) and other Asian countries – to meet demand from some 600 buyers, mainly from North America and Europe. Some of the group's subsidiaries can also assume customised supply chain solutions. For instance, one of Li & Fung's subsidiary-IDS Logistics International- acts as regional distributor for Asia for Timberland and other non-Asian firms (Li & Fung Research Centre 2003). The firm's role is sensitive not only to the availability of port and other transport facilities for connectivity, but also to the trading environment that is affected by the domestic regulations of countries involved as well as various international agreements on trade. Most of the latter are of bilateral nature and therefore country-specific. Firms like Li & Fung best function in such *gateway* as optimal places where such turn-key suppliers and GSC integrators can operate seamlessly and enjoy high-performing transport infrastructure. Hong Kong has been such an ideal place for Li and Fung and the alike to bridge all the suppliers, to have a tax-free and procedure-free inventory, and to finalise all the specifics of a product before sending it for a designated buyer.

We suggest the example of Li & Fung in Hong Kong as a case of interactive port-city development in China because Hong Kong has been a true free port, a large FEZ, or an international enclave for more than half a century. Because more and more cargo from China is redirected away from from Hong Kong and is captured by nearby Shenzhen and other Mainland ports as a result of lower total transport costs (port charges and land trucking by Hong Kong drivers in particular), some GSCs may leave Hong Kong permanently. The virtual manufacturers such as Li & Fung, however, may stay and keep their core operations in Hong Kong. This post-industrial port-city may turn itself into a GSC management centre: only high value-added logistics and management of GSCs stay for networking functions, while physical production and movement of cargo occurs in other locations. The real FTZ development with other major hub ports in China may in fact accelerate the change of Hong Kong toward such a centre, as there has been a downward trend of total cargo volume (without double counting transhipment) there for two consecutive years.

4. Supplier-driven GSC Port-cities: Synchronised Development

The synchronisation between supplier-driven GSC and port development is becoming common in China because a large number of firms in heavy industries are relocating either from inland to the coast, in order to access high quality raw materials supplied globally, or from newly industrialised countries such as South Korea where land and labour cost become high. Bulk cargo terminals are often a component of producer goods chains and do not rest on the same set of conditions than container ports (e.g. call frequencies, connectivity, service quality, SCM software tools, etc.). Based on transaction cost economics, asset specificity in specialised bulk production is sufficiently high to necessitate full integration of the chain. It is thus common to witness single state-owned corporations in China (and elsewhere) assume the integrity of the transport, distribution and processing of specialised bulk-based goods through networks of specialised subsidiaries.

Shougang Group is a case in point. As a state-owned corporation, Shougang is the largest corporation in Beijing with a yearly capacity of 4 million tonnes of steel production and employs 135,000 workers. Due to environmental pressures resulting from the 2008 Beijing Olympic Games, the company is moving permanently to a small island (Caofeidian) on the margins of Tangshan City (a coastal city of Hebei Province 225 km from Beijing and 100 km from Tianjin; see Figure 12.4). Shougang is investing 50 per cent of total capital expenditures to reclaim the island while Tangshan City is assuming the balance. It is believed that the savings for the reduced land transportation of imported ores to Beijing within the first three years of operation will be enough to cover the reclamation cost for a land link. Caofeidian is the only deepwater site in Hebei province, some 18 km away from the seashore and 70 km from the existing port of Tangshan (see small map B in Figure 12.4).

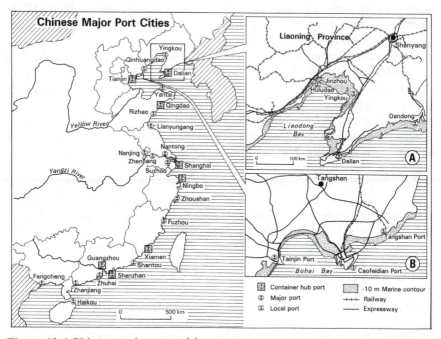

Figure 12.4 Chinese major port cities

The new facilities will allow the company to handle greater volumes of ore and coal than its current terminals capacity. In addition, a crude oil terminal will be built. The massive specialised port complex is likely to become one of China's leading energy and natural resources processing centres and will act as a growth pole for Hebei Province to accommodate firms like Shougang and supplier-driven GSC requirements. Hebei Province thus considers it as its number one priority project in China's recent 11th Five-Year Plan. As a result, much more bulk handling capacities are being built at the new Caofeidian site, indicating the aggressiveness of provincial and city governments in taking this advantage of central government approval in order to expand a user terminal into a huge seaport.

Figure 12.5 Caofeidian Port under construction (photo taken December 2005)

5. Government Roles in Steering Insertion of GSCs into Chinese Port-cities

So far, we have mainly presented the linkages between ports, their host cities and GSCs as a result of aggregate corporate decisions. However, it is essential to highlight the role of the State and municipal governments in providing an enabling policy framework in the context of China. The FEZ-port bundles are key articulation mechanisms between international and domestic spaces that result from active participation on the part of port-city governments in China in order to attract – or partly lock-in – GSCs. The case of Caofeidian is an excellent example on the precise role of government.

Heavy industries that use imported raw materials and produce products for both domestic and international markets are not only located within secondary port cities. Major cities have also been actively fighting to attract them. Tianjin, Shanghai, Ningbo, Qingdao, Dalian, Xiamen and Guangzhou all have petrochemical plants near their port areas. According to recent findings, 30 port-cities have been constructing large-scale petrochemical complexes at deepwater sites simultaneously since the early 2000s (Li 2006). State-owned corporations Sino Petrochemical and Petro China are largely behind such build-up. A major incentive for the local government to invest in port and related transport infrastructure is to get more 'GDP generators' within its own jurisdiction to stimulate the local economy as well as its tax base (Li 2006), seizing the opportunity of 'receiving heavy industries that are globally relocating to low cost countries' (Liaoning Government 2006). In China, ports are considered strategic tools for port-cities to compete regionally, nationally and internationally and, in turn, enhance the status of municipalities, provinces and the State respectively.

   To secondary port-cities, the key point is that they have not been able to establish containerised cargo base for large container port. The environmental sensitivity and less demanding conditions for trade environment such as customs clearance and international banking and other buyer services are also important reasons for these cities focusing on attracting supplier-driven chains. The case of Caofeidian in Hebei reveals a national strategy to assist the weakest coastal province (Hebei) in this region (in between Beijing and Tianjin), and a provincial strategy to refocus development toward its only coastal city. Indeed, green-field specialised terminal construction can *a priori* be seen as an action from a specific supplier (i.e. Shougang in the Caofeidian case), but it is often the case that in many coastal cities in China infrastructure development of such magnitude is directly or indirectly subsidised by the government to raise the city's economic competitiveness. For example, we found through interviews with the local port authority in Qingzhou port of Guangxi province that 90 per cent of the cost for dredging the deepwater channel came from provincial and city governments.

   As a result, China is witnessing a broad geographical spread of supplier-driven developments along its coast, in contrast to buyer-driven manufacturing activities, which are largely concentrated around seven designated hub ports. To test this statement, we investigated the case of Liaoning Province in Northeast China. Liaoning is endowed with six ports: Dandong, Dalian, Yingkou, Jinzhou, Panjin, and Huludao (see small map (A) in Figure 12.4). Data presented in Figure 12.6 shows that in 2005 Dalian, the regional hub, handled 71 per cent of total provincial container throughput. For international trade, its share reaches 94 per cent, indicating a very high concentration of activities related to manufacturing buyer-driven GSCs in a single port-city. In the liquid bulk category, although Dalian is still dominant, a much more diversified situation is present with other ports playing a role in foreign trade. A similar situation is found in dry bulk and break bulk categories, where Dalian captures only 29 per cent and 47 per cent of provincial and international trade respectively.

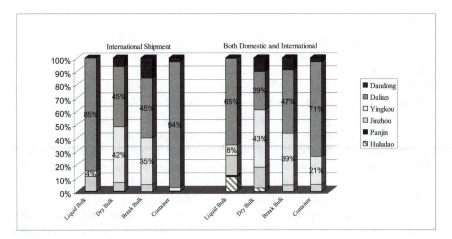

Figure 12.6 Liaoning ports in 2005: Percentage distribution of port throughput by cargo type

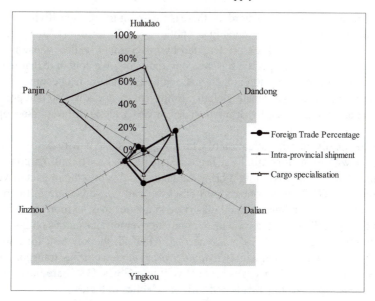

Figure 12.7 Liaoning Ports: Internal and external relationship by shipment, 2005

When investigating the case further, we find that the six ports have a very clear pattern in three dimensions, as shown in Figure 12.7: port specialisation in a single commodity category, foreign trade percentage in the total throughput, and intra-provincial-port shipments. The two weakest ports Huludao and Panjin have the most specialised port activities, namely petroleum products, and none of the ports have extensive connections through shipments with any nearby ports, even as a feeder port. This situation in Liaoning reveals an apparent diversification among port-cities that are forced to choose different GSCs. This results in the lack of an effective hierarchical structure in the regional port system, as GSCs tend to be associated vertically with their components in other cities outside the region.

6. Conclusion

This chapter has presented a deliberate 'port-city-centric' view of evolving GSCs. Port-cities entering the 'logistics era' must find innovative ways to insert themselves into broader supply chain strategies. Our analysis shows the problem is multi-scalar and multi-stakeholder: from local port authorities to national government, and from small local factories to powerful state-owned enterprises and transnational interests. This chapter presents an exploratory examination of how port-cities could be theoretically and empirically inserted into GSC paradigms.

Evidence leads us to believe that Gereffi *et al.*'s (2005) GSC governance model holds interpretative power in the context of China's role in the global economy, but it falls somewhat short in the area of government support to the functioning of GSCs. While it is true that GSCs are first and foremost the product of inter-corporate arrangements across national borders, there is a case for greater sensitivity to the role of various government levels, notably at a policy level. Reforms in China reveal how specific components of GSCs are targeted by government bodies whose role is to provide port-cities with specific business environments. We conclude that in China, port is a tool for port city to compete nationally, and port-cities become a tool for the province or state to compete globally. Empirical cases show also that port-cities in China are being driven by different types of GSCs along different development paths.

Theoretically, our investigation of China suggests some new research directions which we wish to put forward. First, more systematic analysis of bulk cargo facilities in China is warranted, as it might bring valuable insights into the impact of vertical integration of GSCs on secondary port-cities. Not all port-cities are fit to enter the containerisation phenomenon and bulk-based strategies may be more sustainable in terms of a spatially balanced growth. Second, more empirical studies on governance aspects for port-cities and GSCs are needed. After all, the key task for port-cities today is not so much to deal with *individual firms* in manufacturing, transport or other services, but to insert themselves productively into GSCs. GSCs are the product of complex inter-firm arrangements and call for eclectic strategies.

Acknowledgements

We would like to express our acknowledgements to the Provisional Contemporary China Studies Council of University of Hong Kong and Hui Oi Chow Trust Fund for its sincere financial support, Cartographic Unit, School of Geography, University of Hong Kong, for map drawing.

Chapter 13

The Economic Performance of Seaport Regions

Peter W. de Langen

1 Introduction

Seaports are often considered as a driver of regional economic development. Investments in seaport infrastructure and hinterland connections are in many cases justified on the basis of economic benefits for the (local) economy. Economic impact studies of ports estimate direct economic effects and employment effects (Waters 1977 and Hall 2004) but they seldom provide an overall analysis on the relation between the presence of a seaport and regional economic development.

In this chapter, this issue is the centre stage. In an introductory section the relevant literature on the relation of port activities and the port-region's economic performance is discussed. Empirical data of seaports and port regions in the United States (US) is used to address these research questions. The third section briefly describes the major ports in the US. The fourth section provides a statistical analysis of the economic performance of economic areas with ports in the US and the fifth section analyses the performances of 'port counties' in the US. A concluding section, in which avenues for further research are discussed, finalises this chapter.

2 The Regional Economic Impact of Seaports; Literature Overview

The regional impact of port activities has been studied by a number of authors, such as Waters (1977) and Davies (1983). Villaverde Castro and Coto Millan (1998) develop a method to analyse economic impacts based on welfare economic principles, and apply it to the port of Santander. These authors focus on *reduced transport costs*, not on employment impacts or contributions to the local economy. This is sensible, because ports may generate employment and value-added, but these are no 'net' economic benefits. Without port activities, the regions would have a different economic structure. Furthermore, Hall (2004) argues that economic impact studies may exaggerate the economic effects of ports.

Studies of Value-Added Generated in Seaports

The regional economic importance of the port is measured mostly with the *value-added* that is created in the port (see Haezendonck 2001).[1] Value-added shows the growth of the *size* of the port. The value-added generated in ports changes over time because the value-added generated by the firms in the cluster changes (for instance because firms invest, fire employees or make more profit, and through entry and exits of firms).

The value-added is calculated in Antwerp and Rotterdam for a number of consecutive years (Nationale Bank van Belgie 2004, figures 2001, Nationale Havenraad 2004, figures 2003).[2]

As a method to approximate the value-added generated in seaports, weighting rules are developed in to 'translate' throughput volume in value-added, based on differences in generated value-added for different commodities. These weighting rules are reviewed by Haezendonck (2001), who develops a rule based on data from large ports in the Hamburg-Le Havre range. The relative weight of the most important commodities is given in Table 13.1.

Table 13.1 The relative weight of various commodities

Commodity	Relative weight
Crude oil	18
Dry Bulk	5
Containers	3
Chemicals (other liquid bulk)	2
Ro-Ro	1
Conventional cargo	1

Source: Haezendonck (2001).

Table 13.1 shows that crude oil generates relatively little value-added: 1 ton of conventional cargo creates as much value-added as 18 tons of crude oil. Thus, large oil ports, such as Rotterdam and Houston, generate relatively little value-added, according to these weighting rules. Such a weighting rule has three serious shortcomings:

- Only the value-added of cargo handling activities is taken into account. This is a serious shortcoming, since in some cases (or: in some ports) terminal operating companies provide warehousing activities, while in another port

---

 1   Such an analysis requires defining the economic activities that are regarded as port-related. De Langen (2004) presents a set of such 'port cluster activities'.

 2   The methods used in these two ports are similar, but not exactly the same.

warehousing is provided by logistics service providers in the vicinity of the port. It is unclear why the value-added should be included in the first case and excluded in the latter case. Furthermore, the fact that only cargo handling activities are included leads to an underestimation of the value-added, compared to studies where port logistics and port-related manufacturing activities are included (see Havenraad 2004 and the National Bank of Belgium 2004).

- The weighting rule assumes a 'mechanic' relation between volume and value-added. The value-added per ton is assumed to be the same in all ports. However, in practice, huge differences exist between ports. Some ports attract logistics activities while other ports do not. For instance, in transhipment ports, such as Algeciras, the value-added per ton is likely to be much smaller than in end-ports such as Antwerp.
- The weighting rule assumes that all cargo of one particular commodity generates more or less the same value-added in the port. This is not always the case. For instance, the loss of some 'packages of containers' to competing ports may cause a huge loss of value-added, while in other cases (for instance transhipment containers) a loss of a similar container volume has a smaller effect on the value-added in the port.

For these reasons, weighting rules to estimate the value-added generated in seaports are not reliable. This conclusion in confirmed by Table 13.2, that shows the shares of the largest Dutch ports in throughput, in value-added following the weighting rule and the value-added calculated by the Dutch National Port Council (NHR).

Table 13.2 Size of Dutch ports according to three measures

Port	Share of port in terms of throughput	Share of value-added according to weighting rule	Share of value-added based on study from NHR
Terneuzen	3%	3%	9%
Vlissingen	3%	7%	5%
Rotterdam	75%	77%	50%
Amsterdam	11%	7%	8%
IJmuiden	4%	4%	9%
Total the Nederlands	100%	100%	100%

Source: Nationale Havenraad, 2005.

For instance, Terneuzen's value-added using the weighting rule is 3 per cent of the total, while the value-added calculated by NHR is 9 per cent the total value-added. Such differences also occur in other ports. Thus, the weighting rule is not reliable. Figure 13.1 shows the changes in the value-added per ton in the four main Belgian ports, between 1999 and 2004.

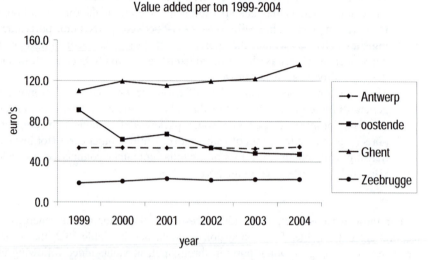

Figure 13.1 Value-added per ton in four Belgian ports
Source: Based on data from Nationale Bank van Belgie (2004).

These figures show that the value-added per ton not only differs between ports, but also changes substantially in a relatively short period. This is not caused by changes in the commodities handled in the port, but because of growth or decline in port-related logistics and manufacturing activities.

Studies of Port Regions

A number of studies have analysed the development of port regions, especially port-cities. Baudouin and Collin (1996) discuss 'The revival of France's port-cities', but their study does not analyse the role of the port in the regional (or urban) economy. Gripaios and Gripaios (1995) show that the impact of the port of Plymouth on the regional economy is substantial. Their analysis is mainly descriptive. The same applies to other papers, such as Todd's (1994) paper on economic growth and port development in Tianjin and Airriess' paper (2001a) on Singapore. Musso *et al..* (2000) suggest a method to calculate employment effects in port-cities but do not address the relation between ports and regional economic performance in general.

On the basis of this overview, it can be concluded that tools to analyse the benefits of ports though reductions of transport costs have been developed. Furthermore, the value-added generated in seaports is calculated in a number of ports. This provides a basis for an analysis of the economic impact of a port. Such studies show the (static) importance of port-related economic activities in the regional economic structure, but do not demonstrate that port regions are better or worse off than other regions. The only comparison of port-cities and 'non-port-cities' is made by Noponen *et al.* (1997) who suggest port-cities in the US no longer derive competitive advantage from their ports, because the introduction of containers has greatly reduced inland transport costs. Their analysis however, is based on rather broadly defined cities and compares manufacturing job growth between port and interior cities. They do not assess whether and to what extent these port-cities are specialised in port activities. Furthermore, they do not present specific data of the port-cities, as ports are not centre stage in their paper.

These conclusions justify more attention for the analysis of the overall economic performance of port regions. The following sections provide a first exploration of this issue.

3 The Port Industry in the US

The US is the largest economy of the world, and a country with a substantial number of seaports. These ports are used for domestic and international trade and handled in total more than 2.5 billion metric tons in 2005 (American Association of Port Authorities 2005). Table 13.3 shows the 39 largest US ports (the gap with nr 40 and below was so substantial that these are not included in the list). The throughput is rounded to million tons for simplicity, while the exact throughput figures are used in the calculations presented later on.

The distribution of these ports over the US is given in Figure 13.2.

Figure 13.2 shows some clusters of ports, such as the lower Mississippi ports, which combined constitute the largest port complex of the US (De Langen 2004), the Houston area ports, the second largest concentration of port activities in the US, the ports around New York and New Jersey, the ports of Los Angeles and Long Beach, generally presented as one port complex, but with separate throughput statistics, and the ports of Tacoma and Seattle, also located in vicinity of each other.

Table 13.3 The largest ports of the US

Port	Throughput 2003 (million ton)	Growth 1996–2003	Port	Throughput 2003 (million ton)	Growth 1996–2003
South Louisiana, LA	199	5%	Philadelphia, PA	33	-21%
Houston, TX	191	29%	St. Louis, MO and IL	32	8%
New York, NY and NJ	146	11%	Pascagoula, MS	31	7%
Beaumont, TX	88	145%	Freeport, TX	31	24%
New Orleans, LA	84	0%	Portland, ME	29	-2%
Huntington-Tristate	78	183%	Paulsboro, NJ	27	9%
Corpus Christi, TX	77	-4%	Port Arthur, TX	27	-27%
Long Beach, CA	69	18%	Portland, OR	27	76%
Texas City, TX	61	9%	Marcus Hook, PA	26	112%
Baton Rouge, LA	61	-24%	Charleston, SC	25	127%
Plaquemines, LA	56	-16%	Boston, MA	25	24%
Lake Charles, LA	53	9%	Savannah, GA	23	33%
Los Angeles, CA	51	12%	Port Everglades, FL	23	22%
Mobile, AL	50	-1%	Richmond, CA	23	5%
Valdez, AK	50	-35%	Tacoma, WA	23	7%
Tampa, FL	48	-2%	Chicago, IL	23	-19%
Pittsburgh, PA	42	-18%	Jacksonville, FL	22	30%
Hampton Roads (Norfolk)	41	-16%	Seattle, WA	19	-17%
Baltimore, MD	40	-8%	Memphis, TN	18	5%
Duluth-Superior, MN & WI	38	-7%			

Source: American Association of Port Authorities (2005).

1 South Louisiana	14 Mobile	27 Port Arthur
2 Houston	15 Valdez (Alaska)	28 Portland
3 New York and New Jersey	16 Tampa	29 Marcus Hook
4 Beaumont	17 Pittsburgh	30 Charleston
5 New Orleans	18 Hampton	31 Boston
6 Huntington Tristate	19 Baltimore	32 Savannah
7 Corpus Christi	20 Duluth-Superior	33 Port Everglades
8 Long Beach	21 Philadelphia	34 Richmond
9 Texas City	22 St. Louis	35 Tacoma
10 Baton Rouge	23 Pascagoula	36 Chicago
11 Plaquemines	24 Freeport	37 Jacksonville
12 Lake Charles	25 Portland	38 Seattle
13 Los Angeles	26 Paulsboro	39 Memphis

Figure 13.2 The most important seaports in the US

The following data are publicly available (and accessible through internet) in the US:

- Throughput figures for of all ports, over a substantial number of years.
- Data on the economic structure and per capita income levels of Economic Areas (EAs), relatively large areas defined based on economic criteria.
- Data on the economic structure of counties, the smallest administrative (and statistical) unit of the US.[3] Available data include per capita income, unemployment and industry structure.

3　There are roughly 3000 counties in the US, but there are large differences in the size of these counties.

These data enable an analysis of the following questions:

- Which industries are overrepresented in counties with seaports?
- How did the counties with seaports perform economically?
- Are changes in per capita income growth in port counties and growth of port throughput related?

These questions are addressed in the following sections.

4 Seaports and Economic Development; an Analysis of Economic Areas

The US is divided in more than 170 economic areas (EAs). Contrary to states, EAs are economically-defined geographical units.[4] The relevant economic areas for all 39 ports were identified. The throughput per inhabitant is calculated as an indicator of the specialisation of economic areas in port activities. Economic areas such as New York-Newark-Bridgeport (EA 118) and Los Angeles-Long Beach-Riverside (EA 97) have very substantial ports, but their population is so large that the throughput per inhabitant is *below* the national average. Thus, such EAs are not specialised in port activities. On the other end of the spectrum, New Orleans-Metairie-Bogalusa (EA 117) and Beaumont-Port Arthur (EA 16) have more than 20 times as much throughput per inhabitant as the national average.

The Average personal income level in EAs is selected as indicator of the economic performance of EAs. Substantial differences in income levels between EAs persist over time (Porter 2003). The relation of the throughput per inhabitant and the average personal income of an EA as a percentage of the national US average personal income was analysed. The results are given in Figure 13.3. Two 'outliers' with a very high throughput per inhabitant are excluded from the calculations but do not alter the results.

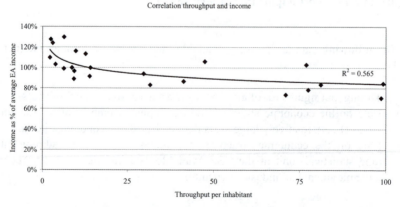

Figure 13.3 The correlation between throughput and average personal income on EA level

---

4   For more information see Johnson and Kort (2004).

Figure 13.3 shows a weak *negative correlation* between per capita income and throughput per inhabitant. These results do *not* support the claim that the presence of a port strengthens the performance of a regional economy. The EAs that are specialised in port activities have on average low personal income levels. The results do not prove that seaport activities have a negative effect on regional economic development. The negative correlation is partly explained because of the effect of EA size on per capita income levels.[5] Furthermore the causality of the relation between throughput per capita and personal income levels is unclear: it may well be that the EAs would be worse off without port activities.

Notwithstanding these limitations, the results do suggest that a high throughput per capita is not in general positively related to economic development. The two specific cases of EAs with a per capita throughput above the US average and a relatively high per capita income, Houston and Anchorage, are rather exceptional: the remote location of Anchorage drives up costs and thus wages while Houston is unique because of its huge petrochemical complex.

Figure 13.4 shows the growth of throughput volumes and the growth of per capita income in all EAs with large seaports, both between 1996 and 2003.

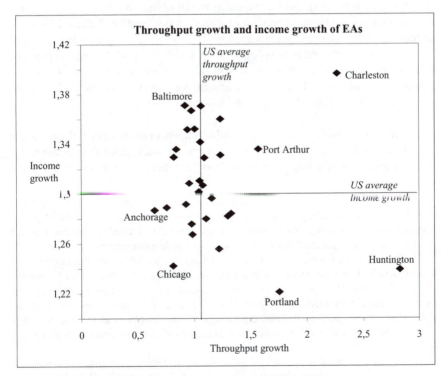

Figure 13.4 Throughput growth and income growth of EAs

---

5   Larger EAs (in terms of population) have higher per capita income levels. Larger EAs also tend to have a lower throughput per inhabitant. The negative correlation also is found for smaller EAs, but is weaker.

Based on the results presented in Figure 13.4 the conclusion can be drawn that *throughput growth and income growth are not related.* Port regions can have different development paths. In some port regions, e.g. Portland and Huntington, the volumes handled in ports grow strongly (compared to the national average), while the income growth lags behind. In other port regions, both volumes and income grow faster than the average (Charleston and Port Arthur), while in a third category, the income growth is relatively high, while volume growth is low (Baltimore). Finally, in some regions both income and throughput growth lag behind (Anchorage and Chicago). This variety of possible trajectories shows that there is no 'automatic' relation between the success of a port and the success of a region. A more detailed analysis is required to understand under which conditions port growth leads to regional growth and under which conditions not.

5 The Economic Performance of 'Port Counties'

A more detailed analysis of the relation between seaports and regional economic development can be made with county data. This analysis starts with calculating four location quotients (LQs) for the cargo handling industry in a county, defined as NAICS code 4883 (support activities for water transportation).[6] These LQs show the relative under- or overrepresentation of 4883 activities in particular counties.[7] The LQs can be calculated for employment and for establishments, and can measure under- or overrepresentation at the state level or at the national level (these are termed LQ^{emp}state, LQ^{emp}US, LQ^{est}state and LQ^{est}US).[8] With the use of these LQs, 'port counties' were defined based on the following criteria.

1. All counties with more than 20 establishments or more than 350 employees in the industry *4883* are considered as port counties, since this demonstrates the presence of a large number of port activities. 37 counties are classified

---

6   This code consists of the more detailed codes *48831* (Port & hardour operation), *48832* (Marine cargo handling), *48833* (Navigational Services to Shipping) and *48839* (Other Support Activities for Water Transportation). These more detailed codes were not analysed because the more detailed the NAICS code, the worse the data availability.

7   These LQs are widely used in regional studies since the 1960s, see e.g. Leigh (1970) for some details. A location quotient calculator is available from the website of the US Bureau of Labor Statistics. The LQ based on employment has to be estimated because employment statistics at the county level mostly provide a range (e.g. 1–19 employees) to ensure no confidential data are publicised. Thus, the national average employment size for this range was taken. In the case of 1–19 employees, the average number of employees is four. The LQ is calculated with this figure.

8   Both geographical scopes are relevant: a county along a river with a few marina's in a landlocked state (without ports) may have a high LQ at the state level, (since there are virtually no *4883* activities in that state) but is not truly a 'port county'. The LQ at the national level of such a county would be low. Also, a county in a state with a large number of port facilities, such as Louisiana, may have low state LQs even though it is specialised in port activities. State level LQs are also relevant because counties clearly specialised in *4883* at a state level can be considered 'port counties'.

as port counties based on this criteria (19 of these have both more than 20 establishments and more than 300 employees, two have more than 20 establishments and 16 have more than 300 employees). The major ports in the US are located in these counties, e.g. Houston (Harris) and LA/Long Beach (county Los Angeles). The average LQs for this group of counties is high; the lowest average LQ for this group is LQ^{est}state and is 5 (which means five times more port establishments than in the state).

2. Second, a group of counties with the following characteristics were defined as port counties:[9]
   - More than one establishment and more than 100 employees, and
   - Three of the four LQs are greater than 1, and
   - LQ^{em}state or LQ^{est}state greater than 3 *or* LQ^{em}US or LQ^{est}US greater than 2.

The condition of three LQs larger than 1 excludes counties without a specialisation in *4883* and the condition of one state LQ greater than 3 or one national LQ greater than 2 excludes counties that are not clearly specialised by at least one LQ indicator. This second group of mostly of smaller counties in population and establishment size consists of 27 counties including counties such as St. Bernard (New Orleans) and West Baton Rouge (Baton Rouge). The average LQs for this group of counties is also high, the lowest LQ is LQ^{est}state, and is 6.8.

The resulting list consists of 64 port counties. Some port counties, such as Plaquemines (Louisiana) are very small (a population of less than 30,000) while others, such as Kings (New York, population about 2.5 million inhabitants) are very large. One county, Cook (Illinois, port of Chicago) is not specialised in *4883* (the unweighted average of all four LQs is smaller than 1). This is because it is a huge county with a population of more than five million people and a very diverse economy. All other port counties are to a greater or smaller extend specialised in port activities. The most specialised port county for LQ^{est}state is Chatham (Georgia, port of Savannah).

As a next step, for each of these port counties, the specialisation in a number of potentially port-related industries was analysed. These industries include for example *325* (Basic chemical manufacturing) and *49312* (Refrigerated warehousing & storage).

For all of these industries, the overrepresentation in port counties was analysed. 13 industries are more than two times overrepresented in port counties, and a larger number of sectors are concentrated to a lesser extent in port counties. These calculations provided the basis for defining *port-related industries*. The industries that are concentrated in port counties are port related industries, while some other industries are also included, because these activities are port-related if they are located in a port county. General freight trucking, local (*48411*) is an example of such an industry; the specialisation of this industry in port counties is low (1.05),

---

9   *Google Earth* was used to locate each of these countries and verify that there are port facilities indeed. One county (Sharp, Arkansas) was omitted as no terminal facilities for freight were found. Some river marinas probably account for the *4883* employment in Sharp.

but the activity is still likely to be port-related. Appendix 13.1 shows the complete list of port-related industries. Further analysis of these port-related activities could address issues such as 'what are the growth expectations for these industries' 'what are wage level developments in these industries' and 'is the per capita income level of counties higher for ports that are specialised in certain port related activities'. These issues are beyond the scope of this chapter.

The ten most seaport-specialised counties in the US, based on an analysis of location quotients of all *port-related economic activities* are given in Table 13.4.[10]

Table 13.4 The ten most specialised port counties in the US for all port industries

Port county	Port	LQ^{emp}US	LQ^{est}US
Valdez Cordova	Anchorage	8.51	3.78
Plaquemines	Plaquemines	8.34	7.22
St James	South Louisiana	7.00	4.72
Jackson	Pascagoula	6.79	0.98
St Charles	South Louisiana	6.33	3.31
St Mary	South Louisiana	6.28	3.10
Aleutians West Borough	Anchorage	6.03	8.77
Lafourche	Fourchon	5.86	4.59
West Baton Rouge	Baton Rouge	5.02	4.28
Hudson	New York	3.95	2.41

These calculations provide a basis for an analysis of the relation between the presence of port activities and the average personal income in port counties. For this analysis, these average personal income levels are expressed as a percentage of the personal income levels in the EA. This provides an indicator of the relative income levels of port counties. On average, the income in the port counties is 2.5 per cent lower than the average county. This demonstrates the underperformance of port counties. Furthermore, the average personal income as a percentage of the EA was related to the specialisation of these counties in seaport-related activities. The results are given in Figure 13.5.

Although the correlation is very weak, this figure confirms the earlier conclusion that if anything, port counties have lower income levels than other counties. As a next step, the changes in the average personal income levels of the port counties from 1969 to 2004 are analysed. Figure 13.6 shows the average personal income in these port counties as a percentage of the income in the respective EAs over the whole period.

---

10 All these counties are relatively small. In small counties, the number of local services (restaurants, supermarkets, car dealers, etc.) is smaller and consequently the LQs tend to be relatively high.

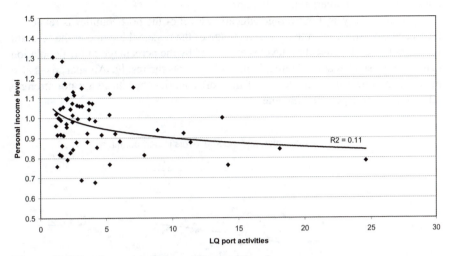

Figure 13.5 Port country LQs and income levels

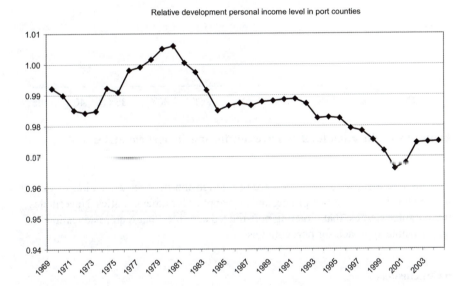

Figure 13.6 Relative personal income levels in port countries

Figure 13.6 shows that the port counties were becoming 'richer' than other port counties in 1970s, but that the personal income growth compared to non-port counties was weak from the early 1980s onwards. As a result, these counties are now worse off than other counties in the same EA. This result also provides opportunities for further investigation, for instance to analyse why some port counties have developed relatively well and others relatively poor.

As a final analysis, the average education level of the port counties is related to the average personal income (as a percentage of the personal income in the relevant EA, as before). The education level is expressed by the percentage of the population that has at least a bachelor degree. Figure 13.7 shows the results. An analysis is also made of the unemployment levels of the port counties, but these are not strongly related to average personal income.

Education and income levels in port counties

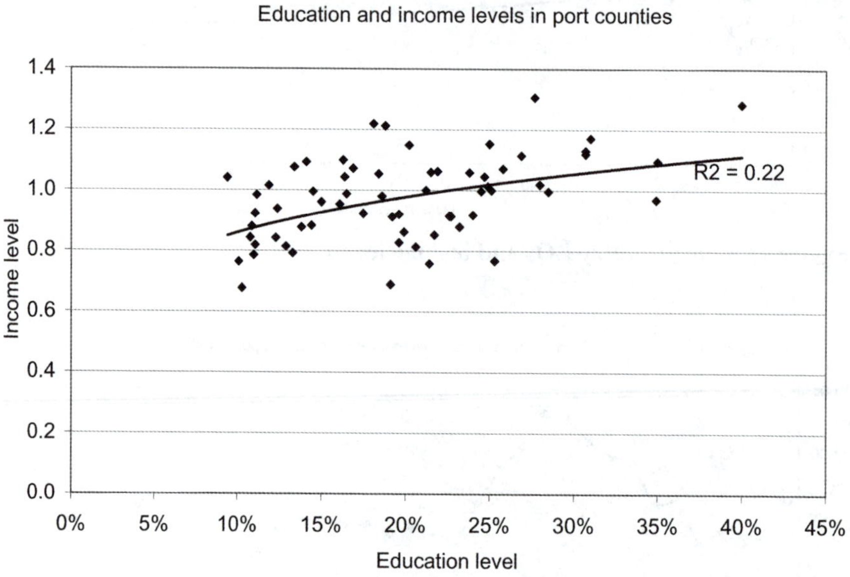

Figure 13.7 Education level and average income in port countries

This figure shows a relatively strong relationship between education level and income level. This is not surprising and also applies for other counties. Nevertheless, these figures suggest that targeting port-related activities that require education may be a sensible approach for port counties.

6 Conclusions

In this chapter, an analysis is made of the relationship between port activities and regional economic development. Existing studies do not provide much insight in this relationship. This issue has been studied with data from the US, because of the size of the country, its many seaports and the availability of rather detailed data. The analysis in this chapter provides a basis for further investigation of the performance of port counties. Furthermore four conclusions can be drawn from the analysis presented in this chapter.

First, both on the level of the EA and on the county level, there is a negative relationship between a specialisation in port activities and the average personal income. These results provide evidence to question the widely made claim that the presence of seaports enhances regional economic development.

Second, it turns out that the performance of ports, measured in the growth of throughput volumes, is not related to the economic development of the port region. Different port regions follow different development paths.

Third, an analysis of economic growth of port counties in the three last decades shows that counties specialised in seaports have underperformed compared to the national average from the early 1980s on. Consequently, counties specialised in ports that used to have somewhat higher average personal incomes than those of the EA as a whole, are now less wealthy than this average.

Finally, it turns out that the personal income levels of specialised port counties are related to the education level in these counties.

These conclusions provide a basis for a further analysis of the relation between seaports and regional economic development. Research opportunities include the development of a typology of port counties and an analysis of the influence of the commodity structure of seaports on regional economic development.

Appendix 13.1 Port-related industries

Component		Industry
Port-related manufacturing	23712	Oil & gas pipeline and related structures construction
	311225	Fats & oils refining and blending
	311412	Frozen speciality food manufacturing
	324	Petroleum refineries
	3251	Basic chemical manufacturing
	3252	Rubber and fibre-manufacturing
	336611	Ship building & repairing
	8113	Commercial & industrial machinery and equipment repair & maintenance
Port-related trade	4235	Metal & mineral (except Petroleum) merchant wholesalers
	42386	Transportation equipment & supplies (except motor vehicle) merchant wholesalers
	42393	Recyclable material merchant wholesalers
	4246	Chemical & allied products merchant wholesalers
	4247	Petroleum & petroleum products merchant wholesalers
	52313	Commodity contracts dealing
	52314	Commodity contracts brokerage
Transport	483111	Deep-sea freight transportation
	483113	Coastal and great lakes freight transportation
	483211	Inland water freight transportation
	48411	General freight trucking, local
	4861	Pipeline transportation of crude oil
	4862	Pipeline transportation of natural gas
	4869	Other pipeline transportation
	492	Couriers & messengers
	48831	Port & harbour operation
	48832	Marine cargo handling
Cargo handling	48833	Navigational Services to Shipping
	48839	Other Support Activities for Water Transportation
	4884	Support activities for road transportation
	4885	Freight transportation arrangement
	4889	Other support activities for transportation
Logistics	49311	General warehousing & storage
	49312	Refrigerated warehousing & storage
	49319	Other warehousing & storage

PART 4
Corporate Perspectives on the Insertion of Ports in Global Supply Chains

Chapter 14

The Success of Asian Container Port Operators: The Role of Information Technology

Daniel Olivier and Francesco Parola

1. Introduction

The supply of port services has undergone deep structural changes in the past decade. The most notable being the sharp increase in private participation in container ports worldwide following general waves of deregulation of national port sectors. This has led in turn to the emergence of powerful transnational corporations (TNC) in the container port industry (Olivier and Slack 2006). Firms such as Hutchison Port Holdings, PSA International and APM Terminals have built impressive international portfolios, owning/operating container facilities across various continents. Yet, little remains known of their internationalisation strategies, in particular the role of micro-managerial responses to technological advances in container terminal operations. Moreover, information technology (IT) is a *sine qua non* condition for successful supply chain management (SCM) as has been mentioned in Chapters 2 and 3, and as these firms increasingly make their way into SCM, it becomes essential to better understand their current engagement with various IT tools.

Meanwhile, a rich literature exists in management studies on the central role of technology in achieving a company's global strategy (Glaister and Buckley 1996; Dussauge and Garrette 1999). While the role of technology in general has long been acknowledged as a deeply influential factor marking developments in the container port industry (especially since containerisation), few studies have attempted to empirically substantiate their net impact on managerial practices at the terminal level. Most studies have discussed the incidence of widespread adoption of technology on managerial strategy either in theoretical terms or in a broad general sense (Airriess 2001a; Notteboom and Winkelmans 2001; Peters 2001). More empirical studies using applied methodologies (Kia *et al.* 2000; Lee-Partridge *et al.* 2000; Airriess 2001a) have better substantiated the benefits of gradual automation of container terminals on managerial performance. Recently, Olivier (2005; 2006) has demonstrated how technology is emerging as a central rationale in the formation of strategic alliances on the port supply side. This lack of empirical focus in academic enquiry sharply contrasts the growing interest found in industry publications on the benefits of terminal automation and the promises held by IT (see among several others Fossey 1998; *Cargo Systems* 2000; 2001; Decker 2003). In sum, while the literature acknowledges the critical role of technological advances in impacting port management practices, much remains unknown as to precisely how firms are concretely tapping into them and the role they play in advancing their internationalisation strategies to become global industry leaders.

This chapter empirically documents the relationship between the adoption of technology as a strategic managerial asset and the success of firms in their international expansion drive. How are leading international operators approaching technology and what role is it playing in their international strategy? More specifically: what type of technologies do they adopt? Under which arrangements? For what purposes? These are the questions concerning us in this chapter. The next section provides a brief overview of institutional changes in container port operations and the resulting rise of TNCs. The impact of East Asia has been particularly profound, as leading in both origin and destination of private capital. Here, the role of private terminal operators in pushing ahead IT-based SCM practices will be highlighted. The third section will justify the critical role of information technology (IT) in container terminal operations and SCM, notably how ports seek to insert themselves in global supply chains. This section will seek to better define what is meant by 'port technology' and IT.[1] Section 4 will provide a theoretical account of governance arrangements of IT among the industry's leading firms. The fourth and final section will substantiate the model with two case studies. We conclude the paper by considering implications for port-cities.

2. The Emergence of Transnational Operators and the Role of Asia

The last decade has been marked by widespread deregulation of port industries worldwide. Reforms have largely facilitated entry of private participants, allowing a number of private players to significantly expand their terminal operations to reach global scales. Indeed, a hallmark of the last decade in the port industry has been the emergence of powerful terminal-operating TNCs (Olivier and Slack 2006). Two types of firms have risen as major players controlling terminal facilities: international terminal operators (ITOs) and ocean carriers, each entering terminal operations with different logistical motivations: carriers invest into container terminals as a way to control cost, reduce turnaround times and secure access to key markets, while ITOs have built international portfolios more on the basis of the exportability of their expertise and the timely seizing of lucrative opportunities opened up by port deregulation.

Two points are worth further consideration in understanding the role of East Asia in this process. First, Asian firms have come to lead the small number of powerful TNCs that now dominate the supply of port services worldwide (Table 14.1). On the strength of their ports, Hong Kong and Singapore in particular have risen to become global headquarters for some of the world's largest port operators and maritime firms. Hutchison Port Holdings (HPH), China Merchants Holdings International, COSCO Pacific and NWS Holdings are all leading ITOs based in Hong Kong and

---

1   For lack of space the focus in this chapter will be narrowed down primarily to IT.

with a strong presence at Kwai Tsing port. PSA International has emerged a top ITO out of the strength of Singapore Port. Meanwhile, Taiwan's Evergreen MC is the ocean carrier with the largest container terminal portfolio.

Table 14.1 Leading 20 TNCs in the container terminal industry, 2005

TNC	Country of origin[1]	Number of terminal projects in operation	Million TEU 2005
1 * Hutchison Port Holdings[2]	Hong Kong	44	51.8
2 * APM Terminals[3]	Denmark	47	42.9
3 * PSA International[2]	Singapore	25	40.3
4 * China Merchants Holdings Int.	Hong Kong	12	24.5
5 * P&O Ports[4]	UK	30	23.8
6 * COSCO Pacific	Hong Kong	20	14.7
7 * Dubai Ports World[3]	UAE	14	12.9
8 * Eurogate/Eurokai Group	Germany	12	12.1
9 # Evergreen Marine Corp.	Taiwan	13	8.7
10 # Mediterranean Shipping Co.	Switzerland	13	7.8
11 * SSA Marine	US	11	7.3
12 * New World Holdings[5]	Hong Kong	6	5.4
13 * Hamburger Hafen LA	Germany	7	6.0
14 # NOL/APL	Singapore	9	5.7
15 * Modern Terminals Ltd.	Hong Kong	5	5.0
16 # Hanjin Shipping	South Korea	11	4.9
17 # OOCL[6]	Hong Kong	6	4.3
18 # NYK Line	Japan	11	4.2
19 * Dragados	Spain	10	3.6
20 # CMA-CGM	France	7	3.4

Notes:
(1) Hong Kong, Taiwan and China are considered separate political entities
(2) PSA International acquired 20 per cent of Hutchison Port Holdings (HPH) in 2006
(3) APM Terminals figures include former P&O Nedlloyd port network
(4) Dubai Ports World acquired P&O Ports in March 2006. Nevertheless, in December 2006, the former P&O Ports North America division (several facilities in the US) was sold out by DPW to a US corporation, AIG Global Investment Group
(5) Data is for 2003
(6) In November 2006 OOIL, parent company of OOCL, sold out North American terminals (except the facility in Long Beach) to a Canadian pension fund company
* = ITOs
# = Ocean carriers
Sources: Drewry 2006; company annual reports; authors own database.

Second, following structural changes in global trade, the largest productivity gains among ports worldwide have generally been recorded in East Asia during the last decade. Whether measured in terms of crane movements per hour, terminal gate flow movements, yard management (e.g. container stacking practices) or even land use efficiencies (TEU/m^2), the greatest productivity gains in container terminal management in recent years have been recorded at East Asian ports (Wang *et al.* 2005; Drewry 2006). In fact, when measured in terminal land area productivity (i.e. TEU/surface), East Asian container ports have shown average land efficiency levels three times that of European ports and four times that of North American ports (Vandeveer 1998; Transystems 2006). Technology-based management innovations have, to a large extent, been at the source of such productivity gains.

Transpacific geographical imbalances are even clearer when considering broader port capacity issues and their implications for global supply chains. In addition to disparities in productivity gains, a clear imbalance exists in the geographical distribution of net additions of greenfield terminal facilities. According to the World Bank (2006), 69.2 per cent of private investments (in value USD) in container terminal facilities worldwide for the period 1984–2004 took place in East Asia. As a consequence, a port infrastructure gap in transpacific containerised trade between East Asian ports and their increasingly congested North American counterparts is now apparent. This gap translates into chronic congestion and delays at major gateway ports which are seriously undermining the performance of global supply chains and even forcing to rethink China-driven global outsourcing (see Chapter 10; Stalk and Waddell 2006).

In sum, fundamental changes in the institutional environment of ports associated with large scale private participation means that an increasing amount of technologies are being developed and deployed under private initiatives at the terminal level: terminal operators have become leading drivers of change in port managerial practices and are spearheading the true insertion of container ports into global supply chains (see Chapter 4 of this book by Slack on the 'terminalisation of ports'). The central point is that private Asian terminal operators have been highly responsive to technological advances in terminal operations to compensate for lack of space. Before discussing such managerial responses, we wish to introduce a simple typology of port technologies and justify the importance of IT in port operations and SCM.

3. IT and Port Operations

Port development has long been recognised as a functional adaptation to advances in naval engineering and ship design (Bird 1963). However, it is an undisputable fact that containerisation has accelerated the rate of technological requirements in contemporary port management practices. Operations at today's leading container terminal facilities rest on a set of sophisticated technologies allowing management of complex box movements. As discussed, East Asian ports have higher productivities than anywhere else in the world and today's largest global port operators have risen out of land-intensive operational requirements. Rapid and widespread adoption of technology-driven management practices in response to capacity constraints has been behind the success of Asian operators (Olivier 2005; 2006). But before further substantiating this claim, it is important to define the scope of what is meant here by 'port technology'. Port technology may be divided into two spheres (Table 14.2): hardware and software equipment.

Managing container movements in material space: Hardware

Container movement at terminals is first and foremost a physical movement in real space. This exercise relies on a set of modern cranes and yard equipment with which contemporary terminals are equipped. Container cranes are generally of two types: (1) ship-to-shore gantries and (2) bridge cranes[2] and display various degrees of automation. Other common terminal machinery include reach-stackers, forklifts and container trucks to accomplish intra-terminal movements of boxes. Thus, the various hardware equipments, ranging from cranes to PCs and wireless devices, is implemented in some specific areas (the 'Xs' in Table 14.2) of container movement and logistics activity. This set of technology and machinery accomplishes actual and real physical movements of containers.

Another set of hardware serves *in situ* real-time container tracking purposes. For instance, wireless, Differential Global Positioning System (DGPS) and Radio Frequency IDentification (RFID) devices may be used (together with PCs and LAN) in the recording of container moves (number 3 in Table 14.2) while quay cranes are related to vessel planning and management (number 2 in Table 14.2). Smart security technologies such as RFID, DGPS, electronic tags and bar coding, e-seals, etc. are becoming the fastest-growing segment of terminal operation hardware.

Managing container movements in virtual space: Software & IT

The highly complex physical movement of containers is supported by softwares enabling flows and exchange of information/data.

A modern container terminal facility presents a spectrum of various activities (numbers 1–10 in Table 14.2), ranging from the planning/management of resources (4) and yard/quay operations (1–3,6,7), to documentation (5), billing and accounting (8), security (9) and customer/supplier interface (10). IT here is defined as a specific set of data management technologies that enable either transactions, information exchange or flows of containers to take place in a virtual space. Across all such areas the role of IT is essential both to improve the productivity and to enhance the reliability of the overall system.

Therefore, any modern container terminal operator is endowed with either custom-designed or generic software packages (see section 4 for such arrangements) to manage/plan the above diverse operations. Such softwares may further fall into two interrelated categories: terminal operating systems (TOS) and Electronic Data Interfaces (EDI). TOS are implemented to manage *in situ* movements of containers, within container terminal space itself (numbers 1–9 in Table 14.2). Such systems can

---

2   Also known as rubber-tired gantries (RTG) or rail-mounted gantries (RMG).

manage thousands of box movements simultaneously: PSA's CITOS can manage up to 40 000 container movements and related data in a single day (see Table 14.3).

Table 14.2 Basic typology of container port technologies

Main IT areas in port terminal operations (software packages)	Hardware				
	cranes, trailers, reach stackers, reefer facilities, scanners, etc.	PCs, servers, LAN networks, etc.	Wireless equipment	DGPS devices	RFID devices
1. Yard management	X	X		X	X
2. Vessel planning/operations	X	X			
3. Operations management Record of container moves by dockers		X	X	X	X
4. Resources management Cranes, human resources, etc.		X			
5. Documentation systems Customs clearance, line instructions, in/out container authorisation, etc.		X			
6. Gate management		X	X		X
7. Rail management	X	X	X	X	X
8. Billing & accounting		X			
9. Security management Container scanning, staff & visitors inspection, etc.	X	X	X		X
10. Electronic Data Interface (EDI)* a) from the carrier to the TO: - stowage instructions - master bay plan - preannouncement of containers b) from the TO to the carrier - stowage plan - discharge & loading report - gate in/out report - rail in/out report - vessel performance report		X			

Notes:
* EDI is essentially related to Vessel operation (2) and Documentation systems (5).
DGPS: Differential Global Positioning System; this device (located on each crane) allows to record the container move from position A to the position B, without providing information on the container itself (ID number, weight, origin/destination, etc.).
RFID: Radio Frequency IDentification; this device allows recognition of each container (ID number and related information) through wireless transmitting/emitting devices. Transmitters are located on individual containers and relay information to local receivers normally using 400 Mhz frequencies.

EDIs and other tracking technologies are used to manage *ex situ* box movements and transactions. EDIs link various players of the supply chain by providing a multi-user internet-based platform where paperless virtual transactions are conducted. EDI (number 10 in Table 14.2) holds a critical importance due to its widespread adoption from terminal operators, the port (or rather the individual terminal) has become an epicentre of innovation in IT SCM solutions.

The relationship between the TNCs and IT is thus central to the understanding of their business strategy: how they develop, purchase or even export such technologies is a core component of their international expansion process. But just how firms develop or access technology is a matter internal to the firms and its management, as there exists a range of IT strategies available to individual firms. The following section presents the various governance arrangements popular among current industry leaders.

4. Governance and Sourcing of IT among Asian Operators

This section introduces a simple governance model of current arrangements under which port IT is being developed and integrated into business practice. Theoretical statements are supported by practical evidence found in the field. Closer scrutiny of organisational aspects of the port-operating TNC reveal four types of relationship operators and carriers entering terminal operations maintain to IT, from external arms-length to complete internalisation strategies (Figure 14.1).

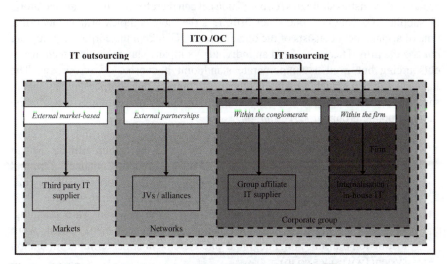

Figure 14.1 Inter-corporate governance arrangements in IT

4.1 In-house IT development

This arrangement consists of the internalisation of technologies developed in-house. Examples include:

- PSA International best illustrates the first relationship. A core strength of PSA International is that the company develops, tests and applies all its IT packages in-house. Its R&D is Singapore-based and its IT packages are first tested at home in Singapore. Successful records of IT management products tested against the world's second busiest container port promises high exportability potential. PSA has taken a lead in branding itself through port logistics and technological solution. The next section will discuss the case of PSA International in detail.
- Another example is CSXWT prior to the Dubai Ports World takeover: the company ran its own terminal management consultancy subsidiary and developed some in-house IT packages.
- Some Japanese carriers have also internalised various segments of terminal IT development and management applications. The sheer size of the Japanese *keiretsu* allows for IT-specialised subsidiaries serving the head firm.

4.2 Intra-conglomerate insourcing

All leading Asian operators belong to broader conglomerates which often carry out group-wide logistics strategies (Olivier 2006). It can therefore occur that an operator's IT supplier is a conglomerate sister firm. It is the most complex arrangement: this type of arrangement consists of the outsourcing of IT *within* the corporate group but *outside* the firm. Therefore, from an individual company standpoint it is technically outsourcing but from a conglomerate standpoint it consists of insourcing. The Japanese *keiretsu* arguably maintains the most complex inter-corporate relations: in some cases such as MOL sourcing of terminal management technology is *within* the same corporate group, or *kigyo shudan*.

- MOL terminals utilise technologies designed by group-affiliate Mitsui Engineering & Shipbuilding Co.'s (MES) patented Container Terminal Management System (CTMS). Through CTMS's various subsystems, MES has been offering 'total packages' for container terminals since 1973, including container data management and documentation, yard planning, ship stowage planning, container handling equipment management, work instruction transmission, integrated gate system container terminal simulation system (www.mes.co.jp).
- The Hyundai group also develops and utilises its own brand of terminal management software: Hyundai Information Technology and Hyundai Intelligence Terminal Operation & Planning System (HI-TOPS). The software is installed in the Busan terminals which the company sold to HPH.
- Another example was in October 2000 when Hutchison International Terminals and ex-Hutchison Whampoa Ltd. subsidiary Orange (sold in 1999)

came together to create a 'mobile terminal message service', a technology that allows tractor drivers to receive real-time instructions on container movements.

4.3 IT-based partnerships

IT can be strong rationale for partnerships. As industry players expand and the industry matures, this has lead to an increasing number of partnerships since the early 2000s. In the container terminal industry, joint ventures remain so far the preferred form of partnership for this type of arrangement. JVs may also bring terminal operators together over efficiency concerns.

- The year 2003 saw the creation of OnePort Ltd., a JV between the three leading terminal operators in Hong Kong: MTL, HIT and COSCO Pacific. It consists of common EDI platform (see Olivier 2005).
- Alternatively, JVs more commonly involve terminal operators with outside IT firms specializing in SCM IT solutions. For instance, in April 2005 HPH formed a JV with US-based Savi Technology Inc.to create an RFID-based network for its global facilities. Elsewhere, HPH and InfoLink Systems created a JV in early 2005 aiming to supply HPH terminals with radio frequency container ID systems. HPH's main logistics subsidiary LINE had previously entered into inter-corporate agreements with some of its largest customers in establishing cargo visibility EDIs: LINE-Evergreen (2000) and LINE-Reebok (2002).
- In June 2004 MTL and Korea's Total Soft Bank formed a JV to modernise MTL's Hong Kong facilities with Modern Terminals Operations System (MOTOS). MOTOS consists of an all-in-one computerised management system including user interfaces and yard management controls, which allows MTL to manage its Hong Kong and mainland China operations from Hong Kong. The system came on stream in December 2004.
- There are other more generic IT firms like Oracle who are also embarking on the development of SCM systems. In 2000, Oracle and HPH came together to create the Global Transport eXchange JV, an online logistics exchange platform.

4.4 Third party IT supplier

The norm within the industry remains by and large the outsourcing of IT management solutions. Computerised management systems are usually outsourced to third party software providers who have specialised in development and export of customised terminal management software. It is precisely those firms that have benefited from the FDI boom in the 1990s to expand their products on an international basis (see Cargo Systems 2000; 2001; Nunan 2001). Market leaders in computer automated terminal operating systems (CATOS) with an international presence include Navis

(US), Cosmos (Belgium), ESC (US, a subsidiary of MTC),[3] Total Soft Bank (Korea), PSA International (Singapore) and Gottwald (Germany). Smaller firms include CMC (India), Maher Terminals (US) and Tideworks (US, a wholly-owned subsidiary of SSA Marine). Yet other firms like Infolink Systems (US) specialise in SCM IT. Examples include:

- Navis supplying terminal software to NYK, HPH and Modern Terminals Ltd. (MTL) (Shekou) (see Table 14.3 below)
- Total Soft Bank to MTL (Hong Kong)
- ESC/CATOS fitting Evergreen's wholly-owned subsidiary Seaside Transportation (Los Angeles & Oakland) and Hanjin's Total Terminals International USWC facilities (Long Beach & Oakland) with its products.

The model highlights the variety of arrangements through which firms approach IT: from arms length to complete vertical integration. It was mentioned earlier how ocean carriers and ITOs enter terminal operations from different strategic angles. While delivery of terminal services constitutes the core activity of ITOs, for carriers it is the provision of container shipping services. This contrast is important as it bears an incidence on their relationship with IT in two ways. First, as evidenced above, ITOs have generally tended to adopt new technologies faster and at larger scales than carriers. For example, leading ITOs have taken the forefront in widescale RFID technology implementation (see Ashley 2006). Productivity-enhancing technologies have been key to their competitiveness. They have leveraged on the strength of their home operations (i.e. home ports) – many of which at the world's largest container ports such as Hong Kong or Singapore – as a base for R&D. Their strategy therefore has been to build a sound management record at home later to be exported and earn them overseas contracts.

Second, ITOs have tended to enter into cooperative forms of arrangements in regard to IT to a larger extent than the carriers. For example, some of the Japanese and Korean carriers have internalised IT development within corporate groupings. ITOs, on the other hand, show greater reach to third-party IT providers. This is also because the leading logistics IT providers have developed independently to emerge as powerful global players in their own right.

We now wish to illustrate these propositions with two practical examples, corresponding in turn to both ends of the governance spectrum: PSA as a case of full internalisation of IT tools and Navis as the leader of third-party terminal software provider.

5. Case Studies

This section will introduce two case firms to illustrate the extreme subcomponents of the governance model introduced in Figure 14.1: PSA as an example of internalised

---

3   Marine Terminals Corp. is a US West Coast terminal operator having terminal JVs with Evergreen, Hanjin and Yang Ming.

in-house technology development and Navis as a third-party market-based supplier of IT packages.

Table 14.3 PSA Corp's IT and logistics products

Product	Corporate Status	Function	Year launched	Partners if any
PSA Logistics	Wholly-owned subsidiary	Manage PSA's logistics businesses	2002	Not applicable
Portnet.com	subsidiary	EDI platform: track & trace, e-submission, berthing space management, e-billing	Developed in 1984, enhanced to global platform in 1999; incorporated as WOS in 2000	Oracle, iPlanet, Origin, Frontline
EZShip	Proprietary technology	Transhipment movement management software	N/A	—
CITOS	Proprietary terminal management software	Electronic Resource Planning System: terminal yard, personnel, equipment and gates management (flow-through gate system)	1988	—
GEMS	Proprietary technology	Global Equipment Management System: e-business solution helping carriers manage their inventory of empties	N/A	—
BoXchange	Proprietary technology	Global container exchange platform	N/A	—
SLOTMAX	Proprietary technology	Worldwide exchange platform on vessel slots availability	N/A	—
Shippers Corner	Proprietary technology	Support website providing shippers with info on vessel schedules, services, and documentation procedures	2000	Singapore National Shippers' Council
N2N Connect	Malaysian incorporated subsidiary	Integrating IT package: Container Reservation System (CRS), Advanced Transhipment Management System (ATM), Track & Trace (T&T)	2000	—
Cargo D2D	subsidiary	EDI Portal. Web-based neutral third party freight reservations system	2000	—

Source: psa.com.sg.

5.1 The case of PSA International

Leveraging on a strong home port, the leading operators have established sound performance records at home, which establishes credibility and further facilitates foreign penetration. Also, they have erected global marketing campaigns around long lists of prestigious performance awards received at home ports. International operators rely heavily on proven domestic track records to regulate their contacts/contracts with international customers and enhance their bargaining power. A key role of home ports have played in the case of ITOs is a geographical base for R&D. Leading ITOs have developed, tried and tested such IT-based tools as electronic data interface (EDI) and sophisticated yard management equipment at their home port before exporting them to their foreign operations. The case of PSA is enlightening in that regard.

Technology is the essence of PSA's brand and identity and the company has become famous for developing its own technology and exporting it. In fact, technology was the driving force of its internationalisation strategy in the mid 1990s. Indeed, PSA's first customer was the Dalian Port Authority (DPA) when in early 1996 it adopted its Portnet technology. The technology proved itself to the extent that the same year the company was awarded a terminal concession: its very first overseas project. Thus, PSA Corp.'s early internationalisation steps were technology-driven and its commitment to IT-based solutions remains a core component of the PSA brand.

Table 14.3 presents the range of computerised management systems developed by PSA. Its CITOS system is among the most advanced in the world in terms of terminal automation and has a proven track record at home having won several awards.

5.2 The case of Navis

A relatively young firm, Navis was launched in 1988 and rose spectacularly to become a world leader in exporting 'supply chain execution software', now used at over 200 marine/intermodal facilities across 44 countries (www.navis.com). From its headquarters in Oakland, Navis had humble beginnings bringing two PhD graduates with backgrounds in the maritime industry who foresaw a niche in terminal automation and corollary IT supporting systems. The firm's early growth followed the development of the company's trademark product SPARCS system (see Table 14.4). Since its origins as a high-tech SME, it has enlarged to about 250 employees worldwide with branch offices in London, Hong Kong, Dubai and Adelaide. Over the years, Navis has expanded to offer a range of IT management products under five headings: (1) marine terminal operations, (2) inland depot operations, (3) shipping line operations, (4) distribution centre operations, and (5) Navis services (e.g. database management, product implementation, consulting, etc.). Although their product base has grown diversified, marine terminal management products remain their core brand (Table 14.4).

Table 14.4 Range of Navis products for marine terminal operations

Product	Function
Navis SPARCS	Comprehensive Terminal Operating System (TOS)
Navis Express	Terminal Operating System (TOS)
Navis Powerstowe	Vessel space management system
Navis Web Access	Web-based EDI platform
Navis PrimeRoute	Dispatch optimisation for terminal tractors

Source: www.navis.com.

In its early days, Navis' primary customers were port authorities wishing to modernise their facilities (e.g. mainly US port authorities such as Houston, Georgia, Newark, Maryland), but increasingly as privatisation unfolded the port-operating TNCs became its primary customers. As the industry leader, Navis supplies its products to both ITOs and ocean carriers' terminal operating subsidiaries among which figure such names as HPH, ECT, ICTSI, DPW (including CSXWT and P&O Ports), NYK, MOL and APL/NOL (Table 14.5). It becomes thus critical for firms like Navis to maintain quality business ties with the operating TNCs. For instance, HPH is one of Navis' main customers. This is because ICTSI fitted all its overseas terminals with Navis software. HPH's acquisition of ICTSI's eight overseas terminals meant HPH inherited Navis-equipped facilities overnight, while at its home terminals HIT is using different technologies.

The case of Navis brilliantly illustrates the resulting booming demand in logistics-based technologies accompanying global trends in qualitative and quantitative port capacity enhancements, in which both ITOs and ocean carriers are undoubtedly playing an active role.

Table 14.5 List of customers and their terminal facilities using Navis products among sampled TNCs, as of August 2005

Product category		
Marine Terminal Operations/yard planning software		Shipping Line Operations / Vessel space management
HPH	• Ningbo • Dar Es Salaam • Bahama Freeport • Veracruz • Buenos Aires • Karachi • Laem Chabang	OOCL
ECT (HPH)	• Rotterdam	APL
MTL	• Shekou	
COSCO Pacific	• Qingdao	
DPW (including ex-CSXWT facilities)	• Puerto Cabello • Puerto Caucedo • Adelaide • Dubai	
APL/NOL: Eagle Marine Services LLC	• Los Angeles • Oakland • Seattle	MOL
APL/NOL: LCIT Co. Ltd:	• Laem Chabang	
NYK: Yusen Terminals Inc:	• Los Angeles • Oakland	
NYK: TIPS	• Laem Chabang	
NYK (Patrick Terminals)	• Sydney Botany Bay	
MOL: TIPS	• Laem Chabang	
HMM	• Kaohsiung	
Yang Ming Line	• Los Angeles • Kaohsiung	

Source: www.navis.com; *CIY, 2005.*

6. Conclusion: Some Implications for Port-cities

IT is a *sine qua non* condition of global supply chains, binding all actors of the chain through information flows. In fact, as demonstrated above, port IT is emerging as a business in itself these days with strong prospects in further automation of container port operations. The primary contribution of this chapter is that it demonstrated how IT expertise has also become an essential ingredient for a successful internationalisation strategy adopted by emerging global operators. Various governance regimes define port-operating TNCs' relations to SCM technologies: some firms embracing IT more aggressively than others. Two of the world's leading ITOs – HPH and PSA – may have very different approaches to their IT strategies but their level of commitment is equally high and they both benefit from strong home ports where they can develop and/or implement technologies.

Domestic market conditions including physical space constraints, the home port factor, capacity constraints and a base for R&D have been singled out as a critical element of a successful internationalisation strategy. ITOs have reaped greater benefits than ocean carriers from the home port factor. In addition, local market conditions have favoured Asian operators: ITOs have best succeeded in emerging economies where land and port capacity shortages have required innovative implementation of productivity-enhancing technological solutions.

Institutional change and the emergence of powerful TNCs in the container port industry have profound consequences. Notably, in the context of this book two key implications for port-cities may be drawn. The first follows from the role of domestic markets in relation to global operators' internationalisation strategy as a base for R&D. The rise of global operators backed by global developments in IT has spatially disjointed the infrastructural, operational and corporate decision-making spaces that traditionally formed the 'port-city'. In other words, the globalisation of port investment and operation through the rise of TNCs in port service supply and global ocean carriers' involvement means that, increasingly, key decisions steering local port projects may be carried out 'at a distance'. Port-cities housing the most powerful operators now increasingly act as 'command-and-control centres' steering port development overseas (see also Rimmer 1999). TNCs are *rescaling* port-cities: as spatial concentrations of corporate headquarters they are extending the outreach of traditional port-cities to global scales of influence via corporate controls.

Second, as ports/terminals engage themselves in SCM, they act as growth poles for complementary logistics activities clustering around them: modern distriparks, warehousing and storage facilities, free trade zones, customs integration, etc. This spatial integration seeks more capacitated greenfield sites and tend to drive away ports from traditional urban areas. As IT underlies the integrated management of such complex activities, it may be further consolidating ongoing spatial dislocation between ports and their host cities by fuelling the migration of container terminals to more capacitated deepwater sites supported by backup land. This dislocation has been a marked feature of the port-city interface in developed economies (Hoyle 2000) and is becoming evident in East Asia (Wang and Olivier 2006; Rimmer 1999; 2004). Further rescaling of the port is also observable at the sub-port level. Terminal operators have their specific set of customers across the chain and as such, within a single port, different terminals may belong to competing supply chains. These inter-firm relations binding the terminal (operator) and various segments of the chain are increasingly defined under a technological environment. It is therefore increasingly difficult to conceive the port as a homogeneous entity since each container terminal may belong to specific chains, possess its own IT environment and function under its own distinctive corporate agenda.

In sum, technologies are where port productivity and security enhancements converge and hold the key to successful SCM practices in a world where global supply chains increase in complexity. While both in theory and in practice this fact is widely recognised, this chapter's originality is in its empirical account of corporate-level strategies and how technology is becoming a central piece to success in the global marketplace in an industry under clear globalising forces. After all, supply chains are the result of aggregate micro-management decisions, at the centre of which smart use of technologies figure prominently.

Acknowledgements

Authors wish to thank Mr. Enrico Rossi Ferrari (EDP manager at the SECH terminal in the port of Genoa) for his useful comments and information on technologies in container terminal operations. We also thank our dear colleague Professor Brian Slack for his insightful comments on earlier drafts of this chapter.

Chapter 15

Which Link, In Which Chain?
Inserting Durban into Global Automotive Supply Chains

Peter V. Hall and Glen Robbins

1. Introduction

In the closing sentence of his call for a new paradigm in port studies, Robinson issues the following challenge: 'the role of ports and the way in which ports position themselves in the new business environments beyond 2001 must be defined within a paradigm of ports as elements in value-driven chain systems, not simply as places with particular, if complex, functions' (2002, 252). Recent research on the maritime shipping industry has focused upon the emergence of more integrated logistics chains, both within the maritime industry itself and between maritime- and land-based transportation modes (Slack *et al.* 2002b). The attention to integration along logistics chains parallels and indeed draws upon the wider literature on global commodity chains (Gereffi *et al.* 2005) and supply chains (Cox *et al.* 2002). Greater integration of logistics chains raises difficult questions for ports and port-cities seeking to secure or maintain dominant positions within global trade flows.

The logistics chain perspective indicates that ports should seek to insert themselves as privileged nodes within particular logistics chains. In this chapter we show that the potential for conflict and uncertainty over goals, roles and actions with respect to supply chain insertion increases significantly when we rescale the analysis in two dimensions: namely, from the port to the port-city and the nation, and from the logistics to the whole supply chain. For clarity we distinguish between logistics chains which deal with the distribution of goods in physical space, and value chains which deal with inter-firm relationships in economic space. We use the term supply chain to encompass both. With some exceptions, few attempts have been made to nest the analysis of logistics chains within the larger supply chains in which they are located. We argue that this analytical bracketing may potentially lead to incorrect policy advice.

Using a case study of the attempts since 1994 to insert Durban into global automotive supply chains, we trace the debate and conflict over what logistics functions to serve in which value chain. We show that this conflict results not only from the tensions within or between competing value and logistics chains, but also from the tensions between parallel local and national decision-making arenas. At the local level, port planning and day-to-day port management are not coordinated with municipal planning and economic development functions (Hall and Robbins 2002), nor is there substantive interaction with major local importers and exporters. At the national level, port policy is caught up in the restructuring and transformation of the national transport agency, while automotive sector policies reflect national industrial goals. This decision-making environment seriously complicates the goal of rapid agreement and alignment around supply chain insertion. This clearly presents challenges for a country such as South Africa which is located at some considerable distance from major global markets.

The chapter consists of a short section which presents the conceptual framework, highlighting the policy challenges raised for ports and port-cities by introducing scale into the supply chain perspective. The bulk of the chapter is devoted to the second section which contains the case study. Here we nest the analysis of automobile imports and exports moving through the port of Durban within the wider port-city and national development context. The chapter ends with a brief conclusion.

2. Conceptual Framework: Logistic, Value and Supply Chains in Scale

The goals of actors operating within supply chains, if not the precise strategies they may employ or the nature of the regimes governing specific chains, are relatively clear. First, actors seek to insert themselves into supply chains. Supply chains provide actors with access to technology, capital, supplies, expertise, and markets, and most importantly, knowledge about these critical resources (Gereffi *et al.* 2005). For ports, the goal of logistic chain insertion has been pursued through improved landside connections, incentives, leases and concessions to attract more port callers, and port networking (Notteboom and Winklemans 2001). Likewise, national and local economies seek to insert themselves into value chains dominated by a decreasing number of global players, especially in the automobile sector.

Second, actors seek appropriate integration along supply chains in order to reduce overall transactions costs and increase efficiency. This implies that actors within a given supply chain should cooperate in order to out-compete other chains. This perspective is the *raison d'être* of supply chain management as a field of practice. Transaction-costs reasoning has been applied to explain vertical integration in the maritime sector (Panayides 2002). Another form of greater integration within supply chains is the upgrading of productive capacity through a variety of (often collective and regionalised) learning, innovating and harmonizing processes (Humphrey and Schmitz 2002; Coe *et al.* 2004).

Third, however, while the heightened integration predicted by the transactions cost approach may be applicable to some parts of the logistics industry, it is insufficient to account for the observed diversity in the governance of supply chains (Gereffi *et al.* 2005). What the so-called 'power perspective' highlights is that supply chain actors will also seek to secure advantage over each other by developing their supply chain capacities. This is because each actor in a supply chain is in some sense in competition with every other actor over the value that may be extracted from what are essentially uncompetitive economic systems (Cox *et al.* 2002). Supply chains are thus inherently unstable, and subject to competition from within as well as from without. Hence, Robinson (2002) asks which critical assets a port must secure in order to enjoy some power when negotiating with steamship lines and other users of port services.

We summarise the three goals of actors with respect to supply chains as *insertion*, *integration* and *dominance*. Our terminology closely matches the notions of value creation, value enhancement and value capture discussed by Coe *et al.* (2004). We use terminology that is more limited in scope, but that seeks to highlight the tensions between and within actors in competing supply chains. In order to understand how this competition plays out in the ports and the city-regions that host them, it seems to us that there are two further challenges. First, we need to rescale the port, and second, we need to pay close attention to the nature of particular supply chains and the specific character of the actors which populate them.

By recognising that ports are elements in supply chains, we are implicitly recognising that they exist in relation to processes that operate within, across and between multiple spatial scales. This is the same challenge which economic globalisation presents to all contemporary spatial-economic analysis and policy (Dicken 2003). For example, global trading regions and the sub-port terminal scale intersect in Olivier and Slack's (2006) argument that the 'global' terminal operating firm is currently a prime agent of 'local' port change. Likewise, Humphrey and Schmitz (2002) ask whether insertion into global value chains leads to upgrading of local industrial clusters, while Coe *et al.* (2004) ask whether regional institutions allow favourable 'strategic coupling' between local firms and global production networks.

The question for ports, and the city-regions that host them, is which chain or chains might they seek to insert themselves into, recognising that there may be trade-offs between different chains. For example, greater port throughput (in a logistics chain) need not necessarily translate into greater local capture of economic activity (in a value chain). The overarching point is that recognising that ports are elements in global supply chains severely complicates the scalar and bounding dimensions of the analytical and policy task. To begin answering the question, which link in which chain, we propose an ideal-typical framework that cuts across three spatial scales (port, port-city and nation), and identifies various strategies employed actors seeking to insert themselves into, integrate activities along, and secure dominance within two types of supply chain (logistic and value chains). The framework is summarised in Table 15.1.

3. Automobiles and Durban: A Case Study

We use the conceptual framework developed in the previous section and presented in Table 15.1 to understand the dynamic relationship between the Port of Durban, municipal and national governments, and the automotive sector in the Durban region and elsewhere in South Africa. The case study illustrates how a variety of actors operating at different scales have used various logistics and value chain strategies to insert Durban into global automobile supply chains. We show that conflict results not only from the tensions within or between competing value and logistics chains, but also from the tensions between parallel local and national decision-making arenas.

Table 15.1 Typology of supply chain strategies at different scales, with examples

		Logistics chains	Value chains
Port (i.e. on- or near-dock and terminal facility)	Insertion	Attract lines through concessions, leases	On- or near-dock value-added activity
	Integration	Improved on-dock information systems	Integrate on-dock with overall supply chain information systems
	Dominance	Specialised and dedicated terminal	Unique on- or near-dock processing facilities
Port-city (i.e. immediate port hinterland)	Insertion	Local road connections	Export promotion
	Integration	Backhaul cooperation	Local cluster strategy
	Dominance	Transport industry cluster strategy	Develop immobile capacities
Nation (i.e. beyond port-city)	Insertion	Long-distance (rail) service and infrastructure	Inward investment attraction
	Integration	Regional corridor strategies	National cluster strategy
	Dominance	Transhipment hub	Strategic trade policy

Three crucial features of the case study should be emphasised at the outset. First, the case is one of a port and a gateway city that enjoy, for the foreseeable future, an effective monopoly over the majority of containerised cargo movements through southern Africa. Second, the Durban port forms part of a national parastatal organisation which remains relatively centralised despite the overall trend towards devolution in post-Apartheid South Africa. And third, the South African state at both national and local levels maintains a developmental stance with respect to the automotive industry.

The case study begins with a brief introduction to the automobile sector in Durban and the development of the port in the city. This is then followed with a discussion of changes in the national economy and in industrial policy with respect to the automotive sector. Finally, the case study looks specifically at automotive logistics and value chain issues that have arisen in Durban in the past decade.

3.1 Background to the auto sector and the Port of Durban

With South Africa's post-World War II industrialisation, the Port of Durban secured substantial and ongoing state investment, and it became the primary port serving the country's economic mining and industrial heartland (in what is today the Gauteng Province). Investment in the port was accompanied by development of a significant industrial base in Durban, including substantial investments from the firm that ultimately became Toyota South Africa. Subsequently, Durban developed a significant cluster of automotive production activities for the domestic market. It is notable that the license conditions under which Toyota South Africa (TSA) operated specifically excluded them from exporting other than to handful of very limited markets in southern and eastern Africa. Nevertheless, by 1981, TSA had established its leadership in the domestic market as the primary producer of passenger and light commercial vehicles, a position that it maintains to this day. Despite the steady growth of localised components suppliers during the period of the 1970s and 1980s, TSA's growing and diverse product offering continued to depend on component imports through the Port of Durban.

What were the logistics and value chain issues in this 'pre-global' context? High import tariffs protected producers and distributors from the price, quality and delivery pressures that are present in today's liberalised global trade environment. Orientation towards relatively uncompetitive domestic markets arguably reduced the attention paid to logistics and supply chain management. There was limited pressure from port users and low responsiveness from port decision-making structures with regard to performance. This situation changed in the late 1980s due to the combined effects of domestic recession and the process of economic reform initiated by the Apartheid government. South African businesses were thrust into an environment of rapidly escalating competition and reduced government protection. This soon led to a much greater appreciation, at least in the private sector, of the importance for firms to insert themselves into, achieving integration efficiencies along, and securing dominance within global supply chains.

3.2 Developments in the SA auto sector since 1990

In the years since the end of Apartheid, South Africa's economic structure has undergone substantial change. Economic restructuring was encouraged through the adoption of an export-oriented policy framework in the context of conservative macroeconomic management. The automotive sector in South Africa was not immune to these changes: duties of 115 per cent in 1995 on completely built-up vehicles are scheduled to reach 30 per cent in 2007 (Barnes and Morris 2004). However, despite trade liberalisation there was also a commitment by the Department of Trade and Industry to avoid pitfalls of de-industrialisation from rapid tariff adjustments (Barnes *et al.* 2004). One of the manifestations of that commitment was the Motor

Industry Development Programme (MIDP), formulated by the government together with key industry players and launched in 1995.

The MIDP encouraged each Own Equipment Manufacturer (OEM) to consolidate domestic production around a reduced range of vehicles, and to harness export-level economies of scale in production. By exporting, OEMs would be entitled to earn duty credits to import a considerably greater range of models from production sites in other parts of the globe. In other words, domestic assemblers were encouraged to insert into global supply chains. And they did: according to Barnes *et al.* (2004), the automobile sector grew rapidly between 1994 and 2002, doubling its export to output ratio and accounting for an increasing share of output value, gross value-added and manufacturing employment.

Figure 15.1 Map of South Africa

Note: The BMW plant is located in Pretoria (Tshwane) and the Toyota plant is located in Durban.

Source: Courtesy of the University of Texas Libraries, The University of Texas at Austin, http://www.lib.utexas.edu/maps/cia06south_adrica_sm_2006.gif, accessed 13 November 2006.

One notable early MIDP beneficiary was Volkswagen (VWSA), which had been exporting Jettas through Port Elizabeth to China since 1991, but perhaps the most prominent MIDP success was BMW. BMW's were first assembled in South Africa from completely knocked down 'kits' in 1968. In 1973 BMW South Africa established the first BMW assembly plant outside Germany in Rosslyn, northwest of Pretoria (see Figure 15.1). In 1994, the first exports were sent to Australia, and in 1996, with a R1bn investment, the plant became 'BMW World Plant, Rosslyn', an integrated part of the BMW global production system. In 1999, a new vehicle distribution centre opened at the plant, and by 2002, approximately 80 per cent of output was being exported. The Port of Durban serves as the main import channel and the primary export channel for BMW.

3.4 The Durban automotive sector

The automotive sector in the greater Durban region was also heavily influenced by these national industrial and trade policy changes. During the mid to late 1990s, local component producers did enjoy some growth in demand from domestic OEMs, and some received orders to supply global production operations. While these benefits were significant, the largest single buyer of components produced in Durban – Toyota – at first did not seek to participate in the MIDP. Barnes and Morris (2004) argue that, apart from Toyota's strategic orientation to the domestic market, their slow response was also due to the fact that the initial MIDP design suited the investment model of the German-owned multinationals and their suppliers rather than that of the Japanese- and American-owned automobile producers. So instead of following a restructuring path, Toyota sourced trade credits on the open market and used these to increase its imports of a greater range of vehicles for sale on the domestic market. However, for much of this period, domestic demand remained very flat, and Toyota found that other importing competitors were cutting into its historic premium in South African small and mid-range passenger car markets.

To take full advantage of the MIDP, TSA had to export. To export, TSA had to renegotiate license agreements with Toyota Motor Corporation (TMC) of Japan. Once this was achieved, TSA stopped producing the Camry, which was now imported from Australia, and began components exports to earn MIDP tariff benefits. In turn, TMC chose in 2000 to acquire a majority stake in TSA and invest in new assembly lines, all geared towards export. This insertion of the local Toyota operation in the firms' global supply chain – achieved by adjusting the licensing and ownership arrangements – was accompanied by a series of actions to integrate, secure and upgrade both value and logistics chains.

In preparation for these changes, TSA made it clear to various levels of government that TMC required certain policy signals before it would invest in additional productive capacity. First, national-level endorsement was required, secured through a series of Japanese and South African government ministerial exchanges and visits from 1998 to 2000. Second, a commitment from local government to be responsive to local infrastructure and land acquisition requests was sought. This was secured through direct contact with the executive of the metropolitan government, expedited planning and building approval for a catalytic converter plant, a private road/bridge link to the rail head, and better signage and street lighting. Third, TSA indicated that they needed a plan for resolving delays in container-handling in the port, and more information about plans for the newly opened automobile terminal. For this, the firm looked to the municipal government to put pressure on the public port authority.

Local Toyota suppliers began working together in 1997 to improve their competitiveness. In 1998 they formed a Benchmarking Club, with financial support from the Department of Trade and Industry, British government, and in 1999, from the Durban Metropolitan Council (Morris and Robbins 2006). One of the priority issues identified by the Benchmarking Club was logistics; a Logistics Working Group was formed to address both maritime and landside issues. The landside concerns are an example of logistics chain integration, and entailed greater coordination on road haulage. Collaboration between Toyota and Durban-based suppliers, who were respectively sourcing and supplying parts in the Eastern Cape Province, resulted in significant back-haul cost savings.

On the maritime side, the Logistics Working Group worked to secure lower and consistent import and export shipping rates for components firms, and to deal with container terminal productivity, lost boxes, damage and delays. In other words, they sought to address matters of both logistics chain integration and dominance. Some success was achieved in negotiations with the shipping lines, but discussions with public-sector terminal operators and the port authority resulted in little or no action.

While we focus on the shipment of fully built-up automobiles in the section that follows, it is important to recognise that containerised components are a critical dimension of Durban's insertion into global automotive supply chains. Growth in container volumes through the late 1990s in excess of 10 per cent per year soon exposed inadequate investment plans and weak management at the Port of Durban. Delays in loading and offloading containers were aggravated by landside congestion problems and the service shortcomings in the rail network. The late 1990s witnessed a number of short-term investment projects by the public port authority, Portnet, and its successor agencies, the National Ports Authority (NPA) and South African Port Operations (SAPO). These involved the expansion of handling facilities at the main container terminal to increase capacity to well over one million TEU. The Port of Durban is projected to handle in the region of 2.3 million TEU in 2006.

3.5 Auto shipments and the Port of Durban

In 1998, a dedicated car terminal designed to handle 90,000 units annually opened in Durban (Arkin 2005). The planning, location, design and scale of the initial automobile terminal reflected BMW's needs as well as those of the increasingly influential vehicle import lobby, but certainly not those of the soon to be exporting Durban-based Toyota. Barnes and Morris (2004) argue that German-owned automobile manufacturers have enjoyed considerable policy influence in post-Apartheid South Africa. Certainly, the new automobile terminal in Durban reflected the ability of BMW, a shipper with its main production activities located over 600 kilometres outside the port-city, to secure preferential access to port planning and investment. As one of the first automobile firms to explicitly adopt the MIDP,

BMW had cultivated close ties with the national government and was able to secure substantial cabinet-level support.

The decision to build the automobile terminal was taken at exactly the same time as two joint port-city planning processes were under way. The Port-City forum, begun erratically in 1997, and the associated South Industrial Basin (SIB, sometimes called the South Durban Basin) planning process were actively developing a grander vision for an automotive logistics park with supply chain value-adding activities (i.e. customisation, accessorisation, and associated space for parts suppliers, etc). The SIB extends from the south end of the port, beyond Durban International Airport, and includes Prospecton, home to Toyota SA. The SIB planning process was funded in part by the national government Department of Trade and Industry, yet Portnet bypassed this process in constructing the new automobile terminal. The case for locating a car terminal at the SIB end of the port is strong, since the SIB accounts for 29.2 per cent of all the automotive components employment in the Province of KwaZulu-Natal, and half of all the firms with turnover of more than R300 million per annum (Barnes and Johnson 2004).

Instead Portnet chose for the automobile terminal a location on the northern side of the port, adjacent to the central business district. Cars for export from Toyota have to go to far side of the port, through the downtown and on public roads, facing insurance concerns, congestion and delays. While the terminal is served by rail, this involves shunting from the rail head adjacent to the SIB. BMW is the only auto terminal shipper that makes use of rail. Finally, the auto terminal soon ran into capacity constraints, necessitating some very expensive additional investments. These involved doubling the number of parking spaces to 7,000 by building a multi-storey parking garage, and the building of a dedicated bridge over the rail lines. These additions were completed in 2004.

Notwithstanding these planning problems, the Durban auto terminal has experienced an increase in unit throughput from just over 40,000 units in 1998, to over 200,000 units in 2004 (or by 79 per cent in seven years). Today, there are over 20 car carrier calls per month, with all major global car carrier lines calling. In general it appears that there has been satisfaction with the performance of the facility (Arkin 2005) although there remains considerable uncertainty about expansions to meet future demand. Land-use and congestion-based conflicts between downtown business interests and local government, and the port, remain unresolved.

3.6 Toyota and the future of auto operations in the Port of Durban

Toyota began to engage the NPA in discussions in 2000 in an effort to gauge responses to the projected increases in export volumes from its Durban plant. Toyota was disappointed with the initial response, and as was the case with container terminal operations, the firm looked to municipal government to put pressure on the port to be more responsive. Indeed, Toyota felt compelled to explore a variety of highly unattractive alternatives, such as using a private terminal on Maydon Wharf amongst bulk and breakbulk cargo, or even placing export cars in containers. During 2004 it became clear that Toyota was serious about ensuring the robustness of its systems when the company announced that it intended to introduce two other export-focused assembly lines at its Prospecton plant. According to an industry expert, the decision has been made to increase Toyota production in Durban to the order of world status, or approximately 250,000 units per year by 2010 (Barnes 2005). Of these, between 120,000 and 140,000 units will be exported, with most going to Europe. It is highly unlikely that the existing automobile terminal port facility will be able to accommodate this growth.

More recently, the NPA acceded to a request from Toyota and the municipality (now the eThekwini Municipality) to set up a joint task team to assess future development options. This was deemed necessary by both Toyota and the municipality due the fact that the location of the present facility close to the commercial centre of Durban's inner city has resulted in congestion problems that would only get worse as Toyota increased its export volume. The NPA has belatedly (in late 2006) agreed to work with the municipality on the construction of a much larger car terminal on the southern side of the port with better access to the industrial areas.

It remains to be seen whether this development heralds a new era of openness and responsiveness in port planning. While the NPA has spent the better part of the last four years developing a Port Masterplan for Durban, it has only been during the course of 2005 that external stakeholders have had limited access to the plan details. The fact that it was developed in isolation from other key stakeholders is reflective of ongoing challenges of a centralised governance system. At the same time the intransigence of the public port authorities reflects, in no small measure, the ports' effective monopoly dominance within the supply chains that are routed through it.

The situation we have described might have been very different if we were dealing with a port authority more responsive to local economic actors. In large part, the scalar tensions playing out on the Durban waterfront are a consequence of the flip-flopping of national ports policy. Successive policy initiatives have all had very little to say about effective action at the local level to address logistics and value chain integration. As currently presented, these strategies appear unlikely to do enough to allow the port and the city of Durban to answer, in a timely fashion, the next time they are asked, which link, in which chain.

4. Conclusions: Reflecting on Supply Chain Issues in the Durban Context

We began this chapter by noting that greater integration of logistics chains raises difficult questions for ports and port-cities seeking to insert themselves into, improve the efficiencies along, and secure dominant positions within these chains. What our case study of inserting Durban in global automobile supply chains has shown is that this is a complex process, involving multiple actors and chains. For this reason we asked which link, in which chain? We have argued for an approach to supply chain insertion which recognises that actors in chains face both internal and external competitive/dominance and cooperative/integrative pressures. We have also argued that supply chain insertion plays out across multiple scales. Hence our conceptual framework differentiates between logistics and value chains, and between port, local and national scale actors and their (often divergent) goals.

In a general sense, we may conclude that supply chains are subject to contests that play out within and across a variety of spatial scales. The port is a central site of this scalar contest. First, we have identified various supply chains in competition with each other to dominate particular (critical) supply chain resource, in this instance the attention and facilities of the national port authority. Second, we have a contest between particular national government and corporate coalitions seeking to insert the port into particular extra-local logistics chains, and a particular port-city and corporate coalition seeking prominence for a value chain embedded in the local economy. And third, we have identified tensions, if not open conflict, between the imperatives of logistics chains tasked with physical goods movements, and the imperatives of value chains tasked with governing economic relations. The shift to a world dominated by supply chains will not eliminate the problems of highly localised tensions between port and city; indeed in some cases it may exacerbate them.

At the end of the day, it makes a difference which supply chains are at play in a particular context. Perhaps Durban is lucky that Toyota is a patient, persistent and growing player in the global automobile industry. Toyota and its suppliers arguably have far more interest in logistics chain insertion and integration because of the way in which Toyota (throughout the world) organises its production. TSA already sources a greater share of it parts locally than any other South African OEM, and as it expands production for export, it is committed to further increasing the share of content sourced locally. In order to improve component quality and quantity the firm has taken an interest in some of its major suppliers, and encouraged others to do so themselves. Furthermore, unlike most other South African OEMs, Toyota does not do preassembly, relying on a more complex 'just-in-time' system that requires close attention to logistics integration. All this provides some grounds for optimism that supply chain problems in Durban will eventually be resolved; at the same time, it certainly raises the stakes.

Chapter 16

Sustainable Development and Corporate Strategies of the Maritime Industry

Claude Comtois and Brian Slack

1. Introduction

Most scenarios of growth in the maritime industry rest on the capacity to manage sustainable development. Occupying critical sites in coastal zones and in day to day transport operations, the dynamics of port and commercial carriers raise concerns for the environment.

A series of issues is raised by these concerns. How is the marine industry assessing environmental conditions? How does legislation answer the industry's requirements posed by sustainable development? How effective are enforcement mechanisms? Above all, how far, and to what extent, is bottom-up approach conducive in controlling the negative externalities of marine transportation facilities and operations?

The initial issue is considered by examining the environmental context which both influences and is influenced by the maritime industry. Attention then centres on the capacity of international legislation to respond to these environmental challenges. Compliance with international conventions is made through a review of enforcement mechanisms. A detailed assessment is then made of the capacity of the marine industry in reducing the environmental impact of its activities. A key feature of the analysis is the focus on the competitiveness of environmental performance. The study begins, however, by reviewing the existing literature.

2. Literature Review

Literature concerning contemporary changes of maritime transport in the perspective of sustainable development is multifaceted. Key issues focus on ocean environment, port development and commercial navigation.

Recent literature on sustainability applied to the marine environment considers the ocean as a strategic (Tangreti 2002) or economic (Miossec 1999; 2001) asset that requires management (Marcadon 1999; Raftopoulos 2001) and international political cooperation (USGAO 1999). Changes are interpreted through the need to provide detailed examination of environmental issues and pollution risks. Interests on port development and the environment focus on the need to establish a common management of environment and port operations (Finney and Young 1995; Poltrack

2000; Wooldridge *et al.* 1999) and on the environmental management linked with the development of new port areas (Bristow and Zhao 1995; Huggett 1998; Abood and Metzger 2001; Amromin *et al.* 2002). Evidence suggests growing concern over quantifying environmental issues and estimating environmental costs. There is an extensive literature considering environmental pollution generated by ships. Research has explored two directions. A first approach considers environmental problems resulting from shipping – ballast waters, air pollution, or dredging operations – marine sediments (Bravard *et al.* 2000; Corbett and Fischbeck 2000; Delouis 2001; Corbett and Farrell 2002). A second approach addresses the relative merits of shipping, notably short sea shipping, in contributing to comprehensive sustainable development strategies applied to transport systems (Giaoutzi and Nijkamp 1993; Callaghan 1998; Hilling 2001; Landaburu and Canu 2002; Saldhanha and Gray 2002; Paixao and Marlow 2002; Donnelly and Mazières 2003). Globalisation and resulting growth in intermodality underpins the comparative advantages of marine transport.

There is a general understanding that a sustainable marine industry is tributary of the environment, port systems and commercial navigation, but mostly of their respective evolution and mutual impact. For the past decade, governments have introduced a variety of rules in different sectors that constitute steps towards attaining a sustainable environment. These laws and rules increase the amount and strength of measures to protect and improve the environment. Examples of legislation include energy consumption, transport development, polluting emissions, protection of ecosystems, etc. There is an important concern on sustainability in terms of rights, obligations and responsibilities (Jenisch 1996; Davos 1998; Bergantino and O'Sullivan 1999; Ringbom 1999; Brusendorff and Ehlers 2002). All partners of maritime industry must be made responsible for the damage they cause to the environment. This can be translated by sanctions, financial obligations or withdrawal of permits. The literature acknowledges the need to elaborate and interpret complex information systems allowing the evaluation of environmental risks and the conception of forecasting models (Post and Lundin 1996; Vandermeulen 1996; Whitehead 2000; Kolb and Wacker 1995; Kageson 1999). Faced with these circumstances, marine transport operations must conform to international regulations and increasingly include an environmental impact assessment satisfying minimum standards of analysis. There has been speculation about the impact of these changes on corporate strategies, but the identification and analysis of corporate sensitivity to environmental issues, the effectiveness of international legislation for sustainable development strategies and the analysis of the emerging corporate practices in sustainable development have been absent in the academic literature.

3. Environmental Profile of the Marine Industry

Environmental conditions can complicate, postpone or prevent the activities of the maritime industry. True, the physical environment has to accept changes. But the physical geography of maritime routes combined with growth in traffic increases the risks of damage to the environment. Maritime transport has an impact on the environment. These impacts on the relation between living organisms and their biophysical milieu are generating costs: environments have been transformed, destroyed or even artificially created to such an extent that it is extremely difficult to identify a pristine reference.

Obviously, the marine industry is confronted with numerous environmental issues, problems and regulations that are related to the objectives of sustainable development. In order to understand the industry's perspective, we have built a data base on the environmental awareness of 800 ports and 120 regular shipping lines for the year 2004. The information pertaining to sustainable development was examined under 17 items. These included the role of legislation, corporate environmental concerns, mission statement, objectives, management, policy, training, programmes, projects, practices, procedures, environmental impact assessment, annual report, development plans, waste management, environmental management system, legislation, resource conservation, community service and distribution system. Data analysis has permitted to classify ports and shipping lines under six categories. This classification reveals some key diagnostic features.

First, approximately 30 per cent of the 800 ports (235/800) provided information on environmental awareness of their activities, but only 11 per cent (85/800) had an environmental management system (EMS) in operation (Figure 16.1). The best practices appear to be found in the world's busiest ports either from developed and emerging economies. There are some champions within the maritime industry whose practices are clearly at the forefront of contemporary concerns of sustainable development. At the international level, the port authorities that demonstrate the best quality of environmental leadership are in Australia, Northern Europe and West Coast of North America.

Second, 34 per cent of the 120 shipping lines (41/120) analysed provided information on the environmental impact of their activities and had an EMS in operation either in-house or certified by EMAS or ISO 14 000. There is thus a marked imbalance between port and shipping lines desire to address these environmental issues. The best practices are found among MOL and NYK in Japan, P&O Nedlloyd in the United-Kingdom and Wallenius Lines in Sweden (Figure 16.2)

Thirdly, the survey has permitted to identify 15 environmental issues preoccupying the industry. The data gives support to the emergence of a certain consensus on the choice and the importance of issues of sustainable development. Table 16.1 indicates that the top five environmental issues identified by port authorities are: water quality (25 per cent); waste disposal (21 per cent); air quality (19 per cent); habitat conservation (19 per cent); and noise (15 per cent). For shipping lines, the most important environmental issues are: air quality (44 per cent), anti-fouling paints (39 per cent), waste waters (22 per cent), ballast waters (20 per cent) and energy consumption (20 per cent). Some issues are common to port authorities and shipping lines (water quality, air quality, waste management, resource conservation, energy consumption, emergency, oil spills, anti-fouling paints, dust emission), while others are either specific to ports (noise, dredging, contaminated).

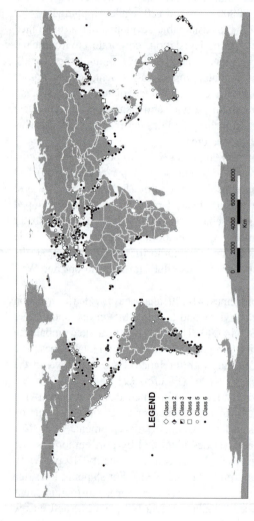

LEGEND

◇ Class 1
◈ Class 2
▧ Class 3
☐ Class 4
○ Class 5
• Class 6

Class 1: uses a certified environmental management system, mentions environmental impact of its activities, has an environmental policy, presents sustainable development objectives and publishes an annual report pertaining to sustainability

Class 2: uses a certified environmental management system, has an environmental policy, mentions environmental impact of its activities, publishes a report;

Class 3: uses a non-certified environmental management system, has an environmental policy, mentions environmental impact of its activities;

Class 4: has an environmental policy and mentions environmental impact of its activities;

Class 5: mentions environmental impact of its activities

Class 6: no information provided

Figure 16.1 Environmental profile of selected ports, 2004

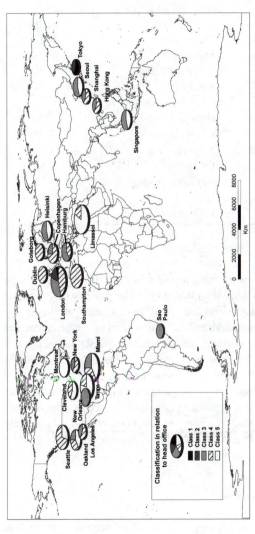

Classification in relation to head office

Class 1
Class 2
Class 3
Class 4
Class 5

Class 1: uses a certified environmental management system, mentions environmental impact of its activities, has an environmental policy, presents sustainable development objectives and publishes an annual report pertaining to sustainability

Class 2: uses a certified environmental management system, has an environmental policy, mentions environmental impact of its activities, publishes a report;

Class 3: uses a non-certified environmental management system, has an environmental policy, mentions environmental impact of its activities;

Class 4: has an environmental policy and mentions environmental impact of its activities;

Class 5: mentions environmental impact of its activities

Figure 16.2 Environmental profile of selected shipping lines, 2004

Table 16.1 Environmental issues of the maritime industry, 2004

Port issues	Frequencies (N = 800)	Shipping lines issues	Frequencies (N = 120)
Water quality	25 %	Air quality	44 %
Waste management	21 %	Anti-fouling paints	39 %
Air quality	19 %	Waste waters	22 %
Habitat conservation	19 %	Ballast waters	20 %
Noise	15 %	Energy consumption	20 %
Emergency	14 %	Waste management	15 %
Dredging	14 %	Solid waste	15 %
Stormwaters	13 %	Resource conservation	12 %
Energy consumption	11 %	Hazardous materials	10 %
Oil spills	10 %	Double hull ships	7 %
Ballast waters	9 %	Ship recycling	7 %
Dust	6 %	Oil spills	5 %
Contaminated soils	6 %	Alternative energy	5 %
Odours	4 %	Dust	2 %
Anti-fouling paints	3 %	Emergency	2 %

Port authorities and shipping lines that do not address these issues or that do not respect the order of priorities to grant to these issues will increasingly be marginalised, because these issues are integrated within the process of economic competitiveness. Already, substandard ships are not allowed to navigate in several regions of the world, while certain inland and coastal waterways, considered too polluted, are abandoned by marine carriers. Environmental legislation is placing increasing restrictions on marine transport activity and the statutory authorities have to respond by developing management systems enabling them to meet these regulatory requirements. Port authorities or shipping companies suffering trade disadvantages as a result of their governments' decisions to accept international environmental regulations (i.e. MARPOL Conventions, KYOTO Protocol) are likely to take retaliatory actions against ports and carriers of non-signatory countries in order to maintain certain equity in terms of competition.

4. Maritime Environmental Legislation

The marine industry is eminently international in terms of property, investment provisions, types of activities and volume of traffic. Marine transport implies global linkages requiring international agreements on shipping lanes and transit routes, ports of call and commercial practices. Contemporary environmental legislation reveals that different international regulations have been adopted on a wide range of environmental issues within the context of sustainable development.

Table 16.2 Selected environmental issues of international marine conventions, 2004

ISSUES COMMON TO THE MARINE INDUSTRY		ISSUES SPECIFIC TO PORTS		ISSUES SPECIFIC TO MARINE CARRIERS	
Issue	Convention	Issue	Convention	Issue	Convention
Water quality	MARPOL 73/78 Annex 2 MARPOL 73/78 Annex 4 IMO Resolution A.868(20) (1997) UNEP (GPA)	**Noise**	KYOTO Protocol MONTREAL Protocol MARPOL 73/78 Annex 6	**Ship recycling**	Basel Convention 1992 IMO A.962(23)
Air quality	KYOTO Protocol MONTREAL Protocol MARPOL 73/78 Annex 6	**Odours**	KYOTO Protocol MONTREAL Protocol MARPOL 73/78 Annex 6	**Hazardous goods**	MARPOL 73/78 Annex 2, 3 IMDG Code
		Dredging	London Convention 1972		
Waste management	MARPOL 73/78 Annex 5	**Contaminated soils**	UNEP FAO World Soil Charter, 1981 Rio Convention 1992 Bonn Memorandum 1999		
Resource conservation	Ramsar, 1971; World Heritage Convention 1972; Washington Convention 1973; Bonn Convention 1979; Rio Convention 1992				
Energy consumption	KYOTO Protocol IEP Chap. 7 WCRE, 2004				
Emergency	ISM Code ISPS SOLAS MARPOL 73/78 Annex 1, 2, 3, 5				
Oil spills	MARPOL 73/78 Annex 1				
Anti-fouling paints	IMO AFS/Conf/36				
Dust	MARPOL 73/78 Annex 2, 3				

Pursuant to the above analysis, consideration has been given to the relationship between environmental issues identified by the marine industry and international legislation. For each issue, we have sought the corresponding international convention, protocol, programme, agreement, charter or rule (Table 16.2). The quality of the international legislative framework was assessed in terms of issue covered, measurement standards, performance indicators and enforcement authority.

First, all the issues identified by the industry are subject to some form of international agreement. The International Maritime Organization (IMO) is the main international organisation responsible for providing mechanisms for intergovernmental cooperation concerning regulations and practices related to all technical aspects affecting international shipping including prevention and control of marine pollution from ships. The analysis raises three remarks. A convention can cover more than one issue. Noise and odours are integrated within the larger context of air quality. Some issues are covered by more than one convention. The MARPOL Convention 73/78 Annex 2 and 3 addresses the issues of emergency, dust emission and hazardous goods. The content of a convention can be determined by other conventions. The IMO procedures on ship recycling makes reference to the Basel Convention on transboundary waste and International Labour Office standards on safety and health at work.

Second, national data on the results of port and shipping activities to meet international environmental obligations are often incomplete, inaccurate or doubtful. Methodologies and guidelines are characterised by vague procedures. There are often no homogenous, exploitable and credible units of measurement that are time referenced with a view to observe the evolution and comparison by sector or at different geographical scales. Data requested do not permit the environmental impacts of transport activities to be quantified continuously. Objectives are often defined in broad terms that do not represent benchmarks for defining strategies of environmental sustainability in different sectors or at different levels. In this context, it becomes extremely difficult to evaluate the extent to which countries are meeting their international environmental obligations (USGAO 1996).

Third, monitoring activities seek to evaluate the compliance of signatory countries with international conventions. Frequent assessments are essential to control the respect of transport operations to the existing environmental legislation. There is a need to establish the minimum standards of quality that are sought from transport operations. These standards must permit to specify the state of environmental quality that is sought and must express the specific environmental status with regards to water, air, soil and all the other components of the physical environment within a precise geographical area. The standards clarify the level of pollution or other impacts that can be supported by people and the environment without any risks. Monitoring activities determine the extent to which governments have integrated procedural compliance of their international commitments into regulations within their respective national legal system. As a result, most monitoring is based on information provided by individual parties to an international agreement. States have shown to be extremely reluctant in compromising their national sovereignty by allowing environmental monitoring to be undertaken by an independent and foreign expertise (Samaan 1993).

Fourth, there are no centralised legislative organisations having the authority or competency to enforce international environmental agreements. International convention on environmental protection provides few mechanisms to enforce environmental legislation. Those that possess such mechanisms can use them rarely or very inefficiently. Decisions by organisations responsible of international treaty on the environment must obtain the consensus of signatory countries, thus giving to each member a right of veto (Ardia 1998). The IMO has no power to enforce the conventions that it help creates. Only contracting governments can enforce the provisions of IMO conventions. Other international organisations only have jurisdictions beyond the 200 nautical miles exclusive economic zones of coastal nations. These agencies often have limited financial resources to fulfil their monitoring responsibilities and do not have the enforcement authority over navigable areas showing the highest traffic density.

5. Enforcement Mechanisms

The enforcement of international environmental conventions is the responsibility of signatory countries or private bodies that can fulfil their obligations through several programmes including control imposed by a coastal state, by a ship's flag state, by a port state or by the industry self regulation.

Coastal State Control

Countries with any amount of coastline are afforded rights under UNCLOS, albeit with some limitations.[1] Countries are permitted to take legal action against any ships that pollute within their territorial seas or EEZs (Exclusive Economic Zones). Prosecution can be very complex as it can involve national and international laws. While certain national laws may raise more constraints than international regulations, evidence shows that nation-states have typically to adjust discharge and concentration standards with those agreed upon internationally. These quantities may be superior to authorised national levels. Coastal states must accept and abide by standards weaker than desired if the IMO agrees to them. Prosecution of those who violate the rules may also become difficult as some pollution incidents are caused by national ships or discharges may take place in open waters where identifying the source is almost impossible except in the case of very important spills.

Flag State Control

Countries that have signed on to the IMO conventions are required to enforce the controls of the conventions on ships which bear their flag. This results in different countries enforcing requirements with varied intensity, and ultimately results in ships registering under a flag of convenience less sensitive to environmental protection, or under a country that is not a party to these conventions. As many ships can register

---

1   See http://www.oceanlaw.net/texts/losc5.htm

in nearly any country, there are a high number of ships registered under these flags of convenience to avoid enforcement from their home countries. They also take advantage of foreign legislation with more lenient labour, safety and fiscal laws. The emergence of port state control is seen as one possible solution to the gaps created by weak enforcement from some flag states.

Port State Control

This form of control is given to port authorities within states that are signatories to the various IMO conventions. The growing use of Port State Control is a reaction by states wishing to protect their waters and ecosystems from substandard ships flying under flags of convenience. Each port authority has the right to inspect any ship for IMO compliance, regardless of their flag, so long as they voluntarily enter that port. While there are currently no global conventions on port state control, many regional agreements have been made to ensure port states are actually exercising their powers within this area.[2]

The main guidelines governing Port State Control include: 1) the criteria required to participate in the process; 2) the inspection of a minimum percentage of vessels entering in ports participating in these regional agreements; 3) the establishment of standards for inspection, detention, and reporting; 4) the development of a ship inspection database; 5) the standardisation of inspection procedures for inspectors; and 6) the regular publication of inspection and detention statistics in the region.[3] The regional approach on these matters has evolved to prevent the development of ports of convenience, where certain port authorities might be more indulgent to substandard ships. These international agreements and MOUs (Memoranda of Understanding) are effective in ensuring compliance in countries that are signatories to the regional efforts. Substandard ships can circulate in areas where there is a lower likelihood of inspection. These ships are increasingly being marginalised and congregate in regions located outside the main maritime trade routes.

Industry Self-regulation

Within the shipping industry there are many bodies that help to enforce international commitments and to insure standards in the daily operations of ports and ships. These industry regulators include the International Chamber of Shipping (ICS),[4] the International Association of Independent Tanker Owners (INTERTANKO),[5] the International Tanker Owners Pollution Federation (ITOPF),[6] the International Group of Protection and Indemnity (P & I) Clubs,[7] the International Association of

---

2   See http://www.imo.org/InfoResource/mainframe.asp?topic_id=406&doc_id=1079
3   See http://www.tc.gc.ca/medias/documents/b02-M016.htm
4   See http://www.marisec.org/
5   See http://www.intertanko.com
6   See http://www.itopf.com
7   See http://www.american-club.com

Classification Societies (IACS)[8] and the Baltic and International Maritime Council (BIMCO).[9] There have been some successes through self-regulation, especially in the increasing strictness for meeting standards required by P & I Clubs and classification societies. Most P & I Clubs are acting out of self-interest to avoid paying for accidents and spills, while classification societies are often motivated to enhance the shipping industry's image, and maintain their own company's integrity. This system of self-regulation is not without serious limitations, as ships which are denied certification by one company may obtain it through another. This is the case with the sinking of the *Erika* in 1999, when the classification society RINA certified the corroded ship, after it was refused by Bureau Veritas.

6. Market Approach to Sustainable Development

International legislation suggests that the environment has become a factor of changes in terms of obligations, responsibilities and competitiveness. This approach recognises the leadership of the international community and governments in focusing efforts on international regulations and their implementation. However, this approach has limitations. Evidence demonstrates that the establishment of international regulations is a slow and contentious process. This suggests that responsibilities of sustainable development blueprint increasingly rest with the marine transport operators that have to develop expertise in environmental management. Given the industry's concern over financial sustainability, the most important challenge for the industry is to implement environmentally sustainable transport within competitive market structures.

In order to measure the extent to which the practices of sustainable development affect the competitiveness of the maritime industry, evidence were drawn from detailed fieldwork with supporting information from trade journals, port and shipping lines annual records and maritime consultants' reports. In depth interviews were conducted in Western Europe, North America and East Asia with members of the industry, governments, research institutes and insurance companies. We wanted to understand the practices in the industry, the environmental management issues, the challenges and the lessons learnt, the economic impact and to relate commercial standards to sustainable development issues that are reshaping the maritime transport industry.

Practices of environmentally sustainable transport increasingly affect the competitiveness of the transport industry around the world. Our analysis suggests that environmental performance has been integrated in the traditional economic considerations of transport enterprises.

- Credit programmes charging different interest rates are being implemented in relation to environmental performance.
- Insurance premiums are being fixed according to green certification.

---

8   See http://www.iacs.org.uk
9   See http://www.bimco.dk

- Environmental components are accounted in the evolution of share values for firms registered in the stock market.
- Green technologies permit firms to achieve important savings.
- Environmental management expertise can be harnessed to become a statutory and even a commercial advantage.
- Legal and compensation costs related to transport project development have an influence in global transactions of mergers and acquisition.

7. Discussions

The research findings provide insights on corporate perspective of sustainable development. Three broad elements deserve discussions. First, the globalisation of markets has been underpinned by the expansion of the world's sea line connections and the importance of hub ports within global logistics networks. The environment plays a constraining effect on the marine industry and rapid technological and scientific progress has permitted to overcome the environment. But evidence shows that the functioning of global trade requires careful consideration of climate, water, air, soil and biodiversity as resources. There is an emerging consensus in the marine industry concerning the typology of environmental issues and impacts. The international overview of sustainable development practices does not make distinctions between varied geographical conditions. Sustainability is global in scope.

Second, environmental regulations are increasing in number and strength. Evidence demonstrates the existence of complex systems of differential charging for environmental purposes (harbour fees, waste management, ballast waters, noise pollution, etc.) that address operations of ships and ports and lead shippers to give emphasis towards sustainability. There is a wide range of responses to environmental legislation. But the practices of sustainable development constitute a sector whose performance increasingly affects the competitiveness of the maritime industry. No longer can port authorities or shipping lines search for pollution permits. They must comply with local/international regulations, factor environmental costs into their business and integrate environmental performance in corporate strategies.

Third, environmental sustainability represents a growing area of responsibility for transport companies, one that is forcing them to acquire expertise in environmental management. The adoption of measures of sustainable development is henceforth considered necessary by the industry in order to maintain its competitiveness both for port and shipping systems. The successes of the policies that are being canvassed towards sustainability largely depend on the privately-owned activities of commercial carriers and terminal operators that are also concerned with financial sustainability. Terminal operators and shipping companies must evaluate the efforts undertaken in terms of resources dedicated to the environment, measure performance over time and communicate their results to the shareholders, local communities and governments. Market economy principles are integrated within environmental management. The increasing links between environmental performance and industry's competition suggest that bottom-up approach giving the operators the assessing rights may be more appropriate than top-down approach in reducing negative environmental externalities.

8. Conclusion

The main dilemma in environmental protection is the conflict between top-down and bottom-up approach. Top-down decision-making recognises public leadership of governments and institutions in focusing efforts on international regulations and their implementation. Bottom-up decision-making acknowledges the role of the business communities in reducing the environmental impact of their activities based on their analysis of operating conditions, environmental assessment, established priorities and organisational capabilities. This study has examined corporate perspective on sustainable development. Arguably, as representative of the private sector, the analysis of change pertaining to sustainable development would not tell as much as state-owned companies would about issues and impact of operations on the environment. This is a misleading proposition as this study focuses on the corporate environmental concerns and strategies has demonstrated. Private ownership does not lead to decision making processes that are radically different from the public sector. The tactics driven by liberalisation and globalisation have changed corporate strategies in such a way that they are integrating sustainability as a competitive asset. This is reflected in their typology of environmental issues and selected corporate actions.

Given the important role that governments can play in the sustainable development process of the maritime industry, efforts in the context of top-down approach must focus on: 1) developing regulation framework concomitant to the main environmental issues of the maritime industry found at the international level; 2) determining issues that would increase the performance of the maritime industry; and 3) supporting corporate leaderships playing a key role in the success of sustainable development practices.

The business community prefers to convince public authorities that their voluntary initiatives based on market mechanisms prove to be successful in implementing effective environmental management practices. Private corporate initiatives can prevent stringent legislation while concomitantly providing the business community the required flexibility in implementing sustainable development practices.

As the above analysis suggests, a key feature facing both government and industry in implementing environmental management consists in maintaining a balance between the environmental, legislative and commercial dimensions of sustainability. Evaluating the trade-off is one of the main challenges facing decision makers.

Acknowledgements

The authors wish to express appreciation for research support from the Québec Ministry of Transport.

References

Abood. K.A. and Metzger. S.G. (2001), 'Green Ports: Aquatic Impact Avoidance, Minimization and Mitigation for Port Development', in Collins (ed.) *Ports 2001 Conference Proceedings*.

Ahlander, K. and Rehling, C. (1999), 'Predator or Prey?', *Containerisation International* 1, 51–3.

Airriess, C.A. (2001a) 'Regional Production, Information-Communication Technology, and the Developmental State: the Rise of Singapore as a Global Container Hub', *Geoforum* 32:2, 235–54.

Airriess, C.A. (2001b), 'The Regionalization of Hutchison Port Holdings in Mainland China', *Journal of Transport Geography* 9, 267–78.

Alphaliner BRS Shipbrokers Group (2005), *Cellular Fleet*, electronic format <http//: www.alphaliner.com>, accessed 5 Oct 2005.

Amato, D. (1999), 'Port Planning and Port City Relations', *The Dock and Harbour Authority* 7:12, 45–8.

American Association of Port Authorities (2005) Statistics available from website <http://www.aapa-ports.org>

Amromin, E. et al. (2002), 'Non-Local Impact of Large-Scale Engineering in Harbors and Gulfs on the Environment', *Ocean Engineering*, 29:7, 739–52.

Appelbaum, R. (2004), *Commodity Chains and Economic Development: One and a Half Proposals for Spatially-Oriented Research*, CSISS/IROWS Specialist Meeting, 7–8 Feb. 2004.

Ardia, D.S. (1998), 'Does the Emperor Have no Clothes? Enforcement of International Laws Protecting the Marine Environment', *Michigan Journal of International Law*, 19, 497–567.

Arkin, T. (2005), *An Examination of the Impact of Infrastructure Provision and Management of the Port of Durban's Car Terminal has had upon the KwaZulu-Natal Auto Industry*. Draft unpublished MA Thesis, School of Development Studies, UKZN.

Armistead, C.G. and Mapes, J. (1993), 'The Impact of Supply Chain Integration on Operating Performance', *Logistics Information Management* 6:4, 9–14.

Armstrong, J. and Overton, T. (1977), 'Estimating Non-response Bias in Mail Surveys', *Journal of Marketing Research* 14:3, 396–402.

Ashar, A. (1999), '2020 Vision', *Containerisation International*, December, 57–61.

Ashar, A. (2000), '2020 Vision', *Containerisation International*, January: 35–9.

Ashley, A. (2006), 'Thinking Out of the Box; Delivering the Goods: How HPH Supports the Global Supply Chain', *Sphere* 15, 16–21.

Atlantic Road and Traffic Management (2003) *Final Report: Downtown Halifax Heavy Truck License Plate Study*. Prepared for Halifax Regional Municipality, Sep 2003.

Baets, W. (1992), 'Aligning Information Systems with Business Strategy', *Journal of Strategic Information Systems* 1:4, 205–13.

Baird, A.J. (1996), 'Containerisation and the Decline of the Upstream Urban Port in Europe', *Maritime Policy & Management* 23:2, 145–56.

Baird, A.J. (2002), 'Privatisation Trends at the World's Top-100 Container Ports', Maritime Policy & Management 29:3, 271–84.

Baird, A.J. (2003), 'Global Strategic Management in Liner Container Shipping'. Presentation at *23rd IAPA World Port Conference*. Durban, 24–30 May 2003.

Baltazar, R. and Brooks, M.R. (2001), 'The Governance of Port Devolution: A Tale of Two Countries', in Park *et al.* (eds) WCTR Conference Proceedings.

Banga, I. (1992), *Ports and their Hinterlands in India 1700–1950* (New Delhi: Manohar).

Banister, D. (1995), *Transport and Urban development* (Oxford: Alexandrine Press).

Banister, D. and Berechman, J. (1993), *Transport in a Unified Europe: Policies and Challenges* (London: Elsevier Science Publishers).

Barke, M. (1986), *Transport and Trade* (Edinburgh: Oliver & Boyd).

Barnes, J. *et al.* (2004), 'Industrial Policy in Developing Economies: Developing Dynamic Comparative Advantage in the South African Automobile Sector', *Competition and Change* 8:2, 153–72.

Barnes, J. (2005) *Personal Communication*. Benchmarking and Manufacturing Analysts.

Barnes, J. and Johnson, J. (2004), *Sectoral Overview of the Automotive Industry in the eThekwini Municipality and Broader KZN Province*. Unpublished research note produced for eThekwini Municipality by B&M Analysts, 2004.

Barnes, J. and Morris, M. (2004), 'The German Connection: Shifting Hegemony in the Political Economy of the South African Automotive Industry', *Industrial and Corporate Change* 13:5, 789–814.

Bastié, J. and Dezert, B. (1980), *L'Espace Urbain* (Paris: Masson).

Basu, D.K. (1985), *The Rise and Growth of the Colonial Port Cities in Asia* (Lanham: University of California).

Baudouin, T. and Collin, M. (1996), 'The Revival of France's Port Cities', *Tijdschrift voor economische en sociale geografie* 87:4, 342–7.

Beddow, M. (2005), 'Mediterranean Vintage', *Containerisation International* February, 36–9.

Benacchio, M. *et al.* (2001), 'On the Economic Impact of Ports: Local vs. National Costs and Benefits', in Park *et al.* (eds) *WCTR Conference Proceedings*.

Bergantino, A. and Veenstra, A.W. (2001), 'Networks in Liner Shipping - Interconnection and Coordination', in Park et al. (eds).

Bergantino, A.S. and O'Sullivan, P. (1999), 'Flagging out and International Registries: Main Development and Policy Issues', *International Journal of Transport Economics* 26:3, 447–72.

Bichou, K. and Gray, R. (2004), 'A Logistics and Supply Chain Management Approach to Port Performance Measurement', *Maritime Policy & Management* 31:1, 47–67.

Bird, J. (1963), *The Major Seaports of the United Kingdom* (London: Hutchinson of London).

Bird, J. (1973), 'Of Central Places, Cities and Seaports', *Geography* 58, 105–18.

Bird, J. (1977), *Centrality and Cities* (London: Routledge Direct Editions).

Blomme, J. (2005), 'Northern Range Port Strategy', in Leggate, Morvillo and Mc Conville (eds).

Boile, M. *et al.* (2006), 'Empty Marine Container Management: Addressing Locally a Global Problem'. Presentation at TRB Annual Meeting, Washington, DC. Paper # 06–2147.

Bonacich, E. (2004), 'Labor and Global Logistics Revolution' Presentation at *Workshop of Time-mapping Globalization in the World-System*, Riverside, CA, 7–8 Feb. 2004.

Borrone, L.C. (2005), 'Sparking the Globalize Trade and Transportation Connection', *Transportation Research Record (TRB)* 1906, 5–16.

Bowersox, D.J. and Daugherty, P.J. (1995), 'Logistics Paradigms: The Impact of Information Technologies', *Journal of Business Logistics* 16:1, 65–80.

Bowersox, D.J. *et al.* (2000), 'Ten Mega-trends that will Revolutionize Supply Chain Logistics', *Journal of Business Logistics* 21:2, 1–16.

Boyer, J.C. and Vigarié, A. (1982), 'Les Ports et L'Organisation Urbaine et Régionale', *Bulletin de l'Association des Géographes Français* 487, 159–82.

Braudel, F. (1979), *Civilisation Matérielle, Économie et Capitalisme* (Paris: Armand Colin).

Bravard, J.P. *et al.* (2000), 'Principles of Engineering Geomorphology for Managing Channel Erosion and Bedload Transport, Examples from French Rivers', *Geomorphology* 31, 1–4, 291–311.

Brenner, A. *et al.* (2006) *Wal-Mart Stores, Inc.*. Report for International Conference on Global Companies – Global Unions – Global Research – Global Campaigns, organized by School of Industrial and Labor Relations, Cornell University New York, NY, USA 9–11 Feb. 2006.

Brewer, A. *et al.* (eds.) (2001) *Handbook on Logistics and Supply Chain Management* (Oxford: Pergamon Press,).

Brinkhoff, T. (2006), *Cities and Agglomerations of the World* <http://www. citypopulation.de/ cities.html>

Bristow, R. and Zhao, X. (1995), 'Some Consequences and Impacts of Port Development – Hong Kong case', *GeoJournal* 37:4, 525–36. From Bristow and Xiaobin to Bristow and Zhao.

Brocard, M. (1994), 'Deux Villes Frontières Portuaires: Le Havre et Southampton', *La Revue d'Ici* 11, 8–12.

Brocard, M. *et al.* (1995a), 'Les Réseaux de Circulation Maritime', *Mappemonde* 1, 23–8.

Brocard, M. *et al.* (1995b), 'Le Chorotype de L'Estuaire Européen' *Mappemonde* 3, 6.

Broeze, F. (1989), *Brides of the Sea: Port cities of Asia from the 16th–20th Centuries* (Honolulu: University of Hawaii Press).

Broeze, F. (1997), *Gateways of Asia: Port Cities of Asia in the 13th–20th Centuries* (London and New York: Kegan Paul International).

Brooks, M.R. and Cullinane, K. (eds) *Devolution, Port Governance and Port Performance* (Oxford: Elsevier).

Brunet, R. (1997), 'Villes Moyennes: Point de Vue de Géographe', in Commerçon and Goujon (eds) 13–25.

Brunn, S.D. and Williams, J.F. (1983), *Cities of the World: World Regional Urban Development* (New York: Harper and Row Series in Geography).

Brusendorff, A.C. and Ehlers, P. (2002), 'The HELCOM Copenhagen Declaration: A Regional Environmental Approach for Safer Shipping', *International Journal of Marine and Coastal Law* 17:3, 351–95.

Callaghan, G. (1998), 'Encouraging Intermodality: Perceptions of Road and Maritime Transport', *Proceedings of the Chartered Institute of Transport* 7:3, 44–56.

Carbone, V. and de Martino, M. (2003), 'The Changing Role of Ports in Supply Chain Management: an Empirical Analysis', *Maritime Policy and Management* 30:4, 305–20.

Carbone, V. and Stone, M. (2005), 'Growth and Relational Strategies Used by the European Logistics Service Providers: Rationale and Outcomes', *Transport Research, Part E*, 41, 495–510.

Cargo Systems (2000), 'Boosting the Capacity', *Cargo Systems* December 2000, 25–7.

Cargo Systems (2001), 'Automatic for the Terminals', *Cargo Systems* May 2001, 21–4.

Cargo Systems (2005), *The World's Top-100 Container Ports*. (London: Cargo Systems - Supplement).

Cariou, P. (2001), 'Vertical Integration within the Logistic Chain: Does Regulation Play Rational? The Case for Dedicated Container Terminals', *Transporti Europei* 7, 37–41.

Carmona, M. (ed.) (2003a), *Globalization and City Ports, Vol. 9: the Response of City Ports in the Northern Hemisphere* (Delft: Delft University Press).

Carmona, M. (ed.) (2003b), Globalization and City Ports, Vol. 10: the Response of City Ports in the Southern Hemisphere (Delft: Delft University Press).

Carr, A.S. and Pearson, J.N. (1999), 'Strategically Managed Buyer – Supplier Relationships and Performance Outcomes', *Journal of Operations Management* 17, 497–519.

Cazzaniga Francesetti, D. and Foschi, A.D. (2002a), 'Mediterranean versus Northern Range Ports. Why Do Italian Containers Still Prefer Routing via the Northern Range Ports? Advice for a New Policy', *IAME Conference Proceedings*.

Cazzaniga Francesetti, D. and Foschi, A.D. (2002b), 'The Impact of Hub and Spokes Networks in the Mediterranean Peculiarity', IAME.

Chaline, C. (1994), *Ces Ports qui Créèrent des Villes* (Paris: L'Harmattan).

Chang, S.E. (2000), 'Disasters and Transport Systems: Loss, Recovery and Competition at the Port of Kobe after the 1995 Earthquake', *Journal of Transport Geography* 8:1, 53–65.

Chang, Y. T. (2003), 'Korea's Strategic Plan to be Northeast Asia's Logistics Hub: Towards the Pentaport Approach', *Korea Observer* 34:3, 437–60.

Chapman, G.P. *et al.* (eds) (2000), *Urban Growth and Development in Asia*, Vol.2 (Aldershot: Ashgate).

Charlier, J.J. and Ridolfi, G. (1994), 'Intermodal Transportation in Europe', *Maritime Policy Management* 21: 3, 237–50.

Chopra, S. and Meindl, P. (2001), *Supply Chain Management: Strategy, Planning, and Operation* (Upper Saddle River, N.J.: Prentice Hall).

Christopher, M. and Lee, H.L. (2001), 'Supply Chain Confidence – The Key to Effective Supply Chains through Improved Visibility and Reliability', *Global Trade Management Conference*, Vestera, Inc.

Christopher, M.G. (1998), *Logistics and Supply Chain Management: Strategies for Reducing Costs and Improving Services* (London: Financial Time Pitman Publishing).

Chu, C.Y. and Huang, W.C. (2005), 'Determining Container Terminal Capacity on the Basis of an Adopted Yard Handling System', *Journal of Transport Reviews* 25:2, 181–99.

Churchill, Jr. G.A. (1979), 'A Paradigm for Developing Better Measures of Marketing Constructs', *Journal of Marketing Research* 16, 64–73.

City of Vancouver (2005), *Clark/Knight Corridor Plan*, Administrative Report from General Manager of Engineering Services and Director – City Plans to Standing Committee on Transportation and Traffic, 15 Mar. 2005.

CLM (2000), *What It's All About* (Oak Brook, IL: Council of Logistics Management).

Coe, N.M. *et al.* (2004), 'Globalizing Regional Development: A Global Production Networks Perspective', *Transactions of the Institute of British Geographers* 29, 468–84.

Collins (ed.) (2001) *Proceedings of the Conference, Ports 2001*. Norfolk. Virginia Port Authority, Naval Facilities Engineering Command, Norfolk, Virginia, 29 Apr.–2 May 2001.

Commerçon, N. and Goujon, P. (eds) (1997) *Villes Moyennes: Espaces, Société, Patrimoine* (Lyon: Presses Universitaires de Lyon).

Comtois, C. *et al.* (1997), 'Political Issues in Inland Waterways Port Development: Prospects for Regionalization', *Transport Policy* 4, 257–65.

Container Management (2004), 'GTOs: The Rise of the Partnership', *Container Management* October, 47–49.

Containerisation International (2005), 'Offshore Container Terminal Planned for the Port of Mumbai', *Containerisation International* 1: 27.

Containerisation International (2006), *Containerisation International Online* <http://www.ci-online.co.uk/>, accessed 12 Oct. 2006.

Containerisation International Yearbook (various years) London: National Magazine Co.

Corbett, J.J. and Farrell, A. (2002), 'Mitigating Air Pollution Impacts of Passenger Ferries', *Transportation Research Part D: Transport and Environment* 7:3, 197–211.

Corbett, J.J. and Fischbeck, P.S. (2000), 'Emissions from Waterborne Commerce Vessels in United States Continental and Inland Waterways', *Environmental Science and Technology* 34:15, 3254–60.

Cox, A. (1997), *Business Success: a Way of Thinking about Strategy, Critical Supply Chain Assets and Operational Best Practice* (Boston: Earlsgate).

Cox, A. (1999), 'A research Agenda for supply chain thinking', *Supply Chain Management: An international journal* 4:4, 209–11.

Cox, A. *et al.* (2002), *Supply Chains, Markets and Power: Mapping Supplier and Buyer Power Regimes* (London: Routledge).

Croom, S. *et al.* (2000), 'Supply Chain Management: An Analytical Framework for Critical Literature Review', *European Journal of Purchasing & Supply Management* 6, 67–83.

Cullinane, K. and Khanna, M. (2000), 'Economies of Scale in Large Containerships: Optimal Size and Geographical Implications', *Journal of Transport Geography* 8, 181–95.

Cullinane, K. and Song, D. (eds) (2007) *Asian Container Ports* (Basingstoke: Palgrave Macmillian).

Cullinane, K. *et al.* (2002), 'A Stochastic Frontier Model of the Efficiency of Major Container Terminals in Asia: Assessing the Influence of Administrative and Ownership Structures', *Transportation Research A* 36, 743–62.

Cullinane, K.P.B. *et al.* (2004,) 'Container Terminal Development in Mainland China and its Impact on the Competitiveness of the Port of Hong Kong', *Transport Reviews* 2004 14:1, 33–56.

Damas, P. (2005), 'Shanghai Grapples Extreme Growth', *American Shipper* 5:90–94.

Damas, P. and Gillis, C. (2005), 'Pacific Trade Frets over U.S. Backups', *American Shipper* 5, 25–6.

Davenport, T.H. (1993), *Process Innovation, Reengineering Work through Information Technology* (Cambridge, MA: Harvard Business School Press).

Davies, C.H. (1983) 'Regional Port Impact Studies: A Critique and Suggested Methodology', *Transportation Journal* 23:1, 61–71.

Davies, H. *et al.* (1995), 'The Benefits of "Guanxi"', *Industrial Marketing Management* 24: 207–14.

Davos, C.A. (1998), 'Sustaining Co-operation for Coastal Sustainability', *Journal of Environmental Management* 52:4, 379–87.

De Langen P.W. (2001), 'A Framework for Analysing Seaport Clusters', in Park *et al.* (eds).

De Langen, P. (2004), 'Analyzing the Performance of Seaport Clusters', in Pinder and Slack (eds) 82–98.

De Martino, M. and Morvillo, A. (2005), 'A Logistics Integration for the Development of the National and Local Economic System: The Case of the Port of Naples', *Proceedings of Logistics and Research Network*, 7–9 Sep. 2005, Plymouth. UK, Logistics Research Network, CILT, 125–130pp.

De Souza, G.A. et al. (2003), 'Liner Shipping Companies and Terminal Operators: Internationalization or Globalization?', *Maritime Economics & Logistics* 5, 393–412.

Debrie J (2004), 'Hinterland Connections and Trans-European Networks' Evolution: the case of South-Western Europe'. Conference Paper 531, WCTR Society.

Decker, N. (2003), 'IT is the Key', *Containerisation International* January 2003, 44–5.

Delouis, A. (2001), 'Sédiments et Navigation en Estuaire', *La Houille Blanche* 8, 62–7.

Dicken, P. (1998), *Global Shift: Transforming the World Economy*, 3rd Edition (New York and London: Guilford Press).

Dicken, P. (2003). *Global Shift: Reshaping the Global Economic Map in the 21st Century*, 4th Edition (New York: Guildford).

Dogan, M. (1988), 'Giant Cities as Maritime Gateways', in Dogan and Kasarda (eds), 30–55.

Dogan, M. and Kasarda, J.D. (eds) (1988), *The Metropolis Era,* Vol.1 (London: SAGE).

Dollfuss, O. *et al.* (1999), 'Trois ou Quatre Choses que la Mondialisation Dit à la Géographie', *L'Espace Géographique* 1, 1–11.

Donnelly, A. and Mazières, J. (2003), *Short Sea Shipping: A Viable Alternative to Overland Transport* <http//:www.amrie.org/docs/shortsea.htm>, accessed 15 Oct. 2004.

Dooms, M., Verbeke, A. (2006), 'An Integrative Framework for Long-term Strategic Seaport Planning: An Application to the Port of Antwerp, in Notteboom (ed.), 173–92.

Drewry (2000), *Mediterranean Container Ports and Shipping. Traffic Growth versus Terminal Expansion - an Impossible Balancing Act?* (London: Drewry Shipping Consultants).

Drewry (2001–2005), *Annual Container Market Review and Forecast* (London: Drewry Shipping Consultants).

Drewry (2003–2006), *Annual Review of Global Container Terminal Operators* (London: Drewry Shipping Consultants).

Drewry (2003), *Global Container Terminals* (London: Drewry Shipping Consultants).

Drewry (2004), *The Drewry Container Market Quarterly*, 5, 2nd Edition (London: Drewry Shipping Consultants).

Drewry, Container and Port Division (2005), *Global Port Congestion – No Quick Fix* (Hamburg: HypoVereinsbank AG).

Ducruet, C. (2003), 'The Trans-scalar Development of Transportation Hubs', *Gyeongsang Nonjib* 18: 2, 171–99.

Ducruet, C. (2004a), 'Comparing European and East Asian port cities: Are Global Databases Relevant Sources for Research?', *Gyeongsang Nonjib* 17:2, 139–59.

Ducruet, C. (2004b), *Port Cities, Laboratories of Globalisation*, unpublished dissertation in geography, Le Havre University.

Ducruet, C. (2005), 'Approche Comparée du Développement des Villes-ports à L'Échelle Mondiale: Problèmes Théoriques et Méthodologiques', *Cahiers Scientifiques du Transport* 48, 59–79.

Ducruet, C. and Jeong, O. (2005), *European port-city interface and its Asian application*, Korea Research Institute for Human Settlements, Research Report 17, Anyang, Korea.

Ducruet, C. *et al.* (2005), 'Air-sea Linkages in European Port Cities', in Fredouet and Rimmer (eds).

Dullaert, W. *et al.* (eds) (2003), *Across the Border: Building upon a Quarter of Century of Transport Research in the Benelux* (Antwerp: De Boeck).

Durand, M.F. *et al.* (1993), *Le Monde Espaces et Systèmes* (Paris: Dalloz).

Durvasula, S. et al. (2002), 'Understanding the Interfaces: How Ocean Freight Shipping Lines can Maximize Satisfaction', Industrial Marketing Management 31, 491–504.

Dussauge, P. and Garrette, B. (1999), *Cooperative Strategy: Competing Successfully Through Strategic Alliances* (Chichester: Wiley).

ECMT (2001), *Land Access to Sea Ports, Round Table 113* (Paris: Economic Research Centre ECMT-OECD).

Eliot, M.E. (ed.) (1974) *Transportation Geography: Comments and Readings* (New York: McGraw Hill).

Ellram, L.M. (1991), 'The Industrial Organization Perspective', *International Journal of Physical Distribution and Logistics Management* 21:1, 13–22.

Evangelista, P. (2002), 'Information and Communication Technologies: A Key Factor in Freight Transport and Logistics', in Morvillo and Ferrara (eds), 15–36.

Evangelista, P. *et al.* (2001), 'Liner Shipping Strategies for Supply Chain Management', in Park *et al.* (eds).

Evangelista P. and Morvillo, A. (2000), 'Cooperative Strategies in International and Italian Liner Shipping', *International Journal of Maritime Economics (IJME)* 2, 1–17.

Fabbe-Costes, N. (2002), 'Evaluer la Création de Valeur du Supply Chain Management', *Logistique & Management* 10:1, 29–36.

Fawcett, J.A. and Marcus, H.S. (1991) 'Are Port Growth and Coastal Zone Management Compatible?' *Coastal Management* 19, 275–95.

Ferrari, C. and Benacchio, M. (2000), 'Market Structure in Container Terminal Operators and Port Services', unpublished paper, *International Association of Maritime Economists Annual Meeting*, Naples, 13–15 Sep., 10pp.

Ferrari, C. *et al.* (2006), 'Southern European Ports and the Spatial Distribution of EDCs', *Maritime Economics & Logistics*, special issue 'Maritime Logistics and Global Supply Chains' 8:1, 60–81.

Finney, N. and Young, D. (1995), 'Environmental Zoning Restrictions on Port Activities and Development', *Maritime Policy and Management* 22:4, 319–29.

Fisher, Marshall L. (1997) 'What is the Right Supply Chain for Your Product?' *Harvard Business Review* 75:2, 105–16.

Fleming, D.K. and Hayuth, Y. (1994), 'Spatial Characteristics of Transportation Hubs: Centrality and Intermediacy', *Journal of Transport Geography* 2:1, 3–18.

Forrester, J.W. (1961), *Industrial Dynamics* (New York: Wiley).

Fossey, J. (1998), 'Terminal Overdrive', *Containerisation International* January 1998: 71–2.

Fossey, J. (2005), 'Turkey's Triumvirate', *Containerisation International – Mediterranean Regional Analysis* November, 23.

Frankel, E. (1999), 'The Economics of Total Trans-ocean Supply Chain Management', *International Journal of Maritime Economics* 1:1, 61–9.

Fredouet, C.H. and Rimmer, P.J. (eds) (forthcoming) *International Transport and Logistics: East Asian and European Experiences* (London: Routledge).

Frémont, A. (2006), 'Shipping Lines and Logistics', *IAME Conference Proceedings*.

Frémont A. and Soppé M. (2004), 'The Evolution of North-European Shipping Networks: From Inter-continental Links to a Global System, 1990–2000', WCTR Society.

Frémont, A. and Ducruet, C. (2005), 'The Emergence of a Mega Port, from the Local to the Global, the Case of Busan', *Tijdschrift voor Econ. En Soc. Geografie* 96: 4, 421–32.

Frémont, A. and Soppé, M. (2003), 'The Service Strategies of Liner Shipping Companies'. Presentation in Research Seminar *Maritime transport, globalisation, regional integration and territorial development*, Le Havre, France, 5 Jun. 2003.

Frémont, A. and Soppé, M. (2004), 'Les Stratégies des Armateurs de Lignes Régulières en Matière de Desserte Maritime', *Belgéo* 4, 391–406.

Freund, W. and Padayachee, V. (eds) (2002), *(D)urban Vortex: A South African City in Transition* (Durban: University of Natal Press).

Frohlich, M.T. and Westbrook, R. (2001), 'Arcs of Integration: An International Study of Supply Chain Strategies', *Journal of Operations Management* 19, 185–200.

Fujita, M. and Mori, T. (1996), 'The Role of Ports in the Making of Major Cities: Self-agglomeration and Hub-effect', *Journal of Development Economics* 49, 93–120.

Fujita, M. *et al.* (1999), *The Spatial Economy: Cities, Regions and International Trade* (Cambridge, London: MIT Press).

Ganeshan, R. and Harrison, T.P. (1995), *An Introduction to Supply Chain Management*, (PA: Department of Management Sciences and Information Systems, Penn State University).

Ganeshan, R. *et al.* (1999), 'A Taxonomic Review of Supply Chain Management Research', *Quantitative Models for Supply Chain Management* <www.business. wm.edu>

Genco, P. and Pitto, A. (2000), 'Transhipment and Liner Networks Restructuring: Opportunities and Threats for Mediterranean Ports', *IAME Conference Proceedings*.

Gentry, J.J. (1995), 'The Role of Carriers in Buyer-supplier Strategic Partnerships: A supply Chain Management Approach', *Journal of Business Logistics* 17:2, 35–55.

Gereffi, G. (2001), 'Shifting Governance Structures in Global Commodity Chains, with Special Reference to the Internet', *American Behavioral Scientist* 44, 1616–37.

Gereffi, G. and Korzeniewicz, M. (1994), *Commodity Chains and Global Capitalism* (Westport, Conn.: Praeger).

Gereffi, G. *et al.* (1994), 'Introduction: Global Commodity Chains', in Gereffi and Korzeniewicz (eds).

Gereffi, G. *et al.* (2005), 'The Governance of Global Value Chains', *Review of International Political Economy* 12:1, 78–104.

Giaoutzi, M. and Nijkamp, P, (1993), 'Waterways as an Alternative Mode', in Banister et al. (eds).

Glaister, K.W. and Buckley, P.J. (1996), 'Strategic Motives for International Alliance Formation', *Journal of Management Studies* 33:3, 301–32.

Gleave, M.B. (1997), 'Port Activities and the Spatial Structure of Cities: The Case of Freetown, Sierra Leone', *Journal of Transport Geography* 5:4, 257–75.

Goss, R.O. (1990), 'Economic Policies and Seaports', *Maritime Policy and Management* 17:3, 207–19.

Gouvernal, E. *et al.* (2005), 'Dynamics of Change in the Port System of the Western Mediterranean', *Maritime Policy & Management* 32:2, 107–21.

Gouvernal, E. (2003), 'Les Lignes Maritimes et le Transport Terrestre: Quelles Enseignements Peut-on Tirer du Cas "Rail Link"', *Cahiers Scientifiques du Transport* 44, 95–113.

Gouvernal, E. and Daydou, J. (2005), 'Container Railfreight Services in North-west Europe: Diversity of Organizational Forms in a Liberalizing Environment', *Transport Reviews* 25:5, 557–71.

Graham, S. and Marvin, S. (2001), *Splintering Urbanism: Networked Infrastructures, Technological Mobilities and the Urban Condition* (London: Routledge).

Greater Vancouver Gateway Council (GVGC) (2003) *Economic Impact Analysis of Investment in a Major Commercial Transportation System for the Greater Vancouver Region.* Prepared by Delcan and Economic Development Research Group, July.

Grinter, M. (2005), 'Hyperbole in Concrete – Port Operators Visit Yangshang', *Lloyds List*, 9 November, 5.

Gripaios, P. and Gripaios, R. (1995) 'The Impact of a Port on Its Local Economy: The Case of Plymouth.' *Maritime Policy and Management* 22, 13–23.

Gripaios, R. (1999), 'Ports and their Influence on Local Economies: A UK Perspective', *The Dock and Harbour Authority*, 235–41.

Guy, E. (2003), *Compétition et Complémentarité Dans l'Évolution des Réseaux Maritimes de Transport de Conteneurs: le Cas de la Façade Est de l'Amérique du Nord*, (Montreal: Montreal University).

Hailey, R. (2005), 'Ports Lagging Behind in Preparation for "Mega Ships" Deliveries', *Lloyds List*, 6 June, 5.

Håkansson, H. and Snehota, I. (1995), *Developing Relationships in Business Networks* (London: Rutledge).

Hall, P.V. (2004), '"We'd Have to Sink the Ships": Impact Studies and the 2002 West Coast Port Lockout', *Economic Development Quarterly - Journal of American Economic Revitalization* 18: 4, 354.

Hall, P.V. and Olivier, D. (2005), 'Inter-firm Relationships and the Evolution of Transportation Systems: The Case of the Car Carriers and Automobile Importers to the United States', *Maritime Policy and Management* 32:3, 279–95.

Hall, P.V. and Robbins., G. (2002). 'Economic Development for a New Era: An Examination of the Adoption of Explicit Economic Development Strategies by Durban Local Government Following the April 1994 Elections', in Freund and Padayachee (eds).

Halldorsson, A. *et al.* (2003), 'Interorganizational Theories behind Supply Chain Management – Discussion and Applications', in Seuring et al. (eds).

Hamel, G. and Prahalad, C.K. (1990), 'The Core Competence of the Corporation', *Harvard Business Review* May-June, 79–91.

Hammant, J. (1995), 'Information Technology Trends in Logistics', *Logistics Information Management* 8:6, 32–7.

Haralambides, H. *et al.* (2001), 'Port Financing and Pricing in the European Union: Theory, Politics and Reality', *International Journal of Maritime Economics* 3, 368–86.

Haralambides, H. *et al.* (2002) 'Costs, Benefits and Pricing of Dedicated Terminals', *International Journal of Maritime Economics* 4:3, 21–34.

Haralambides, H.E. (2000), 'Maritime Logistics: The Emerging Global Approach to the International Transport of Containers', Presentation at *Conference Puertos y Actividades Logisticas: Restos y Oportunidades* , Santander, 5–7 Jul. 2000.

Hautreux, J. and Rochefort, M. (1963), 'Physionomie Générale de L'armature Urbaine Française', *Annales de Géographie*, 406, 660–677.

Hayuth, Y. (1981), 'Containerisation and the Load Centre Concept', *Economic Geography* 57, 160–176.

Hayuth, Y. (1982), 'The Port-urban Interface: An Area in Transition', *Area* 14:3, 219–24.

Hayuth, Y. (1987), *Intermodality: Concept and Practice* (London: Lloyd).

Hayuth, Y. (1988), 'Rationalization and Deconcentration of the U.S. Container Port System', *Professional Geographer* 3, 279–88.

Hayuth, Y. (2005), 'Globalization and the Port-urban Interface: Conflicts and Opportunities', *International Workshop on New Generation Port-Cities and Their Role in Global Supply Chains*, Hong Kong, 12–14 Dec. 2005.

Hazendonck, E. (2001), *Essays on Strategic Analysis for Seaports* (Leuven: Garant).

Heaver, T. (2002), 'The Evolving Roles of Shipping Lines in International Logistics', *International Journal of Maritime Economics* 4, 210–230.

Heaver, T. *et al.* (2001), 'Co-operation and Competition in International Container Transport: Strategies for Ports', *Maritime Policy and Management* 28:3, 293–305.

Heaver, T.D. (1995), 'The Implications of Increased Competition among Ports for Port Policy and Management', *Maritime Policy & Management* 22:2, 125–33.

Heaver, T.D. (1996), 'The Opportunities and Challenges for Shipping Lines in International Logistics'. Presentation at *the 1ˢᵗ World Logistics Conference,* Ramada Hotel, London Heathrow.

Heaver, T.D. (2001), 'Perspectives on Global Performance Issues', in Brewer., Button and Hensher (eds.).

Helders, S. (2006), *The World Gazetteer*. <http://www.world-gazetteer.com/home.htm>, accessed 12 Oct. 2006.

Helling, A. and Poister, T.H. (2000), 'U.S. Maritime Ports: Trends, Policy Implications, and Research Needs', *Economic Development Quarterly – Journal of American Economic Revitalization* 14:3, 298.

Hendersen, J. *et al.* (2002), 'Global Production networks and the Analysis of Economic Development', *Review of International Political Economy* 9:3, 436–64.

Herfort, R. *et al.* (2001), 'Port Selection for Integration in Logistics Supply Chains in Europe: A Case Study of Automobile Transport through Ports'. Presentation at *Logistics Research Network, 6th Annual Conference.*

Hershman, M. *et al.* (1978), *Under New Management, Port Growth and Emerging Coastal Management Program* (Seattle: University of Washington Press).

Hesse, M. and Rodrigue, J. (2004), 'The Transport Geography of Logistics and Freight Distribution', *Journal of Transport Geography* 12:4, 171–84.

Hilling, D. (2001), 'Waterborne Freight. The Neglected Mode', *Logistics and Transport Focus* 3:8, 30–33.

Hoyle, B.S. (1989), 'The Port-city Interface: Trends, Problems, and Examples', *Geoforum* 20:4, 429–35.

Hoyle, B.S. (2000), 'Global and Local Change on the Port-city Waterfront', *Geographical Review* 90:3, 395–417.

Hoyle, B.S. and Pinder, D. (1992), *European Port Cities in Transition* (London: Belhaven).

Hoyle, B.S. and Pinder, D.A. (eds) (1981), *Cityport Industrialization and Regional Development* (Oxford: Pergamon).

Hoyle, B.S. and Hilling, D. (1984), *Seaport Systems and Spatial Change: Technology, Industry, and Development Strategies* (Chichester: Wiley).

Hoyle, B.S. *et al.* (eds) (1988), *Revitalising the Waterfront: International Dimensions of Dockland Redevelopment* (London: Belhaven).

Huggett, D. (1998), 'Future Port Development and Nature Conservation in Great Britain', *Dock and Harbour Authority* 79:886, 18–21.

Humphrey, J. and Schmitz, H. (2002) 'How Does Insertion in Global Value Chains Affect Upgrading in Industrial Clusters?' *Regional Studies* 36:9, 1017–27.

Huybrechts, M. et al. (2002), *Port Competitiveness: an Economic and Legal Analysis of the Factors Determining the Competitiveness of Seaports* (Antwerpen: De Boeck).

IAME (International Association of Maritime Economists) (2000) *IAME Conference Proceedings.* 13–15 Sep. 2000, Naples, Italy.

IAME (2002) *IAME Conference Proceedings on 'Maritime Economics: Setting the Foundations for Port and Shipping Policies'.* Panama City, Panama, 12–15 Nov. 2002.

IAME (2005) *Proceeding of the IAME Conference*, 23–25 Jun. 2005, Limassol, Cyprus.

IAME (2006) *IAME Conference Proceedings on 'Ports, Shipping, Infrastructure and Supply Chains: Critical Issues'* (CD-rom). 12–14 Jul. 2006, Melbourne, Australia.

ICLSP (International Conference on Logistics Strategy for Ports) (2004) Proceedings of 1st International Conference on Logistics Strategy for Ports. Dalian, China, 22–26 Sep. 2004.

Institute of Shipping and Logistics (2001), *Shipping Statistics Yearbook* (Bremen: ISL).

International Transport Journal (2006), *International Register of Logistics and Forwarding Agents.* <http://195.65.73.10/itz/irflaNeu/e/ irfla_suche.asp>, accessed 12 Oct. 2006.

Introna, L.D. (1993), 'The Impact of Information Technology on Logistics', *Logistics Information Management* 6:2, 37–42.

IRSIT (L'Institute de Recherche en Strategie Industrielle et Territoriale) (2004), *Les Villes Portuaires en Europe, Analyse Comparative* (Montpellier: CNRS).

ITJ Daily (2005), *Germanische Lloysand Hyundai design 13,000 teu containership*, electronic format at http//:www.transportjournal.ch.e.daily/index.php, accessed October 6, 2005.

Jenisch, U.K. (1996), 'The Baltic Sea: The Legal Regime and Instruments for Co-operation', *International Journal of Marine and Coastal Law* 11:1, 47–67.

Johnson, J.L. (1999), 'Strategic Integration in Distribution Channels: Managing the Interfirm Relationship as a Strategic Asset', *Journal of the Academy of Marketing Science* 27:1, 4–18.

Johnson, K.P. and Kort, J.R. (2004), *Redefinition of BEA Economic Areas, Survey of Current Business* (BEA publications, U.S. Government).

Joly, O. (1999), *La Structuration des Réseaux de Circulation Maritime*, unpublished dissertation in territorial management, Le Havre University.

Jones, T.C. and Riley, D.W. (1984), 'Using Inventory for Competitive Advantage through Supply Chain Management', *International Journal of Physical Distribution and Materials Management* 15, 16–26.

Journal de la Marine Marchande (1970–2000), *Bilan Annuel des Ports du Monde* (Rueil Malmaison: Wolters Kluwer France & Groupe Liaison SA).

Kageson, P. (1999), *Economic Instruments for Reducing Emissions from Sea Transport*, Air Pollution and Climate Series 11 (Goteborg: The Swedish NGO Secretariat on Acid Rain).

Kalwani, M.U. and Narayandas, N. (1995), 'Long-term Manufacturer-Supplier Relationships. Do they pay?', *Journal of Marketing* 59:1, 1–16.

Keeling, D.J. (1995), 'Transport and the World City Paradigm', in Knox and Taylor (eds).

Kenyon, J.B. (1974), 'Elements in Inter-port Competition in the United States', in Eliot (ed.)

Kia, M. *et al.* (2000), 'The Importance of IT in Port Terminal Operations', *International Journal of Physical Distribution and Logistics* 30:3/4, 331–44.

Kidwai, A.H. (1989), 'Port Cities in a National System of Ports and Cities: A Geographical Analysis of India in the 20th Century', in Broeze (ed.).

Knight, F.W. and Liss, P.K. (1991), *Atlantic Port Cities: Economy, Culture and Society in the Atlantic World, 1650–1850* (Knoxville: University of Tennessee Press).

Knox, P.L. and Taylor, P.J. (eds) (1995), *World Cities in a World System* (Cambridge: Cambridge University Press).

Koch, C. (2005), 'Remarks of the President & CEO of the World Shipping Council'. Presentation at *Annual Spring Conference*, Washington, D.C., 5 Apr. 2005. The American Association of Port Authorities.

Kolb, A. and Wacker, M. (1995), 'Calculation of Energy Consumption and Pollutant Emissions on Freight Transport Routes', *Science of the Total Environment* 169:1–3, 283–8.

Konvitz, J.W. (1978), *Cities and the Sea: Port City planning in Early Modern Europe* (Baltimore and London: John Hopkins University Press).

Konvitz, J.W. (1994), 'The Crisis of Atlantic Port Cities, 1880 to 1920', *Comparative Studies in Society and History* 36:2, pp. 293–318.

Kraman, M.A. (ed.) (1998) *Proceedings of the Conference Ports '98*. American Society of Civil Engineers. Long Beach, California, 8–11 Mar. 1998.

Kreukels, T. and Wever, E. (eds) (1998), *North Sea Ports in Transition* (Assen: Gorcum).

Kuipers, B. (2005), 'The End of the Box?', in Leggate, Morvillo and Mc Conville (eds.).

Kuipers, B. and Eenhuizen, J. (2004), 'A Framework for the Analysis of Seaport-based Logistics Parks', *ICLSP Conference Proceedings*, 151–71pp.

Lahmeyer, J. (2006), *Population Statistics* <http://www.library.uu.nl/wesp/populstat/ populhome.html>, accessed 12 Oct. 2006.

LaLonde, B.J. (1997), 'Supply Chain Management: Myth or Reality?' *Supply Chain Manangement Review* 1, 6–7.

LaLonde, B.J. (1998), 'Building a Supply Chain Relationship', *Supply Chain Management Review* 2:2, 7–8.

Lamming, R. (1996), 'Squaring Lean Supply with Supply Chain Management', *International Journal of Operations & Production Management* 16:2, 183–96.

Landaburu, K. and Canu, P. (2002), 'Cabotage et Ferroutage: Vers des Autoroutes de la Mer', *La Vie du Rail* 219, 6–15.

Lawton, R. and Lee, R. (2002), *Population and Society in Western European Port Cities, c. 1650–1939* (Liverpool: Liverpool University Press).

Lee, S. and Song, D. (2005), 'Hong Kong and Singapore: Port Cities or City Ports?', *IAME Conference Proceedings*.

Lee, S.W. (2005), *Interaction between City and Port in Asian Hub Port Cities*, unpublished dissertation in urban planning, Seoul National University.

Lee, S.W. *et al.* (2005), *A Study of Port Performance related to Port Backup Area in ESCAP Region* (Seoul: Korea Maritime Institute).

Lee, S.W. *et al.* (2006), 'A Tale of Asia's Global Hub Port Cities: The Spatial Evolution in Hong Kong and Singapore', *Geoforum (forthcoming)*.

Lee, T.W. and Cullinane, K. (eds), *World Shipping and Port Development* (Hampshire: Palgrave Macmillan).

Lee-Partridge, J.E. *et al.* (2000), 'Information Technology Management: The Case of the Port of Singapore Authority', *Journal of Strategic Information Systems* 9: 85–99.

Leggate, H. *et al.* (eds) (2005), *International Maritime Transport: Perspectives* (London: Taylor & Francis).

Leigh B.B. and Cuttino J.C. (2003). 'Measuring the Economic and Transportation Impacts of Maritime-related Trade', *Maritime Economics & Logistics* 5:2, 133–57.

Leigh, R. (1970), 'The Use of Location Quotients in Urban Economic Base Studies', *Land Economics* 46:2, 202–5.

Lever, W.F. (1994), 'Regional Economic Growth and Port Activities in European Cities'. Presentation at *Portes Océanes et Développement des Territoires*

Intérieurs, 5th International Conference Cities and Ports, Dakar, Senegal. Nov. 2005.

Lewis, I. and Talalayevsky, A. (1997), 'Logistics and Information Technology: A Coordination Perspective', *Journal of Business Logistics* 18:1, 141–57.

Lewis, M.W. and Wigen, K. (1997), *The Myth of Continents: a Critique of Metageography* (Berkeley: University of California Press).

Li & Fung Research Centre (2003) *Supply Chain Management: the Practice of Li & Fung Group in Hong Kong* (in Chinese) (Beijing: People's University of China Press).

Li, P.P. (2003) 'Toward a Geocentric theory of multinational evolution: the Implications from Asian MNEs as Latecomers', *Asia Pacific Journal of Management* 20, 217–42.

Li, X. (2006) *Comments on Zhuhai Gaolan Port Zone Plan* (draft), a panel discussion at a seminar held on 1 Dec. 2006, Zhuhai, China.

Liaoning Government (2006) *Development Plan for Transportation Infrastructure in the 11th Five-Year Plan*, an internal document, prepared by the Commission for Development and Reforms and Transportation Commission of Liaoning Province.

Littlejohn, P. (2003), 'New Capacity in the Eastern Mediterranean – How will it Impact Existing Trade Patterns?. *Proceedings of the Terminal Operation Conference* (TOC), Genoa, 10–12 Jun. 2003.

Lloyd, P.J. (1992), *Regionalisation and world trade*, OECD Economic Studies, No.18.

Lloyd's List (2001), *Ports of the World 2002* (London: Informa UK Ltd).

Lloyd's List (2005), *Lloyd's Maritime Atlas* (London: Informa UK Ltd).

Lowry, N. (2005), 'China Shipping Tips Cretan site as "Ideal" Mediterranean Hub', *Lloyds List*, 14 November, 1.

Malthus, T.R. (1798), An Essay on the Principle of Population.

Marcadon, J. (1995), 'Ports et Flux de Conteneurs Dans le Monde, 1983–1992', *Mappemonde* 1, 29–34.

Marcadon, J. (1999), 'Les Ports de Commerce, L'environnement et la Gestion Intégrée du Littoral', *Bulletin de l'Association des Géographes Français* 2, 204–11.

Marinova Consulting (2005) *Halifax Trucking Options Study*, presented to Halifax Regional Municipality and Halifax Port Corporation, Jun. 2005.

Marlow, P.B. and Paixao, A. C. (2003a), 'Fourth Generation Ports. A Question of Agility?' *International Journal of Physical Distribution & Logistics Management* 33:4, 355-76.

Marlow, P.B. and Paixao, A.C. (2003b), 'Measuring Lean Ports Performance', *International Journal of Transport Management* 1, 189–202.

Marshall, Macklin, Monaghan (2004) *Final Report: Railway Cut Investigation Study*, prepared for Halifax Regional Municipality, Feb. 2005.

Matsuno, K. *et al.* (2000), 'A Refinement and Validation of the MARKOR Scale', *Journal of the Academy of Marketing Science* 28:4, 527–39.

McCalla, R. (1999), 'Global Change, Local Pain: Intermodal Seaport Terminals and their Service Areas', *Journal of Transport Geography* 7:4, 247–54.

McCalla, R.J. (1999), 'From St. John's to Miami: Containerisation at Eastern Seaboard Ports', *Geojournal* 48:1, 21–8.

McCalla, R.J. (2004), 'From "Anyport" to "Superterminal": Conceptual Perspectives on Containerization and Port Infrastructure', in Pinder and Slack (eds).

McGee, T. (1967), *The Southeast Asian City: a Social Geography of the Primate Cities* (London, G. Bell & Sons).

McKinsey & Co. (2005), *Revitalizing the Hong Kong Sea-trade Sector via Trucking Initiatives*, a discussion document presented at Li and Fung Group on 4 Oct. 2005.

Meersmaan, H. *et al.* (2005), 'Ports as Hubs in the Logistics Chain', in Leggate *et al.* (eds).

Mentzer J.T. *et al.* (2001), 'Defining Supply Chain Management', *Journal of Business Logistics* 22:2, 1-25.

Microsoft (2006), *Mappoint Geographical Atlas* <http://wwwmappoint.com>, accessed 12 Oct. 2006.

Midoro, R. *et al.* (2004), 'The Evolving Role of Mediterranean Ports in the Deep-sea Trade Patterns', *ICLSP Conference Proceedings*, 553–67pp.

Midoro, R. *et al.* (2005), 'Maritime Liner Shipping and the Stevedoring Industry: market structure and competition strategies', *Maritime Policy & Management* 32:2, 89–106.

Miossec, A. (1999), 'Les Estuaires Français entre Développement Économique et Protection de L'environnement', *Bulletin de l'Association des Géographes Français*, 2, 101–7.

Miossec, A. (2001), 'L'évolution de la Géographie des Océans et des Littoraux Face aux Perspectives du Développement Durable au 21e Siècle. Quelles Hypothèses Envisager?', *Annales de Géographie* 621, 509–26.

Monczka, R.M. *et al.* (1998), 'Success Factors in Strategic Supplier Alliances: The Buying Company Perspective', *Decision Sciences* 29:3, 5553–77.

Mongelluzzo, B. (2004) 'Playing with Fire', *Journal of Commerce Online* (published online 10 May 2004), accessed 11 Sep. 2005.

Mongelluzzo, B. (2005), 'Big Ships Mean Big Shake-ups', *Journal of Commerce Online* (published online 28 Feb. 2005), accessed 6 May 2005.

Moriconi-Ebrard, F. (1994), *Geopolis, pour Comparer les Villes du Monde* (Paris: Economica).

Morris, M. and Robbins, G. (2006). 'The role of government in creating an enabling environment for inter-firm cluster co-operation: Policy lessons from South Africa', forthcoming in *Clusters in Africa: Pattern Practice and Policies for Innovation and Upgrading* (INTECH, UNU).

Morvan, M. (1999), *Villes portuaires: les moyens d'un développement solidaire dans une Europe ouverte*, Conférence des Villes Portuaires Périphériques, Brest.

Morvillo, A. and Ferrara, G. (eds) (2002) *Training in Logistics and the Freight Transport Industry* (London: Ashgate).

Murphey, R. (1989), 'On the Evolution of the Port City', in Broeze (ed.).

Muscara, C. and Poli, C. (eds) (1983), *Transport Geography Facing Geography* (I.G.U. Working Group on Geography of Transport).

Musso, E. and Benacchio, M. (2002), 'Demaritimisation o Remaritimisation? L'evoluzione dello Scenario Economico nelle Città Portuali, in Soriani (ed.).

Musso, E. *et al.* (2000), 'Ports and Employment in Port Cities', *International Journal of Maritime Economics* 2:4, 283–312.

Musso, E. *et al.* (2001), 'Co-operation in Maritime and Port Industry and its Effects on Markets Structure', in Park *et al.* (eds) *WCTR Conference Proceedings*.

Narasimhan, R. and Carter, J.R. (1998), 'Linking Business Unit and Material Sourcing Strategies', *Journal of Business Logistics* 19:2, 155–71.

Narasimhan, R. and Das, A. (1999), 'An Empirical Investigation of the Contribution of Strategic Sourcing to Manufacturing Flexibilities and Performance', *Decision Sciences* 30:3, 683–718.

Narasimhan, R. and Jayaram, J. (1998), 'Causal Linkages in Supply Chain Management: An Exploratory Study of North American Manufacturing Firms', *Decision Sciences* 29:3, 579–605.

Narasimhan, R. and Kim, S.W. (2002), 'Effect of Supply Chain Integration on the Relationship between Diversification and Performance: Evidence from Japanese and Korean firms', *Journal of Operations Management* 20, 303–23.

National Chamber Foundation (2003), *Trade and Transportation; a Study of North American Port and Intermodal Systems* (Washington D.C.: U.S Chamber of Commerce).

Ness, G.D. and Tanigawa, K. (1992), *Population Dynamics and Port City Development: Comparative Analysis of Ten Asian Port Cities* (Kobe: Asian Urban Information Center).

Noin, D. (1974), 'Les Activités Spécifiques des Villes Françaises', *Annales de Géographie* 459, 531–44.

Noin, D. (2000), 'La Population des Littoraux du Monde', *L'Information Géographique*, 2, 65–73.

Noponen, H. *et al.* (1997) 'Trade and American Cities: Who has the Comparative Advantage?', *Economic Development Quarterly* 11:1, 67–87.

Norton, R.D. (1986), 'Industrial Policy and American Renewal', *Journal of Economic Literature* 24:1, 1–40.

Notteboom, T.E. (1997), 'Concentration and Load Centre Development in the European Container Port System', *Journal of Transport Geography* 5:2, 99–115.

Notteboom, T.E. (2002), 'Consolidation and Contestability in the European Container Handling Industry', *Maritime Policy and Management* 29:3, 257–69.

Notteboom, T.E. (2004), 'Container Shipping and Ports: An Overview', *Review of Network Economics* 3:2, 86–106.

Notteboom, T.E. (2006), 'Concession Agreements as Port Governance Tools', in Brooks and Cullinane (eds).

Notteboom, T.E. (ed.) (2006), *Ports are More than Piers* (Anwerp:De Lloyd).

Notteboom, T.E. and Winkelmans, W. (2002), 'Stakeholders Relations Management in Ports: Dealing with the Interplay of Forces among Stakeholders in a Changing Competitive Environment', *IAME Conference Proceedings*.

Notteboom, T.E., and Rodrigue, J.P. (2005), 'Port Regionalization: Towards a New Phase in Port Development', *Maritime Policy and Management* 32:3, 297–313.

Notteboom, T.E., Winkelmans, W. (2001), 'Structural Changes in Logistics: How will Port Authorities Face the Challenge?', *Maritime Policy and Management* 28:1, 71–89.

Notteboom, T.E., Winkelmans, W. (2003), 'Dealing with Stakeholders in the Port Planning Process', in Dullaert, Jourquin and Polak (eds).

Novack, R.A. *et al.* (1995), *Creating Logistics Value: Themes for the Future* (Oak Brook, IL: Council of Logistics Management).

Nunan, J. (2001), 'The Allure of Automation', *Container Management*, February 2001, 28–30.

O'Brien, C. and Head, M. (1995), 'Developing a Full Business Environment to Support Just-in-time Logistics', *International Journal of Production Economics* 42:1, 41–50.

O'Connor, K. (1989), 'Australian Ports, Metropolitan Areas and Trade-related Services', *Australian Geographer* 20:2, 167–72.

O'Leary-Kelly *et al.* (2002), 'The Integration of Manufacturing and Marketing/ Sales Decisions: Impact on Organizational Performance', *Journal of Operations Management* 20:3, 221–40.

Ocean Shipping Consultants (2003), *World Containerport Outlook to 2015* (Surrey, UK: Ocean Shipping Consultants Ltd).

Ocean Shipping Consultants (2005), *Marketing of Container Terminals* (Surrey, UK: Ocean Shipping Consultants Ltd).

Okuno, S. (2000), 'Urban Policies of Some Port Cities in the Asia-Pacific Corridor', in Chapman, Bradnock and Dutt (eds).

Oliver, D. *et al.* (2005), 'The Timescale of Internationalisation: the Case of the Container Port Industry'. Presentation at the International Workshop on Port Cities, Hong Kong, Dec. 2005.

Olivier, D. (2005), 'Private Entry and Emerging Partnerships in Container Terminal Operations: Evidence from Asia', *Maritime Economics and Logistics* 7:2, 87–115.

Olivier, D. (2006), *The Globalisation of Port Business: an Asian perspective*, Ph.D. dissertation, University of Hong Kong, June 2006.

Olivier, D. and Slack, B. (2006), 'Rethinking the port', *Environment & Planning A*. 38:8, 1409–27.

Oram, R.B. (1968) 'The Three Principles of Mechanisation', *The Dock and Harbour Authority* 50, 194–95.

Orkney Islands Council (2005), 'Scapa Flow Container Transhipment Terminal' <http//:www.scapaflowhub.com>, accessed 31 November 2005.

Paixao, A.C. and Marlow, P.B. (2002), 'Strengths and Weaknesses of Short-Sea Shipping', *Marine Policy*, 26:3, 167–78.

Paixão, A.C. and Marlow, P.B. (2003), 'Fourth Generation Ports – A Question of Agility?' *International Journal of Physical Distribution and Logistics Management* 33:4, 355–76.

Panayides, P. M. (2001), 'Antecedents and Consequences of Mergers and Acquisitions in Liner Shipping: A Synthesis and Research Agenda', in Park *et al.* (eds) *WCTR Conference Proceedings*.

Panayides, P.M. (2002), 'Economic Organization of Intermodal Transport', *Transport Reviews* 22:4, 401–14.

Park, C. *et al.* (eds) (2001) *Proceedings of 9th World Conference on Transport Research*, 22–27 Jul. 2001, Seoul, Korea. WCTR Society (The World Conference on Transport Research Society).

Patier-Marque, D. (ed.), *L'intégration des marchandises dans le système des déplacements urbains* (Lyon: Laboratoire d'Economie des Transports).

Paul, J. (2005), 'India and the Global Container Ports', *Maritime Economics & Logistics* 7:2, 189–92.

Perpillou, A. (1959), *Géographie de la Circulation, Vol.1.* (Paris: Les cours de Sorbonne).

Peters, H.J.F. (2001), 'Developments in Global Seatrade and Container Shipping Markets: Their Effects on the Port Industry and Private Sector Involvement', International Journal of Maritime Economics 3:1, 3–26.

Pinder, D. and Slack, B. (eds) (2004), *Shipping and Ports in the Twenty-first Century* (London and New York: Routledge).

Poltrack, S. (2000), 'The Maritime Industry and our Environment: The Delicate Balance of Economic and Environmental Concerns, Globally, Nationally, and within the Port of Baltimore', *University of Baltimore Journal of Environmental Law* 1, 51–78.

Porter M.E. (1985), *Competitive Advantage. Creating and Sustaining Superior Performance* (New York: The Free Press).

Post, J.C. and Lundin, C.G. (eds) (1996), *Guidelines for Integrated Coastal Zone Management*, Environmentally Sustainable Development Studies and Monographs Series 9 (Washington: the World Bank).

Prajogo, D.I. and Sohal, A.S. (2006), 'The Integration of TQM and Technology/ R&D Management in Determining Quality and Innovation Performance', *Omega* 34, 296–312.

Pumain, D. and Saint-Julien, T. (1976), 'Fonctions et Hiérarchies des Villes Françaises', *Annales de Géographie* 470, 385–440.

Raftopoulos, E. (2001), 'Relational Governance for Marine Pollution Incidents in the Mediterranean: Transformations, Development and Prospects', *International Journal of Marine and Coastal Law* 16:1, 41–76.

Reck, R.F. and Long, B.G. (1988), 'Purchasing: A Competitive Weapon', *Journal of Purchasing and Materials Management* 24, 2–8.

Reeves, P. (1989), 'Studying the Asian Port City', in Broeze (ed.).

Research & Markets (2005), *Investment Study in China's Port Industry 2005–2006*, <www.researchandmarkets.com>.

Restall, T. (2005), 'Special Report Free Trade Zones', *Port Strategy* June, 34–35.

Ridolfi, G. (1999), 'Containerisation in the Mediterranean: Between Global Ocean Routeways and Feeder Services', *GeoJournal* 48:1, 29–34.

Rimmer, P.J. (1967), 'The Search for Spatial Regularities in the Development of Australian Seaports 1861–1961/2', *Geografiska Annaler* 49:1, 42–54.

Rimmer, P.J. (1998), 'Ocean Liner Shipping Services: Corporate Restructuring and Port Selection and Competition', *Asia-Pacific Viewpoint*, 39:2, 193–208.

Rimmer, P.J. (1999), 'The Asia-Pacific Rim's Transport and Telecommunications Systems: Spatial Structure and Corporate Control since the Mid-1980s', *GeoJournal* 48, 43–65.

Rimmer, P.J. (2004), 'Marketing Incheon: Gateway for Seoul, Northeast Asia and the World', *Journal of International Logistics and Trade* 2:2, 99–121.

Ringbom, H. (1999), 'Preventing Pollution from Ships – Reflections on the "Adequacy" of Existing Rules', *Review of European Community and International Environmental Law* 8:1, 21–8.

Robinson, R. (1970) 'The Hinterland-Foreland Continuum; Concept and Methodology', *The Professional Geographer* 22:6, 307–10.

Robinson, R. (1998), 'Asian Hub/Feeder Nets: The Dynamics of Restructuring', *Maritime Policy & Management* 25:1, 21–40.

Robinson, R. (2002), 'Ports as Elements in Value-driven Chain Systems: The New Paradigm', *Maritime Policy and Management* 29:3, 241–55.

Saldhanha, J. and Gray, J. (2002), 'The Potential for British Coastal Shipping in a Multimodal Chain', *Maritime Policy and Management* 29:1, 77–92.

Samaan, A.W. (1993), 'Enforcement of International Environmental Treaties: an Analysis', *Fordham Environmental Law Journal* 5, 261–83.

Savvides, N. (2003), 'Med Moves', *Containerisation International* September, 74–5.

Schumpeter, J. (1939), *Business Cycles: a Theoretical, Historical and Statistical Analysis of the Capitalist Process* (New York: McGraw-Hill).

Seuring, S. et al. (eds) (2003), *Strategy and Organization in Supply Chains* (Physica Verlag: Heidelberg).

Shirokawa, S. (2000), 'From Maturity to Growth — Current State of Liner Shipping: Aiming for New Horizon of Growth', in Mitsui O.S.K. Lines Company Report *Current State of Liner Shipping 1999–2000*, Tokyo.

Sim, A.B. and Pandian, J.R. (2003), 'Emerging Asian MNEs and their Internationalization Strategies – Case Study Evidence on Taiwanese and Singaporean Firms', *Asia Pacific Journal of Management* 20:1, 27–50.

Singapore Economic Research Committee (2002), *Developing Singapore into a Global Integrated Logistics Hub*, Report of the working group on logistics <www.erc.gov.sg/pdf/ERC_SVS_LOG_MainReport.PDF>, 21pp.

Slack, B. (1989), 'Port Services, Ports and the Urban Hierarchy', *Tijdschrift voor Econ. En Soc.Geografie* 80:4, 236–43.

Slack, B. (1993), 'Pawns in the Game: Ports in a Global Transportation System', *Growth and Change* 24, 579–88.

Slack, B. (1999), 'Satellite Terminals: A local Solution to Hub Congestion?, *Journal of Transport Geography*, 7:4, 241–6.

Slack, B. and Comtois, C. (2004), 'Innover L'autorité Portuaire au 21e Siècle: Un Nouvel Agenda de Gouvernance', *Les Cahiers Scientifiques du Transport* 44, 11–24.

Slack, B. and Wang, J.J. (2002), 'The Challenge of Peripheral Ports: An Asian Perspective', *GeoJournal* 56:2, 159–66.

Slack, B. et al. (1996), 'Shipping Lines Agents of Change in the Port Industry', *Maritime Policy and Management* 23:3, 289–300.

Slack, B. *et al.* (2000), 'Les Systèmes Portuaires et les Villes: Comparaisons entre Diverses Régions du Monde', in Patier-Marque (ed.).

Slack, B. *et al.* (2002a), 'Logistics and Maritime Transport: a fundamental transformation', *Annual Meeting of the American Association of Geographers*, Los Angeles.

Slack, B. *et al.* (2002), 'Strategic Alliances in the Container Shipping Industry: A Global Perspective', *Maritime Policy and Management* 29:1, 65–76.

Sletmo, G.K. (1989), 'Shipping's Fourth Wave: Ship Management or Vernon's Trade Cycle?, *Maritime Policy & Management* 16:4, 293–303.

Sletmo, G.K. (1999) 'Port Life Cycles: Policy and Strategy in the Global Economy', International *Journal of Maritime Economics* 1:1, 11–37.

Song, D. (2002), 'Regional Container Port Competition and Co-operation: The Case of Hong Kong and South China', *Journal of Transport Geography* 10, 99–110.

Song, D. (2003), 'Port Co-opetition in concept and practice', *Maritime Policy & Management* 30:1, 29–44.

Soriani, S. (ed.) (2002), *Porti, Città e Territorio Costiero* (Bologna: il Mulino).

SSA Marine (2004), *U.S. Port Capacity Situation* (Seattle: SSA Marine, Carrix).

Stalk, G. Jr. and Waddell, K. (2006), *The China Rip Tide: Threat or Opportunity?*, Boston Consulting Group <www.bcg.com.>

Steck, B. (1995), 'Les Villes Portuaires Dans le Réseau Urbain Français', *Vivre et Habiter la Ville Portuaire*, Plan Construction et Architecture, Paris, Rouen, Le Havre, 12–14 Oct. 1994.

Stefansson, G. (2002), 'Business-to-Business Data Sharing: A Source for Integration of Supply Chains', *International Journal of Production Economics* 75:1–2, 135–46.

Stern, E. and Hayuth, Y. (1984), 'Developmental Effects of Geopolitically Located Ports', in Hoyle and Hilling (eds).

Stevens, G.C. (1989), 'Integrating the Supply Chain', *International Journal of Physical Distribution and Materials Management* 19:8, 3–8.

Stevens, H. (1999), *The Institutional Position of Seaports* (Boston: Kluwer).

Taaffe, E.J. *et al.* (1963), 'Transport Expansion in Underdeveloped Countries: A Comparative Analysis', *Geographical Review* 53:4, 503–29.

Talley, W.K. (1988), 'Optimum Throughput and Performance Evaluation of Marine Terminals', Maritime Policy & Management 15:4, 327–31.

Tan, K.C. *et al.* (1998), 'Supply Chain Management: Supplier Performance and Firm Performance', *International Journal of Purchasing and Materials Management* 34:3, 2–9.

Tangreti, S.J. (ed.) (2002), *Globalization and Maritime Power* (Washington D.C.: National Defense University Press).

Teurelincx, D. (2000), 'Functional Analysis of Port Performance as a Strategic Tool for Strengthening a Port's Competitive and Economic Potential', *International Journal of Maritime Economics* 2:2, 119–40.

The World Bank Group (2005), *Prospects for the Global Economy* (Washington: The World Bank).

Todd, D. (1994) 'Changing Technology, Economic Growth and Port Development: The Transformation of Tianjin', *Geoforum* 25:3, 285–303.

Tongzon, J. (2005), 'Key Success Factors for Transhipment Hubs: The Case of the Port of Singapore', in Lee and Cullinane (eds).

Tongzon, J. and Heng, W. (2005), 'Port Privatization, Efficiency and Competitiveness: Some Empirical Evidence from Container Ports (Terminals)', *Transportation Research A* 39:5, 405–24.

Tower, C. (2005) 'Vancouver Strike in Third Week', *Journal of Commerce Online* (published online 11 Jul. 2005) <http://www.joc.com/20050711/sections/logis/ w76728.asp>, accessed 12 Jul. 2005.

Towill, D.R. (1997), 'The Seamless Chain – The Predator's Strategic Advantage', *International Journal of Technology Management* 13:1, 37–56.

Transystems (2006), 'Emerging Canadian Port & Intermodal Opprtunities: A Capacity Assessment'. Presentation at the Canada-Asia Maritime Conference, Vancouver, Canada, 2–3 Oct. 2006.

Trotta, M. (2000), 'Mediterranean and Northern terminals: How is the Competition Developing?', *International Journal of Maritime Economics* 4: 351–4.

UNCTAD (United Nations Conference on Trade and Development) (1999), 'Technical Note: The Fourth Generation Port', *Ports Newsletter* 19, 9–12.

UNCTAD (2002), *Review of Maritime Transport* (Geneva: United Nations).

United States General Accounting Office (1996), *Global Warming: Difficulties Assessing Countries' Progress Stabilizing Emissions of Greenhouse Gases* (Washington D.C.: USGAO).

United States General Accounting Office (1999), *International Environment: Literature on the Effectiveness of International Environmental Agreements* (Washington D.C.: USGAO).

Vallega, A. (1979), 'Fonctions Portuaires et Polarisations Littorales Dans la Nouvelle Régionalisation de la Méditerranée, Quelques Réflexions', in Vigarie (ed.).

Vallega, A. (1983), 'Nodalité et Centralité Face à la Multimodalité: Éléments pour un Relais entre Théorie Régionale et Théorie des Transports', in Muscara and Poli (eds).

Valleri, M.A. and Van de Voorde, E. (1992), 'Do Mediterranean Ports Have a Future?', *Journal of Regional Policy* 12:2, 411–30.

Van Hooydonk, E. (2006), *The Impact of EU Environmental Law on Ports and Waterways* (Antwerp-Apeldoorn: Maklu Publishers).

Van Niekerk H.C. and Fourie, Y.(2002), 'An analysis of maritime supply chains in South Africa', *IAME Panama 2002 Conference Proceedings* www.clml.org, definition of SCM, 1986.

Vandermeulen, J.H. (1996), 'Environmental Trends of Ports and Harbours: Implications for Planning and Management', *Maritime Policy and Management* 23:1, 55–66.

Vandeveer, D. (1998), 'Port Productivity Standards for Long-Term Planning', in Kraman (ed.) *Ports '98; Conference Proceedings*, 79–89pp.

Verlaque, C. (1979), 'Inductions Portuaires: Le Cas Sétois', in Vigarie (ed.).

Vernon, R. (1966), 'International Investment and International Trade in the Product Cycle', *Quarterly Journal of Economics*, 80:2, 190–207.

Vickery, S.K. *et al.* (2003), 'The Effects of an Integrative Supply Chain Strategy on Customer Service and Financial Performance: An Analysis of Direct Versus Indirect Relationships', *Journal of Operations Management* 21:5, 523–39.

Vigarié, A. (1968), *Géographie de la Circulation*, Vol. 2 (Paris: Genin).

Vigarié, A. (1979), *Ports de Commerce et vie Littorale* (Paris: Hachette).

Vigarie, A. (ed.) (1979) *Villes et Ports, Développement Portuaire, Croissance Spatiale des Villes, Environnement Littoral* (Paris: CNRS).

Villaverde Castro, J. and Coto-Millan, P. (1998) 'Port Economic Impact: Methodologies and Applications to the Port of Santander', *International Journal of Transport Economics* 25:2, 159–79.

Wallis, K. (2005), 'Hutchison Joins Venture to Expand Yantian Box Berths', *Lloyds List* 10 November, 14.

Walter, A. (1975), 'Marginal Cost Pricing in Ports', *The Logistics and Transportation Review* 11, 297–308.

Wang, J.J. and Slack, B. (2000), 'The Evolution of a Regional Container Port System: The Pearl River Delta', *Journal of Transport Geography* 8:4, 263–75.

Wang, J.J. and Olivier, D. (2003), 'La Gouvernance des Ports et la Relation Ville-port en Chine', *Cahiers Scientifiques du Transport* 44, 25–54.

Wang, J.J. and Slack, B. (2004), 'Regional Governance of Port Development in China: A Case Study of Shanghai International Shipping Center', *Maritime Policy & Management* 31:4, 357–73.

Wang, J.J. *et al.* (2004), 'Port Governance in China: A Review of Policies in an Era of Internationalising Port Management Practices', *Transport Policy* 11:3, 237–50.

Wang, T. *et al.* (2005), *Container Port Production and Economic Efficiency* (Hampshire, UK: Palgrave-Macmillan).

Wang, J.J. and Olivier, D. (2006), 'Port-FEZ Bundles as Spaces of Global Articulation: The Case of Tianjin, China', *Environment & Planning A* 38:8, 1487–504.

Wang, J.J. and Olivier, D. (2007a), 'Hong Kong and Shenzhen: The Nexus in South China', in Cullinane and Song (eds).

Wang, J.J. and Olivier, D. (2007b), 'Shanghai and Ningbo: In Search of an Identity for the Changjiang Delta Region', in Cullinane and Song (eds).

Waters, R.C. (1977), 'Port Economic Impact Studies: Practice and Assessment', *Transportation Journal* 16:3, 14-18.

WCTR Society (2004) *Proceedings of 10ᵗʰ World Conference on Transport Research*, 4–8 Jul. 2004, Istanbul, Turkey.

White, H.P. and Senior, M.L. (1983), *Transport Geography* (Hong Kong: Longman).

Whitehead, P. (2000), 'Environmental Management Framework for Ports and Related Industries', *Terra et Aqua* 80, 22–30.

Wijnolst, N. *et al.* (1999), *Malacca-Max – The ultimate container carrier – Design Innovation in Container Shipping* (Delft: Delft University Press).

Wijnolst, N. *et al.* (2000) *Malacca-Max – Container Shipping Network Economy* (Delft: Delft University Press).

Winkelmans, W. (2005), 'EU Transport Politics for Ports' Presentation at *International Conference on the Role of the Freeport of Riga in creation of the new European Logistics Platform*, Riga, 1 Jun. 2005.

Wisner, J.D. and Stanley, L.L. (1999), 'Internal Relationships and Activities Associated with High Level of Purchasing Service Quality', *The Journal of Supply Chain Management* 35:3, 25–32.

Witherick, M.E. (1981), 'Port Developments, Port-city Linkages and Prospects for Maritime Industry: A Case Study of Southampton', in Hoyle and Pinder (eds).

Wooldridge, C.F. et al. (1999), 'Environmental Management of Ports and Harbours-Implementation of Policy through Scientific Monitoring', *Marine Policy* 23:5, 413–25.

World Bank (1992), *Port Marketing and the Challenge of the Third Generation Port* (Geneva: World Bank).

World Bank (2006), *Private Participation in Infrastructure (PPI) Database* <http://rru.worldbank.org/PPI/>

World Shipping Council (2006), 'Liner Shipping Facts and Figures' <http://www.worldshipping.org/ind_facts.html>, accessed 15 December.

Yeung, H.W. (2004), *Chinese Capitalism in a Global Era: Towards Hybrid Capitalism* (London: Routledge).

Zaheer, A. *et al.* (1998), 'The Strategic Value of Buyer – Supplier Relationships', *International Journal of Purchasing and Materials Management* 34:3, 20–26.

Zohil, J. and Prijon, M. (1999), 'The MED Rule: The Interdependence of Container Throughput and Transhipment Volumes in the Mediterranean Ports', *Maritime Policy & Management* 26:2, 175–93.

Index